Taylan Özgür Kaya is Assistant Professor in the International Relations Department at Necmettin Erbakan University, Konya, Turkey. He holds a PhD from the Department of International Relations at the Middle East Technical University, Turkey.

THE MIDDLE EAST PEACE PROCESS AND THE EU

Foreign Policy and Security Strategy in
International Politics

TAYLAN ÖZGÜR KAYA

I.B. TAURIS

LONDON · NEW YORK

Published in 2013 by I.B.Tauris & Co Ltd
6 Salem Road, London W2 4BU
175 Fifth Avenue, New York NY 10010
www.ibtauris.com

Distributed in the United States and Canada
Exclusively by Palgrave Macmillan
175 Fifth Avenue, New York NY 10010

Library of European Studies 20

ISBN 978 1 84885 982 1

A full CIP record for this book is available from the British Library
A full CIP record for this book is available from the Library of Congress

Library of Congress catalog card: available

Typeset by Newgen Publishers, Chennai
Printed and bound by CPI Group (UK) Ltd, Croydon, CR0 4YY

To Aslı with love

CONTENTS

ACKNOWLEDGEMENTS

This book is based on my PhD thesis, which I submitted at the Middle East Technical University (METU) in 2010. It is a pleasure for me to express my gratitude to those who made this book possible with their contributions. First of all, I wish to express my sincere gratitude to my PhD thesis supervisor at the Department of International Relations, METU, Associate Professor Sevilay Kahraman for her supervision, comments, criticism and guidance, which helped me refine my ideas and arguments.

I am grateful to Professor Hüseyin Bağcı and Associate Professor Pınar Bilgin for taking time out of their busy schedules to participate in the meetings of my thesis supervising committee and their invaluable comments, criticisms and guidance.

I wish to acknowledge my debt of gratitude to METU for providing me a stimulating academic environment and excellent research opportunities without which this book would not have been possible.

I am indebted to Professor Adrian Hyde-Price and the University of Leicester for providing me an invaluable opportunity to spend an academic year as a research student at the Politics and International Relations Department. I am also grateful to the British Council for awarding me the British Chevening Scholarship, which enabled me to conduct my PhD research at the University of Leicester.

I owe a special debt of gratitude to my interviewees in Brussels, who took time out of their busy schedules to answer my questions and provide me very insightful information about the EU's role in the Middle East Peace Process.

Special thanks go to my editors at I.B.Tauris, Maria Marsh and Nadine El-Hadi, for all their kind help and invaluable comments and guidance through the book production process. I express my sincere appreciation to Pat Fitzgerald for copyediting and proofreading.

I owe my deepest gratitude to my parents, Tuna and Cevdet. I remain eternally grateful to them for their unwavering support, encouragement, love and confidence in me.

Words fail me to express my appreciation to my wife, Aslı to whom this book is dedicated. Her unfaltering support, encouragement, patience, enduring love and confidence in me have proven invaluable. This book would not have been possible without her support and encouragement.

Finally, I would like to thank everybody who supported me in any respect during the completion of this book, as well as expressing my apologies to all whom I could not mention personally one by one.

LIST OF TABLES

LIST OF ABBREVIATIONS

ASEAN	Association of Southeast Asian Nations
CFSP	Common Foreign and Security Policy
CIA	Central Intelligence Agency
EC	European Community
ECU	European Currency Unit
EMP	Euro-Mediterranean Partnership
ENP	European Neighbourhood Policy
EOM	European Union Election Observer Mission
EPC	European Political Cooperation
ESDP	European Security and Defence Policy
ESS	European Security Strategy
EUBAM Rafah	European Union Border Assistance Mission for the Rafah Crossing Point
EU	European Union
EUCOPPS	EU Coordinating Office for Palestinian Police Support
EUFP	European Union Foreign Policy
EUPOL COPPS	European Union Police Mission for the Palestinian Territories
EUSR	European Union Special Representative for the Middle East Peace Process
Fatah	Harakat al-Tahrir al-Watani al-Filastini (Palestinian National Liberation Movement)

GAERC	General Affairs and External Relations Council
GMP	Global Mediterranean Policy
Hamas	Harakat Al-Muqawama Al-Islamiya (Islamic Resistance Movement)
IMF	International Monetary Fund
MEDA	Mesures d'Accompagnement (Accompanying Measures)
MEPP	Middle East peace process
MERCUSOR	Mercado Comun del Sur (Southern Common Market)
MFO	Multinational Sinai Force and Observers
NATO	North Atlantic Treaty Organization
NGO	Non-governmental Organization
OPEC	Organization of Petroleum Exporting Countries
PEGASE	Palestino-Européen de Gestion et d'Aide Socio-Economique (European Mechanism of Support to the Palestinians)
PLO	Palestine Liberation Organization
REDWG	Regional Economic Development Working Group
SFOR	Stabilization Force in Bosnia Herzegovina
SME	Small and Medium-Sized Enterprises
TEU	Treaty on European Union
TIM	Temporary International Mechanism
UK	United Kingdom
UN	United Nations
UNIFIL	United Nations Interim Force in Lebanon
UNRWA	United Nations Relief and Works Agency
US	United States
USA	United States of America
USSR	Union of Soviet Socialist Republics

CHAPTER 1

INTRODUCTION

Since 1999, EU Member States have striven to consolidate the EU's CFSP and the EU has become an important foreign and security policy actor in international politics. At the Cologne European Council on 3–4 June 1999, the defence dimension of the EU's foreign and security policy, the ESDP was introduced. In the post-9/11 era, the CFSP and the ESDP have gained substance and momentum. Jolyon Howorth and John T.S. Keeler (2003: 15) have put forward the opinion that 9/11 made the case for the ESDP even more compelling. In this area, significant elements of integration emerged. Institutional struggles were left behind and a range of EU actors and agencies started to work together to develop a coherent political approach to the crises (ibid.). In the post-9/11 era, the EU started to become one of the key foreign and security policy actors in the international arena with the ability to use a full range of instruments including military ones in addition to civilian ones for crisis management and conflict prevention. Michael Smith called this the process of hardening of European foreign and security policy. He argued that particularly since the late 1990s, there was a process of hardening which has led to an injection of hard as opposed to soft security into the European foreign and security policy process, particularly through the elaboration of the ESDP (Smith 2006: 40).

In the post-9/11 era, the ESDP was operationalized. Several operations in the framework of the ESDP have been carried out since 2003.

Until the time of writing, 23 operations had been carried out under the aegis of the ESDP and more are under consideration and planning.

These operations demonstrated that, in the post-9/11 era, the EU became more deeply committed to crisis management and post-conflict rehabilitation efforts in different parts of the world including Africa, the South Caucasus, the Western Balkans, the Middle East and Asia by using its civilian and military instruments (Bono 2006: 14). This demonstrated that, as Michael Smith (2006: 40) put forward, in the post-9/11 era, there is a widening of the geographical scope of European foreign and security policy which means that more regions have become entangled in European foreign and security policy.

In the post-9/11 era, the EU and its Member States officials' efforts to increase the coherence of the EU's foreign and security policy instruments have increased. Intensification of the coordination between the EU and its Member States officials in terms of external deployment of resources including development aid, humanitarian aid, judges, diplomats, military forces etc. in their relations with the so-called 'failed states' or post-conflict-states such as Bosnia, Kosovo, Afghanistan, Democratic Republic of Congo, has been observed (Bono 2006: 28). The threat of terrorism was identified as one of the main reasons for the acceleration of the coherence of the EU instruments for external action (ibid.). In the post-9/11 era, European Council's suggestion that all the activities carried out under the CFSP could be considered as a contribution to long-term actions for the prevention of terrorism represented a radical departure from the notion that was at the heart of the EU that external economic development had to be fostered for the benefit of humanity and be geared to principles of need and removing of regional and global inequalities (ibid.). In the post-9/11 era, the link between external economic development and European security was increasingly highlighted by the EU.

In the post-9/11 era, the EU's first-ever security strategy, 'A Secure Europe in a Better World, European Security Strategy', was prepared by the High Representative for the CFSP Javier Solana and adopted by the EU leaders at the Rome European Council on 12–13 December 2003. In Peter Van Ham's words (2004), the ESS has offered an *acquis stratégique* by establishing priorities and setting clear policy goals. The document primarily offers a common view of the nature of current international security environment (post-Cold War and post-9/11 international security contexts), the EU's role within it, the shared perception of the most serious threats, the most important opportunities in that security environment and appropriate policy responses that the EU should adopt in dealing with them.

In the ESS, terrorism, proliferation of weapons of mass destruction, regional conflicts, state failure and organized crime were identified as key threats to European security in the post-Cold War and post-9/11 international security context. In the ESS, a comprehensive approach to security is identified as the most effective way to manage these security threats. The comprehensive security approach refers to the combined use of full range of available security policy instruments, including both civilian and military (Rieker 2004: 370; Biscop 2003: 185). As a part of its comprehensive security approach, the EU recognizes that transnational threats cannot be dealt with by using traditional security instruments such as military force, these threats have root causes and military force is not an appropriate means to manage their root causes. In the post-9/11 era, the EU prefers a security strategy which combines civilian and military instruments and addresses the root causes of transnational threats.

It was noted in the ESS that the new threats in the post-Cold War and post-9/11 period are not purely military and they cannot be tackled by purely military means; each needs a mixture of instruments. In addition to that, it is stated that European states need to use the full spectrum of instruments for crisis management and conflict prevention at their disposal, including political, diplomatic, military and civilian, trade and development activities in pursuing their strategic objectives. It is also noted that the European states need to develop a strategic culture that fosters early, rapid, and when necessary, robust intervention, to be able to undertake operations involving both military and civilian capabilities. Javier Solana (27 January 2006) also argued that the EU's comprehensive approach to security, that is part civilian, and part military, corresponds to the needs of today's complex security crises.

The nexus between security and development, which was developed in the 1990s and was manifested in an increasing interest in the human security agenda, has assumed a new dimension since 9/11 (Bono 2006: 28). In the ESS, for the first time in the EU's history, underdevelopment in non-European states was identified as a threat to the security of Europeans (ibid.). In the post-9/11 era, underdevelopment, which provides a breeding ground for insecurity, is identified by the EU as one of the contemporary challenges to European security.

In the ESS, it is also stated that European security and prosperity increasingly depend on an effective multilateral system. The development of a stronger international society, well functioning international institutions and a rule-based international order is accepted as the objectives of EU Member States. The latter are committed to upholding and developing international law. The UN Charter is considered as the fundamental framework for international relations, and the consolidation of the UN's international role and responsibilities remains a European priority. It is also noted that EU Member States demand international organizations, regimes and treaties to be more effective in confronting threats to international peace and security, and must be ready to act when their rules are broken. The document also emphasizes that it is a condition of a rule-based international order that law evolves in response to developments such as proliferation, terrorism and global warming. It is acknowledged that EU Member States have an interest in further developing existing institutions such as the World Trade Organization and in supporting new ones like the International Criminal Court. Furthermore, spreading good governance, supporting social and political reform, dealing with corruption and abuse of power, establishing the rule of law and protecting human rights are regarded as the best means of strengthening the international order.

In the ESS, key threats to European security are identified as common threats, shared with all the EU's closest partners. By relying on this, building multilateral cooperation in international organizations and partnerships with key actors is identified as a necessity for dealing with these threats and pursuing the objectives of EU. In the ESS, it was stated that the EU needed to develop an effective and balanced partnership with the USA, since transatlantic relationship is identified as indispensible for the EU. It was also noted that the EU needs to continue to develop closer ties with Russia which is identified as crucial for security and prosperity of the EU. It was pointed out that the EU has to develop strategic partnerships with Japan, China, Canada and India and with all those countries that share the same goals and values with the EU.

In order to implement the defence aspects of ESS, Britain, France and Germany proposed the formation of EU 'Battlegroups' in February 2004.[1] At the Brussels European Council on 17–18 June 2004, EU Member States agreed on Headline Goal 2010, which also included the EU 'Battlegroups concept'. At the 22 November 2004 Military Capabilities Commitment Conference convened in Brussels, EU Member States agreed on the formation of 13 'EU Battlegroups' and it was decided that first Battlegroups would reach full operational capability in 2007. It was also decided that Battlegroups would be employable across the full range of Petersberg tasks as listed in the TEU Art.17.2 and those identified in the ESS, in particular in tasks of combat forces in crisis management, bearing in mind their size. Battlegroups have to be sustainable until mission termination or until relief by other forces. They should be sustainable for 30 days initial operations, extendable to 120 days, if re-supplied appropriately.

It is within this context that this book aims to investigate the congruity between the role that the EU aspires to play as a foreign and security actor and its actual foreign and security policy actions and decisions in a specific case of the MEPP in the post-9/11 era. The correspondence between EU's foreign and security policy rhetoric and the EU's foreign and security policy behaviour will be examined in this book.

The Purpose and the Research Questions of the Book

The overall purpose of this book is to identify the EU's foreign and security policy role conceptions defined in the post-9/11; to examine the congruity[2] between the EU's role conceptions and its role performance in a specific case of the MEPP in the post-9/11 era; and to assess the consequences of (in)congruity between the EU's role conceptions and role performance on both the EU's profile as a foreign and security policy actor and the MEPP. This book aims to analyze the level of congruity between self-conceptualization of 'what the EU is' (role conception) and 'what the EU does' (role performance) and the impact of (in)congruity between the EU's role conceptions and role performance on the EU's profile as a foreign and security policy actor.

This book addresses three main research questions:

1. which role(s) does/do the EU define for itself as a foreign and security policy actor in the post-9/11 era;
2. is there a congruity or incongruity between the EU's self-defined role conceptions and its actual role performance in a specific case of the MEPP in the post-9/11 era;
3. what are the outcomes/consequences of (in)congruity between the EU's role conceptions and role performance on both the EU's profile as a foreign and security policy actor and the MEPP.

Organization of the Book

This book consists of six chapters. It begins with this introductory chapter, which outlines the necessary background to understand and conceptualize this book. This introductory chapter begins with an overview of the context and background that frames the study, which makes an analysis of the EU as a foreign and security policy actor in the post-9/11 international security context. This chapter presents the purpose and accompanying research questions of the book, which demonstrates what the main objectives of the book are and the questions the book seeks to answer.

Chapter 2 presents the theoretical framework for analysis of the book, a review of the literature on the analysis of the European foreign policy and the research design and methodology which will guide the research in this book, and is organized in three parts. In the first part, the theoretical framework for analysis, on which this book is based, will be presented. In this part, application of role theory in analyzing foreign policy and why the role theoretical approach was selected as theoretical framework for analysis and two key concepts, which are associated with role theory and used to inform the analysis in book (role conception and role performance) will be evaluated. The second part provides a review of the literature on the analysis of the European foreign policy, which presents the main approaches in the analysis of the European foreign policy, and describes potential contributions of this book to the existing literature in order to locate this book in the literature on the analysis of European foreign policy. The final part specifies the research design and methodology which will guide the research in this book. This part of the chapter demonstrates how qualitative content analysis has been applied for identifying the EU's foreign and security policy role conceptions and why the speeches delivered by three principal EU foreign and security policy officials concerning foreign and security policy of the EU, and the EU official documents concerning foreign and security policy of the EU were selected as source of data collection for identification of the EU's foreign and security policy role conceptions. Furthermore, this part of the chapter presents why the MEPP was selected as a specific case study and why the period extending from 11 September 2001 to 31 December 2006 was selected as the focus of analysis.

Chapter 3 presents the EU's foreign and security policy role conceptions in the post-9/11 era. In this chapter, the EU's foreign and security policy role conceptions in the post-9/11 era will be identified by analyzing the content of the general foreign policy speeches delivered by the principal EU foreign policy officials during the period extending from 11 September 2001 to 31 December 2006 and selected EU official documents concerning foreign and security policy of the EU. As a result of content analysis, seven role conceptions have been identified: 'force for good', 'force for international peace, security and stability', 'promoter of its values and norms', 'the provider of development aid', 'promoter of effective multilateralism', 'partner for the UN' and 'builder of effective partnership with key actors'. This chapter provides an outline of main roles at work within the EU's role set in the post-9/11 era.

Chapter 4 provides a historical overview of the EU's involvement in the MEPP in the pre-9/11 era, which will help to understand better and to analyze the EU's role performance in the MEPP in the post-9/11 era. This analysis enables to reveal the change and continuity in the EU's policy towards the MEPP. This chapter is organized in three parts which respectively provide a historical overview of the evolution of the EU's policy towards the MEPP from the 1970s up to 1990s.

Chapter 5 provides an analysis of the level of congruity between EU's role conceptions and role performance in the MEPP in the post-9/11 era. It is divided into two parts. The first part provides a general overview of the EU's involvement in the MEPP in the post-9/11 era. After a general overview, the congruity between EU's role conceptions and role performance in a specific case of the MEPP and the consequences of (in)congruity between the EU's role conceptions and role performance on both the EU's profile as a foreign and security policy actor and the MEPP in the post-9/11 era will be analyzed.

Finally, chapter 6 provides the summary of the book and conclusions obtained from this research.

CHAPTER 2

THEORETICAL FRAMEWORK FOR ANALYSIS

The objective of this chapter is to present a theoretical framework for analysis for this book, a review of the literature on the analysis of the European foreign policy and the research design and methodology which will guide the research used in the book. The chapter is organized into three parts. In the first part, application of role theory in analyzing foreign policy and why the role theoretical approach was selected as the theoretical framework for analysis and role conception and role performance, its two key concepts, which are associated with role theory and used to inform the analysis in the book, will be evaluated. The second part provides a review of the literature on the analysis of the European foreign policy and describes the book's potential contributions to the existing literature in order to locate it in the literature on the analysis of European foreign policy. The final part specifies the research design and methodology which will guide the research used in the book. This part of the chapter demonstrates how qualitative content analysis was applied to identify the EU's foreign and security policy role conceptions and why the speeches delivered by three principal EU foreign and security policy officials concerning foreign and security policy of the EU, and the EU official documents concerning foreign and security policy of the EU, were selected as sources of data collection for identification of the EU's foreign and security policy role conceptions. Furthermore, this part of the chapter presents why the

MEPP was selected as a specific case study and why the period extending from 11 September 2001 to 31 December 2006 was selected as the focus of analysis.

Role Theory in Analyzing Foreign Policy

This book uses a theoretical framework for analysis based on role theory. What this effectively means is that the role of the EU as a foreign and security policy actor in a specific case of the MEPP in the post-9/11 era has been analyzed by using role theory as theoretical framework for analysis.

In this part of the chapter I will summarize the key features of role theory. In particular, I clarify the meaning of the key concepts which are associated with role theory and are used to inform the analysis: role conception and role performance.

Stephen Walker (1979: 176) argued that as a scientific explanation of social phenomena, role theory tends to be conceptually rich and methodologically poor. He further asserted that role theory has served more as a conceptual framework within which scholars from various disciplines have conducted research using range of methodologies (ibid.).

Bruce Biddle (1979: 16) also argued that role theory shows the promise of relevance, richness of conceptual structure, and the vigour of empirical research. Christer Jönsson and Ulf Westerlund (1982: 124) identified role theory as a research orientation or framework. According to Bruce J. Biddle, role theory concerns one of the most important features of social life, characteristic behaviour patterns or roles. It explains roles by presuming that persons are members of social positions and hold expectations for their own behaviours and those of other persons (Biddle 1986: 67). Biddle identified role theory as a science concerned with the study of behaviours that are characteristic of persons within contexts and with various processes that presumably produce, explain, or are affected by those behaviours (Biddle 1979: 4).

Role theory has its origins in the discipline of social psychology. The concept of role, which was borrowed from theatre, referred to certain characters in a story rather than to the actors or players who played them (Walker 1979: 173). The utility of the concept of role and its connotations for understanding real world behaviour as well as behaviour on the theatrical stage depends on the resemblance between the two arenas (ibid.). For the social psychologists whose observations are guided by the concept of role, the object of study is the enactment of the role by persons in social settings (Sarbin and Allen 1968: 489). Role theory provides a perspective for discussing or studying many social issues (Biddle 1986: 68). Role theory has been employed by social scientists for studying social phenomena because it provides many concepts, enabling investigators to study different and competing explanations for human conduct and, as many of the terms appearing in role theory are drawn from the common language, they seem natural and easy to measure (Biddle 1979: 13). Carl Backman argued that role theory as used in behavioural sciences has descriptive, organizational and explanatory value. For him, the concept of role has helped to integrate knowledge relevant to three levels of abstraction: culture, social structure and personality. He posited that research and study at each of these levels suggest some interesting analogues, possibly helpful for making sense of international relations (Backman 1970: 311).

Role theory was borrowed from social psychology and applied to foreign policy analysis by Kalevi Jacque Holsti in 1970 with his seminal study, 'National Role Conceptions in the Study of Foreign Policy'. In his cross-national study, Holsti analyzed the general foreign policy statements of highest-level policy-makers in order to form a typology of national role conceptions. He built a typology of role conceptions including 17 role conceptions identified by content analysis of speeches and statements of the highest-level policy-makers of 71 states during the period extending January 1965 to December 1967. In his study, he adopted an inductive strategy for the identification of role conceptions. He adopted a bottom-up perspective rather a top-down one. What this effectively means is that instead of building an 'ideal type' role concept and using it to explain and understand the international role of states, he preferred to construct a role typology by content analyzing the speeches and statements of the highest-level policy-makers of states.

Holsti focused on national role conceptions, which he defined as the policy-makers' own definitions of the general kinds of decisions, commitments, rules and actions suitable to their state, and of the functions, if any, their state should perform on a continuing basis in the international system or in subordinate regional systems (Holsti 1970: 245–46). According to Holsti, national role conceptions are context bound. They are bound to the social-psychological context of the policy-makers. National role conceptions reflect policymakers' own perceptions of their states' position, functions and behaviours in international system. In his analysis, social context is 'international system' and states are members of social positions and holding expectations for their own behaviours within the system. Highest-level policy-makers identify social position of their state and expectations for the behaviour of their state within the international system. Holsti focused on the 'subjective' dimension of foreign policy rather than a universally applicable vision of international relations commonly held by all international actors (Aggestam 2006: 11). Holsti argued that actual role performance (foreign policy actions and decisions of states) in international politics principally stemmed from the policymaker's role conceptions, domestic needs and demands and critical events or trends in the external milieu (Holsti op cit.: 243). Holsti's analysis was based on the assumption that role performance results from and is consistent with policy-makers' conceptions of their nation's directions and duties in international system or regional systems (Walker 1979: 244–45). Thus, for Holsti, national policy-makers will act consistently with what they perceive and conceive as appropriate for their states' position, functions and behaviours in international system or regional systems.

As Carl Backman argued, Holsti's study illustrated the explanatory value of the role theory in analyzing foreign policy. He argued that Holsti's study demonstrated how the concept of role can be used in explaining regularities in relations between basic analytical units of international system, the governments (Backman 1970: 311). According to Naomi Bailin Wish, since most of the previous studies focusing on decision-makers' perceptions comprise only perceptions of the external environment, especially enemy characteristics and actions, and very few examine decision-makers' perceptions of their own, Holsti's focus on self-defined role conceptions to study foreign policy fills a gap in the foreign policy analysis literature (Jönsson and Westerund 1982: 131).

Naomi Bailin Wish argued that although Holsti hypothesized that national role conceptions are strongly related to role performance, he examined only the relationship between role conceptions and one type of foreign policy behaviour, the level of international involvement or participation. She further argued that Holsti never tested his hypothesis with a systematic measure of participation or involvement in the international system (Wish 1980: 535). She put forward the argument that in cases of systematic categorization, national role conceptions, which she defined as foreign policy-makers' perceptions of their nations' positions in the international system, can be a powerful tool for explaining variations in many types of foreign policy behaviour (ibid.). She noted that national role conceptions provide norms, guidelines, and standards which affect many aspects of decision-making (ibid.: 533). Wish set out to find the relationship between national role conceptions and foreign policy behaviour and determine the factors underlying the entire set of role and behaviour variables by using quantitative techniques. As a consequence of her analysis, she concluded that many national role conception characteristics are strongly related to foreign policy behaviour (ibid.: 546). Through her analysis, she found greater similarities among role conceptions expressed by leaders from the same nations than from differing nations, although they were in power at different times and therefore experienced a changing international system. For her, this brings longevity and stability to the role conceptions. By relying on research results, she concluded that these results showed the value of analyzing role conceptions which provide long-standing guidelines or standards for behaviour (ibid.: 547). She argued that longevity and stability of role conceptions are assets when trying to explain long-term patterns of foreign policy behaviour rather than single decisions (ibid.). She argued that her findings demonstrated the potential utility of national role conceptions for explaining and possibly eventually predicting patterns in foreign policy behaviour (Wish 1987: 95).

Stephen Walker (1987d: 271) argued that Holsti's inductive strategy for the identification of role conceptions differed from the efforts of previous studies, which deduced roles from the implications of classical balance of power theory and its derivatives. Walker suggested that an apparent gap emerged between idiosyncratically based or domestically based national role conceptions and the role expectations consistent with a balance of power system. Holsti identified the reason behind this incongruity as the previous international politics theorists' tendency to focus on the activities of the major powers and ignore regional systems outside Western Europe where cooperative ventures were very significant (ibid.). Walker argued that balance of power theory was insufficient in scope and required to be modified or replaced with a theory that would include the variety of foreign policy phenomena exposed by Holsti's use of role as a concept to study foreign policy (ibid.).

In addition to Stephen Walker, Lisbeth Aggestam argued that Holsti's inductive strategy for the identification of role conceptions differed from traditional approaches in international relations theory, especially realism. In realist approach, the sources of roles are predominantly systemic and based on material factors, thus the state's general role is studied deductively in terms of the state's position within a structure (Aggestam 2006: 13). According to Aggestam, the novelty with Holsti's study was that roles are not unfolded from abstract theoretical discussions, but analyzed inductively in terms of the roles perceived and defined by policy-makers (ibid.). Aggestam emphasized that Holsti's approach has great strengths in the sense that it set out to take careful account of political reality as it is experienced by the policy-makers, who construct it in a dynamic interaction between rules and reasons (ibid.). Holsti's study demonstrated that the practitioners of foreign policy have defined different and numerous roles than general roles stipulated deductively by academics.

Philippe Le Prestre (1997a: 13), while elaborating on the utility of the concept of role in analyzing foreign policy, made a similar evaluation with Walker and Aggestam and stated that using the concept of role enables to go beyond the traditional or realist, explanation of foreign policy, which is based on security or on national interest defined by prudent quest for power. For Le Prestre, roles help define national interests and divorce them from power. Le Prestre also suggested that role conception can help explain the general direction of foreign policy choices. The expression of a national role reveals preferences, operationalizes an image of the world, generates expectations and effects the definition of the situation and of the available options. He also suggested that the concept of role helps to explain visible anomalies in the conduct of states. What this effectively means is that the concept of role can help to explain why some states conduct their foreign policy in a manner contradictory to their national interests. According to Le Prestre, the concept of role enables the explanation of foreign policy behaviours which structural realism, that asserts that capacities are the only determinate factor for the definition of a role, remains inadequate to explain. Le Prestre gave the example of structural realism's failure to explain Japan and Germany's choice not to bear greater responsibilities through a leadership role commensurate with their power. Le Prestre argued that in anarchic system roles impose obligations on states and help shape their interests. Thus, the concept of role helps us expand the definition of national interest beyond more basic geopolitical factors that are linked to national survival. In addition to Le Prestre, Richard Adigbuo (2007: 90) also argued that the concept of role helps explain visible anomalies in the conduct of states. Adigbuo gave the example of the impossibility of explaining decision of the Nigeria, which had one of the lowest incomes per capita in the world, to send aid to the Soviet Union or sponsor liberation movements abroad through its national interest. He argued that this example showed that a role can lead a state to act contradictorily with its national interest – thus enabling analyst to separate interests from power (ibid.: 90).

Moreover, Le Prestre posited that the concept of role enables the reconciliation between different levels of analysis (the individual, the society and the system) and provides a means of assessing the interaction between internal and external variables. Role conceptions can also help explain foreign policy continuities. As Naomi Wish argued, role conceptions, which provide long-standing guidelines or standards for behaviour, help explain long-term patterns of foreign policy behaviour.

Stephen Walker (1979: 204) argued that some important foreign policy questions can be examined by using a combination of concepts

from role theory and methods inspired by cognitive dynamics literature. Walker (1987b: 2) put forward three reasons for utilizing role
analysis for analyzing foreign policy behaviour: its descriptive, organizational and explanatory value. Descriptively, the concepts associated
with role analysis provide a vocabulary of images which can focus
upon foreign policy behaviour at the national level of analysis, shift
down the individual level of analysis and also move up to the systemic level of analysis. He suggests that the ability to make a distinc-
tion between coherent and incoherent foreign policy across different
levels of foreign policy decisions shows the potential descriptive and
normative utility of role theory in monitoring and assessing the conduct of foreign policy (Walker 1979: 204). Christer Jönsson and Ulf
Westerlund also emphasized the multilevel descriptive power of role
theory. By relying on the assumption that the international political
system is stratified like other social systems, they noted that in international politics research, role theory can be applied at state, interstate
and systemic levels (Jönsson and Westerlund 1982: 128). The concept
of role not only has a multilevel descriptive power, but also a multi-
dimensional scope in its application to foreign policy behaviour. Role
conception goes beyond the narrow conceptualization of foreign policy
behaviour as a continuum of cooperative and conflictual behaviour.
Organizationally, the concepts associated with role analysis enable to
adopt either a structure-oriented or a process-oriented perspective. It
is possible, to focus on the structure of a set of roles at the national
level of analysis or on the structure of a set of roles which define the
relations among a group of nations. Concerning role theory's explanatory utility and its potential for providing policy-makers with a policy-
relevant theory, Walker argued that the explanatory value of role theory depends on whether its concepts are theoretically informed either
by an appropriate set of self-contained propositions and methods, or
by the specification of an appropriate set of supplementary limiting conditions and rules linking these conditions with role concepts.
Appropriateness is a function of context defined as a particular domain
of behaviour. Although Walker noted that its explanatory utility and
its potential for providing policy-makers with a policy-relevant theory
are less clear, he argued that role theory's focus on cues and expectations

as sources of influence on a nation's foreign policy may eventually produce empirical generalizations that can be translated into short-term policy prescriptions (Walker 1979: 204). Moreover, he asserted that role theory possesses potentially a high value as an analytical tool for linking individual and systemic generalizations (ibid.: 205).

James Rosenau argued that role theory has organizational value in analyzing foreign policy. He put forward that the concept of role meets the need for a unifying dimension across the source variables for international action – individual, governmental, societal and systemic (Rosenau 1987: 45). According to Rosenau, in his study, 'Pre-theories and Theories of Foreign Policy', although the role concept was a central feature of the formulation, its scope was limited to the attitudes, behaviours and expectations that attach to top positions in the foreign policy-making process. The various role variables were considered as competing with individual, governmental, societal and systemic source variables for international action. In the Pre-theory, role variables have been discussed primarily at the level of individual decision-makers and been contrasted with idiosyncratic or personality variables (Jönsson and Westerlund 1982: 128). For him, this kind of formulation seemed too vague as a means of achieving a theoretical link between micro and macro-phenomena. The main problem as he sees it is the lack of common dimensions across source variables which could provide a basis for comparing among them. He stated that in the Pre-theory, societal and systemic variables consist of forces operating on top officials; governmental variables involve institutional practices to which they must accommodate; individual variables are comprised of pre-acquired values which predispose them in certain directions; the various sources, practices and values are in endless tension among themselves and with the expectations attached to the top roles. The concept of role provides a common dimension for all these source variables for international actions. For Rosenau, adopting role concept as the unit of analysis enables to achieve a theoretical link between micro and macro-phenomena (Walker 1987a: 244). As Gauvav Ghose and Patrick James (2005: 429) argue, role theory has a descriptive, organizational and explanatory value. For them, role theory has considerable potential to be utilized to explain foreign policy decisions and outcomes by connecting different levels and units and, in the process, provides a unified analysis (ibid.).

Charles F. Herman also emphasized explanatory value of the role theory in analyzing foreign policy. He suggested that role concept, which he defines as decision makers' expectations about the pattern or configuration of foreign policy activity that their government will pursue in certain situation in support of their beliefs, enables us to explain and predict foreign policy actions and decisions of national governments (Hermann 1987: 220). He noted that national governments have certain roles that they assume in world affairs and if we have knowledge about these roles, which national governments actually act to fulfil, the actions and decisions of those governments can be predicted and explained (ibid.: 219).

Lisbeth Aggestam emphasized the analytical utility of role theory for analyzing EU foreign policy. She asserted that role theory is potentially a very productive analytical tool for analyzing EU foreign and security policy. She defined role conception as the normative expectations that the role be-holder expresses towards itself, that is, the ego-part's own definition (Aggestam 2006: 19). According to her, a role conception defines responsibilities and obligations in foreign policy (Aggestam 2004a: 64). Role conceptions belong to the subjective dimension of foreign policy (Aggestam 2006: 19) rather than a universally applicable vision of international relations commonly held by all international actors. Role conceptions show the intention and motives of foreign and security policy actors (ibid.). When analyzing EU foreign policy, a role conception refers to images that foreign policy-makers hold concerning the general long-term function and performance of the EU in the international system (ibid.: 20). Aggestam emphasized the explanatory value of role concept in analyzing EU foreign policy and argued that a role conception provides a clearer view of the reasons for the EU's adoption of a particular orientation and approach in international relations (ibid.: 21). Just like Philippe Le Prestre, Aggestam argued that focusing on the concept of role enables us to transcend the traditional or realist explanation of foreign policy as the prudent quest for power. For her, the concept of role helps understand obligations and commitments that an actor perceives beyond only considerations to maximize its material interests. In her view, a European role conception reflects norms about the purpose and orientation of the EU as an actor in the international system (ibid.: 25).

In this book, two key concepts, which are associated with role theory are to inform the analysis: role conception and role performance.

Role Conception: In the context of this book, the concept of role conception refers to the EU's own conception and definition of its general long-term responsibilities, obligations, functions and orientations as a foreign and security policy actor in the post-9/11 international security context, which has been extracted from the speeches delivered by three principal EU foreign and security policy officials including the High Representative for the CFSP of the EU/Secretary General of the Council of the EU, Javier Solana (1999–2009) and the EU Commissioners for External Relations and European Neighbourhood Policy, Chris Patten (1999–2004) and Benita Ferrero-Waldner (2004–2009) concerning foreign and security policy of the EU, and the EU official documents (belonging to the period extending from 11 September 2001 to 31 December 2006) concerning foreign and security policy of the EU, including ESS, statements of the Council of the European Union, European Commission's communications and Founding Treaties of the European Union.

Role Performance: Role performance refers to the decisions and actions of a foreign and security policy actor (in this case, the EU). In the context of this book, the concept of role performance refers to actual foreign and security policy behaviour of the EU in a specific case of the MEPP in the post-9/11 international security context. The EU's role performance during the period extending from 11 September 2001 to 31 December 2006 has been investigated.

In this book, role theory is selected as a theoretical framework for analysis for three main reasons. The first is the conceptual richness of role theory which enhances its explanatory and analytical utility in analyzing foreign policy. Two key concepts associated with role theory (role conception and role performance) help explain and analyze the EU foreign and security policy in this book. As previously noted, Aggestam has argued that EU foreign and security policy role conceptions have provided a clearer view of the reasons for the EU's adoption of a particular orientation and approach in international relations. The EU's foreign and security policy role performance could provide a clearer picture of how effectively the EU has carried out its adopted foreign and security policy orientation and approach in international relations. Analyzing the congruity between the EU's role conception and role performance enables us to assess the effectiveness, efficiency and credibility of the EU as a foreign and security policy actor in a more precise way.

In addition to Aggestam, Naomi Bailin Wish also emphasized on the explanatory and analytical utility of role theory in analyzing foreign policy. As previously noted, Naomi Bailin Wish has argued that role conceptions provide long-standing guidelines or standards for behaviour, and longevity and stability of role conceptions are assets when trying to explain long-term patterns of foreign policy behaviour rather than single decisions. By relying on this argument, it can be said that studying EU's role conceptions has potential utility in explaining and possibly eventually predicting the general direction of foreign policy choices of the EU and long-term patterns of EU's foreign policy behaviour.

The second reason is that role theoretical analysis of foreign policy enables us to transcend traditional explanation of foreign policy which facilitates the analysis and explanation of a non-traditional and unique foreign policy actor, the EU, whose foreign policy cannot be explained through traditional approaches in international relations theory, especially realism.

The third reason is that as Lisbeth Aggestam has argued, the inductive strategy, which was firstly used by Holsti and then adopted by other scholars studying role conceptions for the identification of role conceptions, has enabled us to take careful account of political reality as it is experienced by the policy-makers, who construct it in a dynamic interaction between rules and reasons when compared to roles that are revealed from abstract theoretical discussions. For this reason, I have selected role theoretical analysis which enables us to take careful account of political reality in analyzing the EU foreign policy when compared to deductive strategy used by academics for constructing 'ideal type' role concepts or conceptual frameworks for explaining and understanding the EU foreign policy. What this means in effect is that inductive strategy used in role theoretical analysis has greater potential in reflecting political reality than deductive strategy used by academics for constructing role concepts.

Role Theory in Analyzing European Foreign Policy

The objective of this part of the chapter is to locate this study in the literature on the analysis of European foreign policy and suggest its potential contributions to the existing literature.

European Foreign Policy Analysis

There are several conceptualizations of European foreign policy and accordingly different conceptual approaches to its analysis. Ole Elgström and Michael Smith (2006: 1) identified this as 'analytical heterogeneity' and asserted that the reason behind this heterogeneity is the EU's status as an 'unidentified international object' with a rather mercurial existence and impact. Studies concerning European foreign policy analysis are more about the EU's actorness in international arena. There are various studies concerning European foreign policy. Some scholars, such as Brian White (1999, 2004) and Elke Krahmann (2003), have a systemic and multilevel understanding of European foreign policy; they have identified European foreign policy as the aggregate of the foreign policy of both Member States and the EU and offered a multilevel and systemic analysis of it. Some scholars, such as Karen Smith (2008) and Hazel Smith (2002), took the EU as an actor which has a foreign policy of its own and offered a single level analysis of European foreign policy, that is, the EU level. In these studies, the unit of analysis is the European Union Foreign Policy. Studies which analyze the EU as a foreign policy actor can be classified under two sets of studies: the first set of studies is those which emphasized the state-like features of the EU and offered the analysis of the EU's foreign policy just like as if it were a nation-state. Such studies can be identified as state-centric analyses of European foreign policy (ibid.); the second set of studies is those which emphasize distinctive and unique characteristics of the EU and offered alternative concepts for the analysis of the EU's foreign policy (see Allen and Smith 1990,

1998; Hill 1993; Bretherton and Vogler 2006; Manners and Whitman 1998, 2003; Duchéne 1972, 1973; Manners 2002).

This book is located in the second set of studies which takes the EU as an actor with a foreign policy of its own, highlights distinctive and unique characteristics of the EU and offers alternative concepts for the analysis of the EU's foreign policy. Brian White (2004: 16–17) identified the studies in this tradition as 'the European Union-as-actor' approach which concentrates on the impact of Europe on world politics. Roy H. Ginsberg and Michael E. Smith (2007: 268) divided studies on EU foreign policy into two essential areas: the internal dimensions and external dimensions of EU foreign policy. These studies focusing on external dimensions of EU foreign policy, which deal with the EU's impact on specific problems outside the EU itself, rather than the internal dimensions of the EU foreign policy which deal with institution building, policy-making and the influence of EU foreign policy on EU Member States, belong to studies examining external dimensions of EU foreign policy.

Brian White (2004: 17) argues that scholars such as David Allen and Michael Smith, Gunnar Sjostedt, Bretherton and Vogler, François Duchéne and Ian Manners and Richard Whitman have moved beyond a state model to identify a distinctive non-state but nevertheless collective entity, with the European Union providing the actor focus of analysis. Ben Tonra (2006: 124) put forward the suggestion that these approaches had striven to deconstruct state-centric views of world politics by shifting analysis away from how state-like the EU's foreign policy is towards analysis of its presence, actorness. These approaches are holistic approaches to an analysis which focuses on singleness and unitaryness of the EU. In these studies, the EUFP has been analyzed at the EU level, so in these studies the EU is taken as the level of analysis. Accordingly, the object or the unit of analysis is the EUFP. In these, the main objective is to find out how the EU's role in international politics can be best conceptualized and characterized. In these studies, deductive strategy was used for identification and conceptualization of the EU's international role. First of all, an 'ideal type' role concept or a conceptual category was constructed and then it was used to explain and understand the international role of the EU. The EU's role literature can be classified as: the EU as a presence, the EU as an actor, the EU as an international identity, the EU as a civilian power and the EU as a normative power. After presenting different conceptual approaches to European foreign policy analysis, the next section will discuss the application of role theory to European foreign policy analysis and describe potential contributions of this book to the existing literature.

Role Theory and European Foreign Policy Analysis

Lisbeth Aggestam (2004) employed role theory for the first time in analyzing European foreign policy. She analyzed the foreign policies of the three largest Member States of the EU: Britain, France and Germany in the post-Cold War Europe. She carried out a comparative analysis of British, French and German conceptions of identity and role in order to find out the role the state performs as an agent of foreign policy action in Europe during the period between 1990 and 1999. On the basis of her comparative role analysis of British, French and German foreign policies, Aggestam found that during the 1990s, as a result of the process of Europeanization, the foreign policy role sets of Britain, France and Germany had been transformed. Thus, she concluded that at the end of 1990s, policy-makers of the three largest Member States of the EU gradually converged on a common role conception of Europe as an ethical power. In her study, the main aim is to investigate the changing role of the state as the agent of foreign policy action; hence she took the state as an agent of foreign policy action in Europe rather than the EU itself.

Following Aggestam, in their study *The European Union's Roles in International Politics* Ole Elgström and Michael Smith applied role theory to the analysis of European foreign policy. Unlike Aggestam's study, their analytical focus is the EU itself. Their study took the EU as an agent of foreign policy for the first time. They argued that previous studies on the analysis of the EU foreign policy had not referred to role theory as deployed in the foreign policy analysis literature as used in Holsti, Walker and Le Prestre's studies (Elgström and Smith 2006: 124). They put forward the idea that role theory has potential analytical utility in analyzing EU foreign policy. Their innovative study showed the utility of role theory as an analytical framework in the analysis of the EU foreign policy and paved the way for further studies.

Drawing upon Ole Elgström and Michael Smith's argument, this book takes the EU foreign and security policy as the object of analysis and role theory as theoretical framework for analyzing it. In this book, the analytical focus is the EU level and the EU is analyzed as an actor which has a foreign and security policy of its own. What this effectively means is that this book examines the EU as an actor which has a foreign and security policy more than the sum of the foreign and security policies of its Member States. For the purposes of this book, the EU's foreign and security policy refers to the official politico-security rhetoric (role conceptions) and actions and decisions (role performance) of the EU formulated and implemented by the authorized agents of the EU (the High Representative for the CFSP and the EU Commissioner for External Relations and European Neighbourhood Policy) and directed towards the external environment of the EU with the purpose of promoting the domestic values and interests of the EU. In this book, as the analytical focus is the EU level discourse, the speeches of principal EU foreign and security policy officials, and the EU official documents concerning foreign and security policy of the EU are analyzed in order to identify role conceptions of the EU. In their study Elgström and Smith have argued that a gap, which they call the 'conception-performance gap', exists between role conceptions and role performance in EU's foreign policy. In this book, the relationship between the EU's role conception and its actual role performance is analyzed and whether there is a 'conception-performance gap' in the EU's foreign and security policy regarding the MEPP in the post-9/11 era is explored.

Since this book focuses on the EU's own definitions of its role as a foreign and security policy actor, the main emphasis is on agency rather than structure or interaction. Drawing on this point, the book focuses on the intentional sources of roles, mainly on the self-defined role conceptions of the EU, rather than structural or interactional sources of roles. Walter Carlsnaes, in his article 'Where is the Analysis of European Foreign Policy Going?' (2004: 505; 2006: 556), mentioned about four perspectives in foreign policy analysis: structural perspective; socio-institutional perspective; agency-based perspective and interpretative actor perspective. For him, interpretative actor perspective is based on the reconstruction of the reasoning of individual or group policy-makers. Carlsnaes (2004: 506) argued that the interpretative actor perspective can be utilized for penetrating the teleological links between intentions and foreign policy actions. This book, which focuses on the relationship between the roles the EU aspires to play and its actual foreign policy decisions and actions, belongs to the interpretative actor perspective among these four perspectives.

When compared to previous studies on the analysis of the EU foreign policy, this book is innovative in terms of its objective and methodology. Unlike previous studies, the aim of the book is not to construct an 'ideal type' role concept or a conceptual category and use it to explain and understand the international role of the EU, but to test congruity between the EU's self-defined role conceptions and its role performance. In this book, as a methodological strategy for the identification and conceptualization of the EU's international role, a bottom-up perspective is preferred to a top-down perspective. The EU's role conceptions and categories are inductively constructed in terms of how the EU's roles are defined in the speeches delivered by three principal EU foreign and security policy officials concerning foreign and security policy of the EU, and the EU official documents concerning foreign and security policy of the EU. What this effectively means is that role concepts, which are identified as appropriate for the EU to perform in international politics, are defined by the EU.

Studying the congruity between the EU's role conceptions and its actual role performance would contribute to the literature on the analysis of the EU foreign policy by diverting the attention from how to best characterize the EU's role in international politics to assessing the effectiveness, efficiency and credibility of the EU as a foreign and security policy actor.

Research Design and Methodology

In addition to Stephen Walker's assertion that role theory has served more as a conceptual framework within which scholars from various disciplines have conducted research using range of methodologies, Bruce Biddle (1979: 2) identified role theory as methodologically neutral; he further argued that role concepts have been studied with nearly all of the methodological tools used by social scientists. In this book, qualitative content analysis and case study method have been utilized as methodological tools.

Content analysis is a method which enables researchers to examine human behaviour in an indirect way, through an analysis of their communications. In content analysis, usually, but not necessarily, the written content of a communication is analyzed. The contents of virtually any type of communication can be analyzed, including essays, newspapers, magazine articles, political speeches, etc. (Fraenkel and Wallen 2006: 483). In this book, content analysis is used as a methodological tool to identify the EU's foreign and security policy role conceptions defined in the post-9/11 era. Content analytic method is appropriate for the identification of role conceptions because, as Carl W. Backman (1970: 311) argued, by referring to Holsti's study, inductive approach through content analysis provided a much richer classification of roles.

There are six main stages in content analysis: determining objectives of the content analysis, defining the population, determining the sample (developing a sampling plan), specifying the unit of analysis, formulating coding categories and interpreting content analysis data.

Accordingly, in the first stage of the research, the objective of the content analysis was determined. Determining the objective is crucial for energy and time saving, because by determining specific objectives we want to accomplish, we can confine our analysis to a certain aspect of communication rather than examining all its aspects (Bilgin 2006: 11). The objective of the content analysis in this book is to find out which role(s) does/do the EU define for itself as a foreign and security policy actor in the post-9/11 era? In other words, the objective is to identify the EU's foreign and security policy role conceptions, the roles that the EU aspires to play as a foreign and security actor, in the post-9/11 era.

In the second stage of the research, the population for the study was defined. The population is the set of units from which the researcher wishes to generalize (Neuendorf 2002: 74). For content analysis, the population, which is often a set of messages, serves as the basis for any sampling (ibid.). In this book, the population from which the sample was drawn was defined as the speeches of principal EU foreign and security policy officials and the EU official documents concerning foreign and security policy of the EU referring to the EU's general long-term responsibilities, obligations, functions, duties and orientations as a foreign and security policy actor and belonging to the period extending from 11 September 2001 to 31 December 2006.

In the third stage of the research, the sample that would be used in the analysis was determined. Determining a sample is the process of selecting a subset of units for research from the larger population (ibid.). By using the method of purposive sampling,[1] the speeches delivered by three principal EU foreign and security policy officials, including the office holder of the High Representative for the CFSP of the EU/Secretary General of the Council of the EU Javier Solana (1999–2009); the office holders of the EU Commissioner for External Relations and European Neighbourhood Policy, Chris Patten (1999–2004) and Benita Ferrero-Waldner (2004–2009) referring to range of foreign and security policy issues rather than speeches referring to specific foreign and security policy issues during the period extending from 11 September 2001 to 31 December 2006 were sampled. In addition to principal EU foreign policy officials' speeches, the EU official documents concerning foreign and security policy of the EU, including ESS, statements of the Council of the European Union, European Commission's communications and Founding Treaties of the European Union were sampled.

In this book, the content of general foreign policy speeches delivered by the principal EU foreign policy officials, Javier Solana, Chris Patten and Benita Ferrero-Waldner, referring to the EU's general roles as a foreign and security actor in international context rather than speeches referring to its role in specific issues during the period extending from 11 September 2001 to 31 December 2006, was reviewed. The speeches examined were limited to pronouncements of these three principal EU foreign policy officials, because they were principal officials in the formation, preparation and the implementation of the EU's foreign and security policy, for the reason that it could be confidently assumed that their speeches tend to reflect general long-term responsibilities, obligations, functions, duties and orientations of the EU in foreign and security policy. To put it another way, it was assumed that their speeches would represent the institutional self-conception and self-definition of the EU's general long-term responsibilities, obligations, functions, duties and orientations as a foreign and security policy actor. As argued by Henrik Larsen, in his article 'The EU: A Global Military Actor', the discourse of the high representative, Javier Solana, was assumed to represent the language of the Council context, because he has acted within the Council sphere as he legally has acted by the delegation of the Council.[2] In a similar way, it can be assumed that the discourse of the EU Commissioner for External Relations and European Neighbourhood Policy represents the language of the Commission context, because he/she has acted within the Commission sphere as he/she legally has acted by the delegation of the Commission. The speeches were obtained mostly from the official homepage of Javier Solana, the official webpage of the European Commission and other internet sources.

Furthermore, the selected sample was confined to general foreign policy speeches setting out broad outlines of the EU's foreign and security policy and embraced a variety of issues, rather than speeches referring to the EU's role in a specific geographical region like the Middle East, the Balkans and Africa, or specific issues like the conflicts in those areas. Moreover, the sample is confined to speeches referring to the EU's foreign and security policy roles in a international context rather than referring to EU's role in international political economy like the EU's role as a model of regional integration and its role as promoter of inter-regionalism.

The EU official documents concerning foreign and security policy of the EU were also sampled in order to complement the principal EU foreign policy officials' speeches. Since the EU's foreign and security policy has an intergovernmental character, the general purpose and orientation of the EU's foreign and security policy is determined by EU Member States by consensus. On foreign and security policy issues, the European Council composed of heads of state and government of EU Member States defines the general policy guidelines for EU's foreign and security policy and GAERC composed of foreign ministers of EU Member States takes the necessary decisions for defining and implementing the EU's foreign and security policy on the basis of the general guidelines defined by the European Council. Because of this, in the EU context in order to identify role conceptions for the EU in the area of foreign and security policy, the content of the EU official documents concerning foreign and security policy was analyzed in addition to speeches of the principal EU foreign policy officials.

I selected the EU official documents concerning foreign and security policy of the EU, such as ESS, statements of the Council of the European Union, European Commission's communications and Founding Treaties of the European Union for identifying role conceptions, because, although these documents are prepared by the EU foreign policy officials, they are adopted by the EU leaders on the basis of consensus and therefore it could be confidently assumed that their contents tend to reflect the role conceptions for the EU shared by all EU Member States. To put it another way, it was assumed that these documents would represent EU Member States' collective or shared conception and definition of the EU's general long-term responsibilities, obligations, functions, duties and orientations as a foreign and security policy actor. It was assumed that the EU official documents represented a common language and understanding in the EU context. Just like the speeches, the selected sample of official documents was limited to general foreign policy documents setting out broad outlines of the EU's foreign and security policy and embraced a variety of issues, rather than documents referring to the EU's role in a specific geographical regions or issues.

In the fourth stage of the research, the unit of analysis was specified. In content analysis, a unit is an identifiable message or message component, which serves as the basis for identifying the population and drawing a sample; on which variables are measured; or which serves as the basis for reporting analysis (Neuendorf 2002: 71). Units can be words, characters, themes, interactions, or any other result of 'breaking up a "communication" into pieces' (ibid.). In this book, words, phrases and sentences referring to the EU's general foreign and security policy roles were specified as units of analysis.

In the fifth stage of the research, coding categories were formulated. In content analysis, there are two means of categorization.

The first is coding data by using predetermined categories. The second is coding data by using categories that emerge as the data are reviewed (Fraenkel and Wallen 2006: 507). In this research, the latter was employed. Since the objective of this research is to identify the EU's self-identified roles, by relying on Kalevi Jacques Holsti and Lisbeth Aggestam's methodology (see Holsti 1970: Aggestam 2005), rather than coding data into predetermined categories, I preferred to develop categories based on the data and then code the data through a preliminary reading of the speeches and official documents. This preliminary reading was carried out by reading speeches and official documents and noting role statements expressed in the speeches and official documents with reference to the EU's general long-term responsibilities, obligations, functions, duties and orientations as a foreign and security policy actor. In this preliminary reading, I sought to single out statements which contained themes giving evidence of the presence of role conceptions. As a result of this preliminary role analysis carried out in the initial stages of research, a basic typology of role conceptions around which analysis revolved emerged. This typology was then refined as the research process progressed, but its basic structure did not fundamentally change. As seen from Table 2.1, for some role conceptions, several alternative role statements were determined and as the research process progressed they were refined and reduced to one role conception. These basic roles constitute the coding categories used in the analysis.

Table 2.1   Basic Typology of EU's Role Conceptions in the Post-9/11 Era Emerging from Preliminary Role Analysis

1. Force for good
2. Force for international peace, security and stability, net exporter of stability, enabler for peace, security and stability
3. Developer, provider of development aid, key donor
4. Promoter of its values and norms, promoter of democracy, human rights, rule of law and good governance
5. Promoter of effective multilateralism
6. Partner for the UN, supporter of the UN
7. Builder of effective partnership with key actors, global ally

In the sixth stage of the research, content analysis data was interpreted. In content analysis, a common mean of interpreting the data is frequency analysis, which is carried out by counting the incidences of certain words, phrases, symbols, or other manifest content and measuring their percentage and/or proportion of particular incidences against total incidences in the selected sample (Fraenkel and Wallen 2006: 491). However, this research does not aim to measure the frequency of the role statements in the speeches and official documents. The objective of this research is to identify the EU's foreign and security policy role conceptions defined in the post-9/11 era. Therefore, frequency analysis of the role statements including counting words or phrases referring to role statements and measuring the percentage of their incidences to total incidences was left out of this research. Rather than focusing on quantitative, proportional or percentage analysis of data, this research focused on qualitative analysis of data.

As a result of the qualitative content analysis of data, seven role conceptions were identified: 'force for good', 'force for international peace, security and stability', 'promoter of its values and norms', 'the provider of development aid', 'promoter of effective multilateralism', 'partner for the UN' and 'builder of effective partnership with key actors'. At this stage, 60 speeches and official documents which included words, phrases and sentences referring to one or more of the above outlined roles were selected and coded. In this analysis, either manifest or latent content of the speeches and official documents were coded.

Manifest content of a communication refers to the obvious, surface content – the words, pictures, images, and so on that are easily discerned by the naked eye or ear. No inferences as to underlying meaning are necessary (Fraenkel and Wallen 2006: 488).

Latent content of a communication refers to the meaning underlying what is said and shown (ibid.: 489). In my analysis, latent content of the speeches and official documents were also coded. The words, phrases and sentences implying the EU's role conceptions rather than obviously referring to them were examined.

While the method of coding manifest content provides the researcher with the advantage of ease of the coding and reliability, another researcher is likely to arrive at the same conclusions (coding manifest content provides high inter-coder reliability[3] scores), the method of coding latent content provides the researcher with advantage of getting at the underlying meaning of what is written or said, but carries the risk of having lower reliability scores, so another researcher would probably arrive at different conclusions (the problem of external coder or inter-coder reliability) (ibid.: 489–90). In order to deal with reliability problem, I utilized both methods and tried to keep the method of coding latent content to a minimum as fas as possible.

After identifying role conceptions, the congruity between EU's self-defined role conceptions and its actual role performance was tested by using case study method. In order to test the congruity between EU's role conceptions and its role performance; the MEPP was selected as a specific case study. In order to analyze the congruity between EU's self-defined role conceptions and its actual role performance, I focused on the EU's role performance in the MEPP during the same period in which role conceptions were defined; the period extending from 11 September 2001 to 31 December 2006.

The MEPP was selected as a specific case study, because the Middle East is a prominent region for both the EU and its Member States. The Middle East, specifically the Arab-Israeli conflict and the subsequent peace process has been a foreign policy priority for the EU since it was first able to act as a (more or less) coherent international actor with the introduction of EPC (Smith 2002). In the ESS, resolution of the Arab-Israeli conflict is identified as the strategic priority of Europe and it is stated that the EU must remain engaged and ready to commit resources to the problem until it is solved. It is identified by the EU officials as 'the mother of all conflicts in the Middle East'.[4] It is considered as a single strategic threat to Middle Eastern security, with which the solution of other conflicts is bound up (ibid.). There are three main reasons for this.

The first one is the geographical proximity of the region to Europe; any social and political instability or insecurity such as the rise of radical Islamism and terrorism in the Middle East would adversely affect the EU's internal social and political stability and security due to spillover effect. In terms of internal social and political stability, the presence of important Jewish and Muslim minorities in some European states results in European concerns about the disastrous impact of any hardening of the Arab-Israeli conflict on internal social cohesion (Schmid et al. 2006: 9). Moreover, uncontrolled migration flow from the region is perceived by Europeans as a challenge to their security and stability. Particularly in the post-Cold War era, EU policy-makers started to consider stability in the Middle East as an integral part of 'security in Europe' (Bilgin 2004: 274). It has been confirmed by EU officials that security in Europe is directly related to security in the Middle East.[5] Accordingly, they have sought to create cooperative schemes with the Mediterranean-rim countries of the Middle East to encourage and support economic development and growth with the expectation of helping to reduce refugee flows from the Middle East to Europe and prevent regional conflicts like the Arab-Israeli conflict being exported to the EU (Bilgin 2004: 274).

The second reason is related to energy security. European states are largely dependent on Middle Eastern oil and natural gas and wanted to ensure a sustained flow of oil and natural gas at reasonable prices (Bilgin 2005: 140).

The third reason is that some of EU Member States, Britain and France have a special relationship with the region because of their status of being former colonial powers in the region. Due to these reasons, preservation of the security, stability and peace in the Middle East is very crucial for EU Member States and the EU. That is why they have sought to be actively involved and play an active role in the Arab-Israeli conflict and the MEPP since early 1970s.

The EU has managed to be actively involved in the MEPP in the 1990s and its involvement has increased in the post-9/11 era. The EU is one of the members of the Quartet on the Middle East, which was designed to mediate the peace process and is composed of the EU, the USA, the UN and Russia. In addition to that, the EU has continued to be the largest donor of financial aid to the Palestinian Authority and the MEPP. The EU supported the reform process of the Palestinian Authority towards the creation of an independent, economically and politically viable, sovereign and democratic Palestinian state. The EU supported the Palestinian reform process in areas of the promotion of judicial independence, promotion of accountability and transparency in the fiscal system, the security sector reform, reform of administration and the executive, holding of free and fair elections, developing a modern education system and media based on peace, tolerance and mutual understanding, the promotion of pro-peace civil society.

The EU also increased its role in the security dimension of the MEPP with the launch of two ESDP operations: EUPOL COPPS and EUBAM Rafah. In the post-9/11 era, the EU remained committed to a negotiated settlement resulting in two states, Israel and an independent, viable, sovereign and democratic Palestinian state, living side by side in peace and security on the basis of the 1967 borders and in the framework of a just, lasting and comprehensive peace in the Middle East, basing on UN Security Council Resolutions 242, 338 and 1515, the terms of reference of Madrid Conference of 2002 and the principle of 'land for peace'. Thus, it can be observed that the EU has been actively involved in the MEPP in the post-9/11 era. Because of this, this issue has been selected as a specific case study in order to test congruity between the EU's self-defined role conceptions and its actual role performance.

Although I focus on the EU's role performance in the post-9/11 era, I also investigate the EU's involvement in the MEPP from the 1970s up to 1990s as a historical overview in order to better understand and analyze the EU's role performance in the MEPP in the post-9/11 era. This historical overview is worth analyzing and evaluating, since it will help to understand better and analyze the EU's role performance in the MEPP in the post-9/11 era as well as to uncover the change and continuity in the EU's policy.

The period extending from 11 September 2001 to 31 December 2006 was selected as the focus of analysis due to several reasons. First of all, during this period, particularly since 9/11, US policy towards the MEPP changed and the USA decided to adopt a multilateral approach to the peace process, with cooperation with European governments (Musu 2007a: 21). As a result, the Quartet on the Middle East, which provided a multilateral framework for the EU's participation in the political and diplomatic dimension of the MEPP, was established. The EU has played an active role in the political and diplomatic dimension of the peace process. Furthermore, during this period the EU started to play a prominent role in the security dimension of the peace process through its ESDP operations. During this period, an increase in international recognition of the EU as a significant player in the political, diplomatic, security dimension of the Middle East conflict has been observed. Secondly, during this period, a revival of peace process which was blocked since the second half of 1990s has also been seen.

Despite continuing mutual violence between the Israelis and the Palestinians especially, since the outbreak of Al-Aqsa Intifada in September 2000, with the launch of the Roadmap by the Quartet in April 2003, the blocked road to the peace in the Middle East opened. Despite the international community's efforts, at the end of 2005, which constituted the deadline set by the Roadmap for the final settlement of the Arab-Israeli conflict, the Roadmap was stuck in gridlock. Israeli unilateral actions, including the construction of Security Fence and Disengagement Plan, and continuing mutual violence between the Israelis and the Palestinians decreased the prospect of the successful implementation of the Roadmap and led it into a dead end. Moreover, in 2006, significant events, which had decisive effects on the MEPP, had taken place. The first was Hamas's sweeping victory in the Palestinian legislative election of 2006, and the Quartet's decision to boycott the Hamas-led Palestinian government when it refused to meet and implement the three principles put forward by the Quartet on the Middle East including non-violence comprising the laying down of arms, recognition of Israel's right to exist and acceptance and fulfilment of existing agreements and obligations, including the Roadmap. The EU also decided to impose sanctions on the Hamas-led Palestinian government and suspend its direct aid. Due to the escalation of violence in the region, the EU's two ESDP operations in the Palestinian Territories were temporarily suspended. The second event was the Israel-Lebanon War of 2006 and subsequent huge military contribution of EU Member States to the expanded UNIFIL by providing the backbone of the force, which enabled EU Member States' significant military presence in the region. All-in-all, this five-year period, in which a revival and then gridlock in the peace process was observed, as well as an increase in the EU's presence, involvement and role in the political, diplomatic, security dimension of the Middle East conflict, was considered as the appropriate period of time in order to test the congruity between EU's role conceptions and its role performance.

CHAPTER 3

THE EU'S FOREIGN AND SECURITY POLICY: ROLE CONCEPTIONS IN THE POST-9/11 INTERNATIONAL SECURITY ENVIRONMENT

The objective of this chapter is to identify the roles that the EU aspires to play as a foreign and security actor in the post-9/11 era. It was carried out by analyzing the content of the general foreign policy speeches delivered by the principal EU foreign policy officials and the EU official documents. The empirical study of roles in this chapter was conducted inductively in terms of how the EU's roles are defined in the speeches delivered by three principal EU foreign and security policy officials and the EU official documents. As a result of content analysis, seven role conceptions were identified: 'force for good', 'force for international peace, security and stability', 'promoter of its values and norms', 'the provider of development aid', 'promoter of effective multilateralism', 'partner for the UN' and 'builder of effective partnership with key actors'. These seven role conceptions provide an outline of main roles at work within the EU's role set in the post-9/11 era (Table 3.1).

Table 3.1   EU's Role Set in the Post-9/11 Era

Force for good
Force for international peace, security and stability
The provider of development aid
Promoter of its values and norms
Promoter of effective multilateralism
Partner for the UN
Builder of effective partnership with key actors

Force for Good

This role conception implies the EU's responsibility and duty to make the world a better place for everybody by making the world freer, more peaceful, fairer, more prosperous, more secure and more stable.

This role conception refers to universal ethics which is the 'global common good' (Aggestam 2008: 6). The High Representative for the CFSP of the EU, Javier Solana in one of his speeches noted that the EU's international role should be to work for the global common good. He pointed out that

> The EU has a responsibility to work for the 'global common good'. That is a fitting way of describing the EU's global role and ambition (Solana, 24 January 2005).

This role conception points to the belief that the foreign policy objectives of the EU are based on the universal promotion of peace, security, stability, democracy, human rights, rule of law and good governance, and multilateralism besides the protection of the EU's citizens and self-interests. Javier Solana emphasized the ambition of the EU to act as a force for good in his speeches. He stated that

> The idealism behind the EU's foundation is vital to defining who and what we are today. And it helps to appreciate the value of the European Union as a force for good in the world. We have carefully built a zone of peace, democracy and the rule of law of more than 500 million people. Now we have to extend that zone further. And to answer the call for Europe to act. To promote

peace and protect the vulnerable. That is the aim of the CFSP. It is also my personal mission. It may be hard for some to imagine that in Asia, Africa and Latin America, people speak with great admiration of the European experience (Solana, 23 November 2006).

This role conception holds that the EU's foreign and security policy should not be understood as altruistic and other-serving or other-regarding. The EU's foreign and security policy as a force for good is not based on altruism and moral absolutism in terms of self-sacrifice at all times, nor is it devoid of interests. Material interests and ethical considerations tend to be interlinked. So, it should be recognized that the EU, like any other international actor, has mixed motives (Aggestam 2008: 8). The motives behind the EU foreign and security policy are both other-serving (other-regarding) and self-serving (self-regarding) and self-interested. The EU, as a force for good, acts for the well-being of both its citizens and others. The EU as a force for good is expected to defend both its citizens and others rather than to defend against others. According to this role conception, while pursuing European interests more cohesively, the EU is also contributing to a better world by strengthening justice (human rights) and order (effective multilateralism). Esther Barbé and Elisabeth Johansson-Nogués argued that in order to be a force for good, there is need for balance and equilibrium between material interests and ethical considerations. There is a need for ethically balanced policy. For them, in order to be a 'force for good', the EU needs to balance member and non-member concerns and satisfy the preferences of all actors involved (2008: 85). The preference equilibrium would result in collective welfare (ibid.). In his speeches Javier Solana has underlined the EU's need to develop ethically balanced policy, in which equilibrium exists between material interests and ethical considerations, as a force for good. He stated that 'the rationale is double: to advance our interests and protect our citizens. But also, and I insist, to have Europe act as a force for good in the world' (Solana, 9 November 2005).

In the article 2.5 of the Treaty of Lisbon Amending the Treaty on European Union and the Treaty Establishing the European

Community, the EU's need to develop ethically balanced policy was emphasized. It was noted that

> In its relations with the wider world, the Union shall uphold and promote its values and interests and contribute to the protection of its citizens. It shall contribute to peace, security, the sustainable development of the Earth, solidarity and mutual respect among peoples, free and fair trade, eradication of poverty and the protection of human rights, in particular the rights of the child, as well as to the strict observance and the development of international law, including respect for the principles of the United Nations Charter (Art. 2.5, Treaty of Lisbon Amending the Treaty on European Union and the Treaty Establishing the European Community).

The EU as a force for good is expected to use its force for the good of the community of peoples as a whole, namely, in the universal pursuit of peace, prosperity, democracy and human rights (Aggestam 2008: 8). This role conception puts emphasis on duties and responsibilities to others. According to article 2.1 of the Treaty of Lisbon Amending the Treaty on European Union and the Treaty Establishing the European Community, the EU's aim is to promote peace, its values and the well-being of its peoples.

The EU as a force for good should work on the basis of the interests of the community of peoples as a whole rather than solely those of its own interests. According to Lisbeth Aggestam (ibid.: 1), the EU's role as a force for good represents a conceptual shift in its role and aspirations from what it is to what it does; from simply representing a power of attraction and a positive role model to proactively working to change the world in the direction of its vision of the global common good. The vision of global common good refers to the EU's duties and responsibilities to make the world a better place for the whole community of peoples, including both Europeans and non-Europeans, by making the world freer, more peaceful, fairer, more prosperous, more secure and more stable. This vision is reflected in the EU's universal promotion of peace, security, stability, prosperity, democracy, human rights, rule of law, good governance and multilateralism.

Force for International Peace, Security and Stability

This role conception first of all refers to the EU's status of being a zone or pole of stability, security and peace in the world. Javier Solana emphasized the EU's status of being a pole of stability, security and peace in his speeches. He pointed out that

> In this new geo-political landscape the European Union is an attractive pole of stability, democracy and prosperity. We have maximized our status as a 'net exporter of stability' by acknowledging legitimate aspirations to join our Union; while emphasizing that this is dependent on a commitment to our common values (Solana, 23 May 2002).

This role conception emphasizes the necessity of exporting the EU's stability, security and peace to both the EU's neighbourhood and the wider world by using the EU's various foreign policy instruments including political, diplomatic, military and civilian, trade and development instruments. In one of his speeches (24 July 2002) Javier Solana stated that the EU has the declared ambition to contribute to peace and stability worldwide through the complementary deployment of a wide array of instruments (trade, aid, technical assistance, police training, etc.) including, where appropriate, military assets.

The scope of the EU's promotion of stability, security and peace is not limited to only EU's near abroad rather it has a global scope. This role conception is expressed in statements of Benita Ferrero-Waldner, the EU Commissioner for External Relations and European Neighbourhood Policy, who argued that the EU has the obligation to export peace, stability and prosperity which Europeans enjoyed in the EU to its Eastern and Southern neighbours, because otherwise in the long run it imports instability from its neighbourhood (Ferrero-Waldner, 14 December 2005). Thus, she asserted that exporting stability, security and peace the EU has enjoyed to its neighbours is in the enlightened self-interest of the EU (ibid.: Ferrero-Waldner, 10 February 2006). This means that while the EU is acting to further the interests of others, ultimately it serves its own self-interest. It is based on the belief that it can 'do well by doing good'.

It is also emphasized in the ESS that it is in the EU's interest that countries on its borders are well-governed and because of this the EU should extend its benefits of economic and political cooperation to its neighbours in the East and tackle political problems there by using the full spectrum of instruments. In the ESS, the EU's promotion of security, stability and peace is identified as some form of self-defence. It is stated that with the new threats in the post-Cold War era, the first line of defence will often be abroad, that is, beyond the EU's borders. The EU's promotion of security, stability and peace is seen as self-serving. The EU's promotion of security, stability and peace refers to a positive-sum and win-win situation in which both the EU and its neighbourhood mutually enjoy peace, security and stability with the EU's promotion of security, stability and peace. This argument is based on the idea that the world is interdependent and the EU should deal with the situations which in the future may adversely affect its security and stability. According to Benita Ferrero-Waldner, enlargement and European Neighbourhood Policy (ENP) are two key tools for promoting the security, stability and peace the EU has enjoyed beyond its borders.

Enlargement is one of the EU's most powerful and effective foreign policy tools for promoting peace, security and stability within Europe. Enlargement is a process which helps the democratic and economic transformation of the candidate countries by encouraging extensive political and economic reforms in candidate and potential candidate countries. With enlargement the EU has successfully used its membership conditionality to export its economic and political models to first Southern Europe in 1980s and then to Central and Eastern Europe in 1990s. The carrot of the EU membership helped to transform Southern Europe and Central and Eastern Europe into modern, stable, prosperous, well-functioning democracies. So, through enlargement by using its transformative power the EU has extended peace, security and stability in Europe. Javier Solana emphasized the importance of enlargement as a policy tool for promoting peace, security and stability within Europe in his speeches. He noted that

> We want to make Europe safer, more stable. The European Union's
> fundamental policy of inclusiveness has made enlargement

inevitable: it has brought peace and prosperity to all countries who have become its members, and has brought stability to the region (Solana, 25 March 2002).

In another speech, he identified the enlargement as vital for promoting peace, security and stability as well. He pointed out that

> Enlargement is essential for stability. This is not only a historical or even 'moral' duty. It is also a process fundamental for stability and security in Europe. Membership of the Union, beyond reforms and economic development, means stability for the countries concerned. The prospect of accession has contributed decisively to stabilizing central and Eastern Europe, which is the primary objective of our policy. Through enlargement the Union creates stability around it by using its force of attraction (Solana, 1 March 2001).

The ENP is a key instrument for the promotion of security, stability and peace in the EU's eastern and southern neighbours, including Eastern Europe, South Caucasus, North Africa and the Middle East. The ENP, which is the EU's newest foreign policy tool, has the objective of sharing the benefits of the EU's 2004 enlargement with neighbouring countries in strengthening stability, security and well-being for all concerned. It is designed to prevent the emergence of new dividing lines between the enlarged EU and its neighbours and to offer them the chance to participate in various EU activities, through greater political, security, economic and cultural cooperation. The ENP is designed to prevent the emergence of a sense of exclusion on the part of the neighbours of the enlarged EU and to prevent enlargement to act as a divisive and destabilizing factor in the enlarged EU's neighbourhood, so it is an inclusionary process which aims to enable the EU's neighbours to utilize some benefits of EU membership without being a full member. It is a policy for encouraging stability, security and prosperity beyond the borders of the EU through regional integration (Kahraman 2005: 2). The ENP aims to improve security at the borders of the enlarged EU and to promote stability and prosperity beyond (ibid.: 15).

The ENP is not about enlargement and thus does not offer the prospect of membership. With the ENP, the EU offers its neighbours a privileged relationship, building on a mutual commitment to common values including the rule of law, good governance, the respect for human rights, including minority rights, the promotion of good neighbourly relations, and market economy principles and sustainable development. The ENP offers a deeper political relationship and economic integration. The level of ambition and pace of development of the relationship between the EU and each partner country will depend on the extent to which these values are effectively shared. In return for commitment to shared values, the EU offered each partner country increased market access and functional cooperation in a wide range of areas (ibid.: 16).

In the ENP, the emphasis is on creating a secure and stable neighbourhood rather than supporting the transition (ibid.: 17). The ENP is based on the logic of stabilization, which is related to the need for secured and properly managed external EU borders (ibid.: 26). The main aim of the ENP is to stabilize the neighbourhood of the enlarged EU. With the ENP, the EU has adopted a stabilization approach based on region-building, progressive economic integration and closer political cooperation, while excluding the prospect of membership (ibid.: 4). In the East where the enlarged EU shares a land border with the new neighbours, the EU is faced with many soft security challenges such as illegal trafficking, organized crime, terrorism and nuclear proliferation, and so needs to manage its external borders (ibid.). EU Member States recognized that they could not fence off instability behind ever tighter borders and this forced them to make a choice: whether to export stability and security to their near neighbours, or risk importing instability from them (Cremona 2004: 3). The security interdependence with the EU's neighbours and the task of extending zone of security, stability and prosperity across Europe is the main driving force behind the launch of the ENP (Kahraman 2005: 26). William Wallace (2003: 19) emphasized the EU's security interdependence with its neighbours and put forward the opinion that the EU's strongest self-interest lies in investing in stability and cooperation around its borders, since the costs of defending the EU from its unstable neighbourhood would be much higher than those of promoting prosperity and security beyond its borders.

Benita Ferrero-Waldner, the EU Commissioner for External Relations and European Neighbourhood Policy emphasized that the ENP serves the enlightened self-interest of the EU. She noted that

> The European Neighbourhood Policy (ENP) is founded on the premise that by helping our neighbours we help ourselves. It provides us with a new framework and new tools for promoting good government and economic development in the EU's neighbourhood. And it utilises the valuable experience we have already gained of assisting countries in transition...ENP is a win-win policy, based on mutual interest and shared values. We share our neighbours' desire to press forward with reform and become more prosperous and stable. We want to increase our security, prosperity and stability, and theirs. And we want to tackle our citizens' most pressing concerns – security, migration and economic prosperity (Ferrero-Waldner, 31 October 2005).

In her Guest Editorial published in *European Foreign Affairs Review*, Benita Ferrero-Waldner (2006) stated that the 'ENP will help make the European Union and its neighbourhood an area of peace, security and stability. And in so doing will bring a brighter future for both our citizens and those of our neighbours'.

In addition to the EU's soft power instruments (enlargement and the ENP) for promoting peace, security and stability, Javier Solana, the High Representative for the CFSP, emphasizes the importance of ESDP civilian and military crisis management operations carried out in different parts of the world such as Africa, the South Caucasus, the Western Balkans, the Middle East and Asia. These operations have demonstrated the EU's commitment to the promotion and protection of international peace, security and stability. Solana emphasized the importance of the ESDP as a policy tool for promoting peace, security and stability within Europe in one of his speeches as follows. He noted:

> Let me be clear: what we are doing is not about replacing NATO. Nor is it about militarizing the Union. It is about effective crisis management. About increasing the role of the European Union as a promoter of stability and security (Solana, 9 November 2005).

In another speech, Solana pointed out that through ESDP operations the EU has been able to act as a key enabler for peace and stability in the world:

> Last year, the European Union conducted 10 operations with around 10,000 men and women serving in them. The global reach and the scope of these different operations is striking. Across three continents, they cover the spectrum from 'pure' military operations – through security-sector reform and institution building – to police and rule-of-law missions. And their impact is significant. From Aceh to Rafah, and from Kinshasa to Sarajevo, the EU is providing the key enablers for peace and stability (Solana, 29 January 2007).

As can be seen, in the post-9/11 era the EU became a capable foreign and security policy actor that can mobilize both civilian and military instruments for promoting peace, security and stability.

The Provider of Development Aid

This role conception refers to the EU's development cooperation which has the aim of eradicating poverty in the context of sustainable development including the pursuit of the UN Millennium Development Goals.[1] This role conception emphasizes the EU's commitment to the UN Millennium Development Goals. It emphasizes the EU's commitment to meet its responsibility as a union of developed countries to help developing countries in their fight to eliminate extreme poverty, hunger, malnutrition and pandemics such as AIDS; in achieving universal primary education; in promoting gender equality and empowering women; in reducing the mortality rate of children; in improving maternal health; in achieving sustainable development, which includes good governance, human rights and political, economic, social and environmental aspects.

In the Joint Statement by the Council and Representative of Governments of the Member States Meeting Within the Council, the European Parliament and the Commission, titled as 'The European Consensus on Development', the central importance of the EU's development policy in the EU's external relations was emphasized as follows:

> Never before have poverty eradication and sustainable develop-ment been more important. The context within which poverty eradication is pursued is an increasingly globalised and inter-dependent world; this situation has created new opportunities but also new challenges. Combating global poverty is not only a moral obligation; it will also help to build a more stable, peace-ful, prosperous and equitable world, reflecting the interdepend-ency of its richer and poorer countries. In such a world, we would not allow 1,200 children to die of poverty every hour, or stand by while 1 billion people are struggling to survive on less than one dollar a day and HIV/AIDS and malaria claim the lives of more than 6 million people every year. Development policy is at the heart of the EU's relations with all developing countries (Council of the EU, 22 November 2005: 4).

This role conception put emphasis on the EU's standing of being the world's greatest donor of financial aid. The EU and its Member States spent an estimated €47 billion in 2006 in public aid to developing countries, of which about €7.5 billion was channelled through the EU (http://europa.eu/pol/dev/overview_en.htm). In his speeches Javier Solana emphasized the EU's status of being the world's largest donor of financial aid:

> The Union and its Member States together represent more than half of all financial aid to developing countries. This aid takes a variety of forms: grants, loans, technical and humanitarian assistance. It has sometimes to be recalled that even the finan-cial assistance paid out by international institutions like the IMF or the World Bank is to a very large extent European money.

> The USA is the largest single member country in these insti-tutions, but the EU is the largest payer. This does not mean that we could not be more generous. We certainly should be

more generous, and the EU has subscribed to the commitment of the Monterrey Conference last March to make finally significant steps towards increasing development assistance (Solana, 16 October 2002).

In addition to Solana, Benita Ferrero-Waldner also referred to the EU's status of being the world's largest donor of financial aid:

> Our soft power promotes stability, prosperity, democracy and human rights, delivering concrete results in the fight to eradicate poverty and in achieving sustainable development. The European Commission alone provides aid to more than 150 countries, territories and organizations around the world. We are a reliable partner over the long term, and as the world's biggest donor we help bring stability and prosperity to many parts of the world (Ferrero-Waldner, 2 February 2006).

As seen in the above quotation, the EU's development cooperation also corresponds to its soft power. The EU's role conception as the provider of development aid is closely connected with its role conception as a force for international peace, security and stability, because peace, security and stability are identified by the EU as indispensible for development and also development is seen as indispensible for them. It is argued that they can best be accomplished through development and development through them. Underdevelopment, which provides a breeding ground for insecurity and instability, is identified by the EU as one of the contemporary challenges to international security. For this reason, the EU grants central importance to development cooperation in its foreign and security policy. Javier Solana emphasized the link between security and development:

> Security is a precondition for development. We must re-double our efforts to combat the great ongoing challenges of extreme poverty, hunger and the new pandemics, breaking the cycles of insecurity and tackling bad governance, corruption and disregard of rule of law (Solana, 26 November 2003).

Besides Solana and the ESS, Benita Ferrero-Waldner also emphasized the link between security and development. She pointed out that

> The philosophy underlying the EU's approach to security, as outlined in the Security Strategy, is that security can best be attained through development, and development through security. Neither is possible without an adequate level of the other (Ferrero-Waldner, 30 May 2006).

As can be understood from the above quotation the ESS can be identified as the framework document which lays down a linkage between security and development:

> Security is a precondition of development. Conflict not only destroys infrastructure, including social infrastructure; it also encourages criminality, deters investment and makes normal economic activity impossible. A number of countries and regions are caught in a cycle of conflict, insecurity and poverty (European Security Strategy 2003).

As was mentioned in the introduction, in the ESS, for the first time in EU history, underdevelopment in non-European states was identified as a threat to the security of Europeans. In the post-9/11 era, underdevelopment, which provides a breeding ground for insecurity, is identified by the EU as one of the contemporary challenges to European security.

In another document, the link between security and development and their indispensability for each other was emphasized by the European Commission. It was stated that

> Development is crucial for collective and individual long-term security: they are complementary agendas and neither is subordinate to the other. There cannot be sustainable development without peace and security, and sustainable development is the best structural response to the deep–rooted causes of violent conflicts and the rise of terrorism, often linked to poverty, bad governance and the deterioration and lack of access to natural resources (Commission of the European Communities, 13 July 2005: 8).

In a Joint Statement by the Council and Representative of Governments of the Member States Meeting within the Council, the European Parliament and the Commission, entitled 'The European Consensus on Development', the link between security and development was emphasized. It was pointed out that

> Insecurity and violent conflict are amongst the biggest obstacles to achieving the Millennium Development Goals. Security and development are important and complementary aspects of EU relations with third countries. Within their respective actions, they contribute to creating a secure environment and breaking the vicious cycle of poverty, war, environmental degradation and failing economic, social and political structures.... Achieving the Millennium Development Goals is also in the interest of collective and individual long-term peace and security. Without peace and security development and poverty eradication are not possible, and without development and poverty eradication no sustainable peace will occur. Development is also the most effective long-term response to forced and illegal migration and trafficking of human beings. Development plays a key role in encouraging sustainable production and consumption patterns that limit the harmful consequences of growth for the environment (Council of the European Union, 2005: 14–15).

In one of its communications (Commission of the European Communities, 12 April 2005: 10) the European Commission reemphasized the link between security and development and noted that 'the EU will treat security and development as complementary agendas, with the common aim of creating a secure environment and of breaking the vicious circle of poverty, war, environmental degradation and failing economic, social and political structures'.

Promoter of its Values and Norms

This role conception put emphasis on the EU's standing of being a community of shared values. This role conception points to the belief that the EU is founded on values and norms such as respect for human dignity, liberty, fundamental freedoms, democracy, equality, rule of law, good governance and respect for human rights and minority rights, which are also at the core of the EU's relations with the rest of the world. These values and norms are not specific to the EU; they are widely shared by liberal democratic states, hence are universal in nature.

The EU's relations with the wider world are informed by these values and norms. The universal promotion of these values and norms through the world is identified as one of the main objectives and priorities of the EU's foreign policy:

> For now let me just reiterate that our goal will remain delivery of concrete achievements – the building blocks of Europe that Schuman spoke of – and promoting what we stand for around the world – global solidarity, multilateralism, democracy and human rights (Ferrero-Waldner, 2 February 2006).

The promotion of these values and norms is accepted to be closely connected with the protection of the security of the EU. This role conception emphasizes the necessity of promoting the EU's values and norms and establishing well-governed democratic states for the protection of the security of the EU and the strengthening of the international order. So, the promotion of the EU's values and norms is seen by the EU as in its enlightened self-interest. The motive behind the EU's promotion of its values and norms is seen as both other-serving and self-serving. In the ESS, the link between the EU's promotion of values and the protection of the security of the EU was emphasized:

> The best protection for our security is a world of well-governed democratic states. Spreading good governance, supporting social and political reform, dealing with corruption and abuse of power, establishing the rule of law and protecting human rights are the best means of strengthening the international order (European Security Strategy 2003).

The EU uses a wide range of instruments, including political, diplomatic instruments, economic instruments, financial instruments, aid and enlargement, for the promotion of its values and norms through the world. Benita Ferrero-Waldner referred to the EU's use of this wide range of instruments for the promotion of its values and norms. She pointed out that

> The respect for universal human rights, the rule of law and the promotion of democracy have for decades been at the very core of EU foreign policy. We use our foreign policy tools – aid, trade, and economic agreements – to promote human rights and good governance in every corner of the globe (Ferrero-Waldner, 1 June 2005).

Besides Ferrero-Waldner, Javier Solana also referred to the EU's use of enlargement for the promotion of democracy. He noted that

> For the European Union, the desire to promote democracy comes natural. The Union is based on a shared attachment to democracy. And through enlargement we have built an ever-widening area of freedom, democracy and stability across Europe. The European Union is also a model of what societies can achieve for their citizens. A source of inspiration, enticing governments to change the way their countries work. To support the momentum towards democratic change, the Union has developed an extensive set of policies and instruments (Solana, 4 May 2006).

Promoter of Effective Multilateralism

Katie Verlin Laatikainen and Karen Smith (2006: 2) put forward that effective multilateralism for the EU seems to imply making international organizations and agreements more effective. According to the European Commission's communication,

> An active commitment to an effective multilateralism means more than rhetorical professions of faith. It means taking global rules seriously, whether they concern the preservation of peace or the limitation of carbon emissions; it means helping other countries to implement and abide by these rules; it means

engaging actively in multilateral forums, and promoting a forward-looking agenda that is not limited to a narrow defence of national interests (Commission of the European Communities, 10 September 2003).

This role conception emphasizes the EU's commitment to the establishment of an effective multilateral system in which a stronger international society, well functioning international institutions and a rule-based international order plays a central role. In one of his speeches Javier Solana emphasized the EU's commitment to the establishment of an effective multilateral system:

> It is not enough to say we support multilateralism. We must be prepared to make it work. Making it work means extending the scope of international law. It means strengthening multilateral institutions. It means developing closer regional cooperation. I passionately believe that the security of the EU in the face of global threats can only be safeguarded if the fundamental values enshrined in the UN Charter and other international regimes and treaties are woven into an extensive web of multilateral instruments. And where international order is based on agreed rules, we must be prepared to ensure the respect of these rules when they are broken (Solana, 26 November 2003).

Benita Ferrero-Waldner also emphasized the EU's ambition of creation of multilateral world governed by multilateral institutions. She maintained that

> Our vision is a world governed by rules created and monitored by multilateral institutions.... This is where I come to the title of today's conference, our contribution to the 'quest for a multilateral world'. However, for a multilateral system to work, multilateral institutions must function properly and must be up to the challenges of the 21st century. So our quest should not only be for a multilateral world, but for effective multilateral institutions to govern it (Ferrero-Waldner, 4 July 2005).

In the ESS, the EU's commitment to the establishment of an effective multilateral system was identified as a necessity for the maintenance of its own security and prosperity. It was noted that

> In a world of global threats, global markets and global media, our security and prosperity increasingly depend on an effective multilateral system. The development of a stronger international society, well functioning international institutions and a rule-based international order is our objective (European Security Strategy 2003).

The EU identified the UN as the main expression of effective multilateralism (Menotti and Vencato 2008: 104). The UN lies at the centre of this multilateral system and it is accepted as the prime multilateral institution. The UN Charter and other international regimes and treaties constitute fundamental values and norms which are used to govern world that is based on an effective multilateral system. Benita Ferrero-Waldner emphasized the EU's commitment to the establishment of an effective multilateral system with the UN at the centre. She stated that

> The EU is convinced that only an effective multilateral system can adequately address the new and complex challenges the international community faces today. For that reason, the EU has made effective multilateralism with the UN at its core a central element of its external action. Effective multilateralism is more essential now than ever, and that is why it is one of the major priorities within my portfolio (Ferrero-Waldner, 8 December 2004).

The EU sees an effective multilateral system as the best means to guarantee its prosperity and security, thus it is committed to the proper functioning of multilateral institutions, which is essential for the working of rule-based order. This role conception holds that the main objective of the EU's foreign policy is to improve the effectiveness of multilateral institutions, predominantly the UN. Effective multilateralism is identified as the guiding principle of the EU's foreign and security policy. In a Communication entitled 'The European Union and the United Nations: The Choice of Multilateralism', the Commission identifies effective multilateralism as the guiding principle of the EU's foreign and security policy:

> The European Union's commitment to multilateralism is a defining principle of its external policy. Taking international cooperation as a precondition for meeting numerous global challenges, the EU has a clear interest in supporting the continuous evolution and improvement of the tools of global governance (Commission of the European Communities, 10 September 2003: 3).

This role conception notes that in order to effectively deal with contemporary global challenges and promote the EU's security, there is a need to cooperate with the EU's strategic partners such as the USA and other regional organizations ASEAN, MERCUSOR and African Union.

Partner for the UN

This role conception is closely connected with the EU's role conception as promoter of effective multilateralism. As the EU is committed to the establishment of rule governed effective multilateral system, the UN is seen by the EU as the most important partner for the establishment of such system. Javier Solana emphasized the importance of the UN for the multilateral system to which the EU is committed to. He stated that

> The European Union, as you know, is an organization that believes in multilateralism and therefore we believe in the United Nations and we are supporters of the United Nations as one of the most important priorities. The centre of gravity, the heart of the multilateral system . . . (Solana, 24 January 2007).

The EU is committed to upholding the universal values, norms, goals and principles enshrined in the UN Charter and supporting and strengthening the UN's efforts for the protection and promotion of regional and global peace, security, stability and prosperity. This role conception emphasizes the EU's responsibility to support and to strengthen the UN in order to fully enable the UN to fulfil its role effectively in seeking multilateral solutions to global problems on the basis of its Charter (European Union 2004). In the ESS, it was noted that

> Strengthening the United Nations, equipping it to fulfil its responsibilities and to act effectively, is a European priority. (...)

> The EU should support the United Nations as it responds to threats to international peace and security. The EU is committed to reinforcing its cooperation with the UN to assist countries emerging from conflicts, and to enhancing its support for the UN in short-term crisis management situations (European Security Strategy, 12 December 2003).

Benita Ferrero-Waldner also emphasized the EU's commitment to the establishment of an effective multilateral system with the UN at the centre. She stated that

> We in the EU believe that the UN lies at the heart of the multilateralism we espouse. It must be fully enabled to play its rightful, pivotal role in seeking multilateral solutions to global problems (Ferrero-Waldner, 8 December 2004: 7).

The EU is devoted to strengthening its partnership with the UN in carrying out its global responsibilities. In his speeches Javier Solana emphasized the strengthening and deepening partnership between the EU and the UN in a range of areas. He noted that

> It is safe to say that our working relations with the United Nations are deeper and closer than ever before. Our presence in Bosnia responds to a request from the UN. It has generated a network of contacts which has deepened and strengthened our partnership at all levels. As the European Union becomes operational in new areas, this partnership can only deepen (Solana, 21 May 2003).

Benita Ferrero-Waldner also emphasized the increasing cooperation between the EU and the UN in a wide-range of areas. She stated that

> The European Commission and the UN have enjoyed increasingly close cooperation over the years, and I would like to see this cooperation intensified during my mandate. Our current cooperation spans the fields of development cooperation and conflict prevention – we support one another's activities in the field; provide financial support (the European Commission contributes some €700 million per annum to the UN's budget); and involve one another in crisis management operations (Ferrero-Waldner, 8 December 2004).

Builder of Effective Partnership with Key Actors

This role conception also is closely connected with the EU's role conception as a promoter of effective multilateralism. It points to the EU's belief that contemporary global and regional problems and threats are common problems shared by the humanity and thus cannot be dealt with through unilateral initiatives. In the ESS, the necessity to develop multilateral cooperation for dealing with contemporary global and regional problems and threats was emphasized. It was pointed out that

> There are few if any problems we can deal with on our own. The threats described above are common threats, shared with all our closest partners. International cooperation is a necessity. We need to pursue our objectives both through multilateral cooperation in international organizations and through partnerships with key actors (European Security Strategy 2003).

This role conception places an emphasis on the EU's preference for pursuing its foreign and security policy objectives through multilateral cooperation in international organizations and through building partnerships with other important global and regional actors. Javier

Solana emphasized the importance of multilateral cooperation with the EU's strategic partners. He stated that

> But improved consistency and capabilities will not be enough unless Europe strengthens relations with its strategic partners. Better cooperation with them is the key to effective multilateralism. Threats are never more dangerous than when the international community is divided. For this reason in particular, the transatlantic link is irreplaceable. Our security and the effectiveness of the common fight against threats depend on the strength and balance of that relationship (Solana, 12 November 2003).

This role conception emphasizes the EU's intention to form global alliances to handle contemporary global problems and threats and also to form regional alliances to handle regional problems with key regional actors and regional organizations. The USA and NATO are identified by the EU as the most important strategic partners for handling the contemporary global problems and threats. The EU grants utmost importance to the transatlantic partnership. Moreover, the EU identifies regional powers Japan, China, Canada, India and Russia, Latin America and regional organizations such as ASEAN, MERCUSOR and African Union as potential strategic partners for dealing with regional problems and threats. The EU also emphasizes the establishment of partnership with the other great geographical centres such as the Arab world and Africa in their search for stability and development. In one of his speeches Javier Solana highlighted the importance of building partnership with regional actors. He pointed out that

> In a world where partnership and cooperation is crucial to success, our relationships will take many forms. In the Western Balkans, with NATO, especially in preparation for the take-over from SFOR. With regional powers such as Japan, China and India; with regional organizations such as ASEAN, MERCOSUR and the African Union. Europe's history, geography and culture connect us globally. In our own neighbourhood, we must work

for closer relations with Russia, building a strategic partnership through respect for common values. Our ambition is a Europe more active and more capable; an articulate and persuasive champion of effective multilateralism; a regional actor and a global ally (Solana, 8 January 2004).

Conclusion

The EU's role set is composed of role conceptions which are not mutually exclusive, but in some cases are closely interlinked. The EU's role conception as a 'force for good' is closely interlinked with role conceptions as a 'force for international peace, security and stability', 'provider of development aid' and 'promoter of its values and norms'. While making the world a better place for everybody as a 'force for good', the EU seeks to promote peace, security, stability and values and norms including respect for human dignity, liberty, fundamental freedoms, democracy, equality, rule of law, good governance and respect for human rights and minority rights through the world and help developing countries in their fight to eliminate extreme poverty, hunger, malnutrition and pandemics such as AIDS and in achieving sustainable development.

Moreover, the EU's role conception as 'provider of development aid' is closely connected with its role conception as a 'force for international peace, security and stability', because peace, security and stability are identified by the EU as indispensable for development and vice versa. It is argued that they can best be accomplished through development and development through them. Underdevelopment, which provides a breeding ground for insecurity and instability, is identified by the EU as one of the contemporary global challenges to global security.

Furthermore, the EU's role conception as 'promoter of its values and norms' is closely connected with its role conception as a 'force for international peace, security and stability', because the promotion of its values and norms and establishing well-governed stable democratic states through the world are identified by the EU as a necessity for the protection of both international security and the security of the EU and the strengthening of the international order.

The EU's role conception as 'promoter of effective multilateralism' is closely interlinked with role conceptions as 'partner for the UN' and 'builder of effective partnership with key actors'. The EU's role conception as 'partner for the UN' is closely connected with its role conception as 'promoter of effective multilateralism'. While the EU as 'promoter of effective multilateralism' is committed to the establishment of rule-governed effective multilateral system with the UN at the centre, the UN is seen by the EU as the most important partner for the establishment of such a system. The EU's role conception as 'builder of effective partnership with key actors' is closely connected with its role conception as 'promoter of effective multilateralism', because according to the role conception as 'builder of effective partnership with key actors', contemporary global and regional problems and threats are common problems shared by all the world thus cannot be dealt with through unilateral initiatives there is a need for multilateral cooperation in international organizations and building partnership with other important global and regional actors to deal with these issues.

In the post-9/11 international security environment, the EU identified itself as a 'benign force' which claims to act on the basis of the interests of the whole community of peoples in the world. This effectively means that in its foreign and security policy, the EU not only claims to act in its own self-interest and the interests of EU citizens, but also to act in the interests of others, non-Europeans. The EU's foreign and security policy is understood as both self-serving (self-regarding) and other-serving (other-regarding). In other words, the EU claims to act for the global common good. While acting to promote the interests of others, ultimately the EU claims to serve its own self-interest. The EU's philosophy in its foreign and security policy is based on the belief that it can 'do well by doing good'. The EU's foreign and security policy can be identified as a 'foreign policy without tears', which effectively means that the EU tries to serve the interests of all but does not want to harm anybody (Aoun 2003: 311).

The EU's role conceptions as a 'force for international peace, security and stability', a 'force for good', a 'promoter of its values and norms' and a 'provider of development aid' are seen by the EU as directly related to the enlightened self-interest of the EU. While promoting stability, security and peace which Europeans enjoy in the EU beyond the

EU's borders; acting to make the world a better place for everybody by making the world freer, more peaceful, fairer, more secure and more stable as a force for good; promoting its norms and values including democracy, rule of law, good governance and human rights beyond the EU's borders; and helping the developing world in its fight to eliminate extreme poverty, hunger, malnutrition, the EU serves both the interests of others and its own interest. First of all, the EU enables others to live in a secure, stable and peaceful environment in which democracy, the rule of law, good governance and human rights prevail and hallmarks of underdevelopment – poverty, hunger and malnutrition – are eliminated. Secondly, as the EU identified underdevelopment and the lack of democracy, the rule of law, good governance and human rights as sources of insecurity and instability, by dealing with these sources, the EU is able to manage the situations which in the future may adversely affect the EU's security and stability due to spillover effect. This refers to a positive-sum and win-win situation.

Another point is that the EU is committed to the establishment of an effective multilateral international system which is governed by rules created and monitored by multilateral institutions. In EU terms, a rule-governed effective multilateral system is a system in which multilateral institutions and international agreements and treaties would become more effective. The EU identifies the UN as the most important multilateral institution and places the UN at the centre of the effective multilateral international system which it is committed to establish. The EU identified the UN as the most important partner for the establishment of an effective multilateral international system. The EU is also committed to the establishment of global and regional partnership and alliances with other important global and regional actors in managing contemporary global and regional problems and threats. This is due to the EU's belief that since contemporary global and regional problems and threats are common problems shared by the entire world and thus cannot be dealt with through unilateral initiatives; there is a need for multilateral initiatives to handle these issues. The EU places multilateral cooperation in international organizations and building partnership with other important global and regional actors at the centre of its conduct of foreign and security policy.

CHAPTER 4

A HISTORICAL OVERVIEW: THE EC/EU'S INVOLVEMENT IN THE ARAB-ISRAELI CONFLICT AND THE MEPP IN THE PRE-9/11 ERA

The Arab-Israeli conflict and the subsequent peace process has been one of the most strongly debated issues by EU Member States since the establishment of EPC in early 1970s (Musu 2007a: 11). The EU has issued numerous joint declarations and adopted joint actions on the Arab-Israeli conflict and the MEPP and they have always been on the top of agenda of the EU's foreign policy (ibid.). The objective of this chapter is to provide a historical overview of the EU's involvement in the MEPP. This historical overview is worth analyzing and evaluating, since it will help better to understand and analyze the EU's role performance in the MEPP in the post-9/11 era as well as to uncover the change and continuity in the EU's policy. The chapter is organized into three parts which provide a historical overview of the evolution of the EU's policy towards the MEPP from the 1970s up to 1990s.

The Quest for a European Common Position in the 1970s

In the 1950s and 1960s, the European states did not have a significant presence either individually or collectively in the region. After the failure of the UK and France, the two prominent European colonial powers in the region, during the Suez Crisis in 1956, the two super powers, the USA and the Soviet Union, became the major powers in the region. In the late 1960s and early 1970s, France and the UK sought to regain their status as major players in the region through their collective efforts under the framework of EPC. EPC was used by the two former colonial powers as a tool to reintroduce themselves into the Middle East (Dieckhoff 1987: 258). France and the UK, the so-called 'Channel Axis', were the two actors within the EC who promoted the EC's political involvement in the Middle East (ibid.: 265).

In the late 1960s, EC Member States adopted divergent positions[1] towards the Arab-Israeli conflict. On the eve of the Six-Day Arab-Israeli War in 1967, the European leaders convened in Rome to discuss the situation in the Middle East. West Germany regarded the Rome Summit as a rare opportunity to speak with a single voice about the tense situation in the Middle East (Smith 2004: 63). The driving force behind the Rome Summit during the 1967 Arab-Israeli War was EC Member States' intention to coordinate their foreign policies, because they differed from each other in terms of their positions on important international issues like the Middle East conflict. The EC had no procedures or mechanisms to coordinate the foreign policy positions of its Member States and occasional intergovernmental summits were the most suitable places for the coordination of EC Member States' foreign policies (ibid.: 63).

During the Rome Summit, despite efforts to make a joint community declaration, EC Member States were not able to agree on a common declaration due to their divergent positions (Ifestos 1987: 420). After the Summit, German Chancellor Kurt Kiesinger said that 'I felt ashamed at the Rome Summit. Just as the war was on the point of breaking, we could not even agree to talk about it' (ibid.: 420; Greilsammer and Weiler 1984: 132). During the war, France supported the Arabs and condemned Israel in the UN debates. Although West Germany declared its neutrality, in fact it supported Israel. Italians were divided amongst themselves – while the Foreign Minister Amintore Fanfani adopted a pro-Arab position, the majority of Christian Democrats, the Socialists and President Giuseppe Saragat backed Israel. Belgium and Luxembourg tried to find a solution in UN institutions. The Netherlands supported Israel (ibid.: 131; Ifestos 1987: 420). Instead of Community deliberations, the French President de Gaulle, in January 1969, offered a four-power summit including France, the USSR, the UK and the USA to discuss a settlement for the Arab-Israeli conflict, but the USA rejected this (Smith 2004: 63). EC Member States' different traditions and interests in the Middle East, different intensity of ties with Israel and with the Arab world, and the failure to agree on a political role for Western Europe beside the USA contributed to EC Member States' failure to agree on a common position (Musu 2007a: 12).

EC Member States' failure to coordinate their positions and policies and respond adequately to a major world crisis, such as the Six-Day Arab-Israeli War, led them to set up mechanisms or procedures for foreign policy coordination and consultation among them. In April 1969, de Gaulle resigned and Georges Pompidou took over the French Presidency and started new initiatives for foreign policy cooperation. Pompidou initiated the Hague Summit on 2 December 1969 to discuss enlargement, economic and monetary union and political union. At the Hague Summit, the leaders of EC Member States decided that they were ready to 'pave the way for a united Europe capable of assuming its responsibilities in the world of tomorrow and of making a contribution commensurate with its traditions and mission' (Smith 2002: 66; Smith 2004: 69; Hill and Smith 2000: 72). At the Summit, the responsibilities of taking steps towards political union by harmonizing foreign policies of EC Member States were discussed (Smith 2002: 27) and the leaders of EC Member States

> ... agreed to instruct their ministers of foreign affairs to study the best way of achieving progress in the matter of political unification within the context of enlargement the ministers would be expected to report before the end of July 1970 (Hill and Smith 2000: 74).

A Committee composed of Political Directors of EC Member States' foreign policies, headed by the Belgian Political Director, Viscount Etienne Davignon drafted the report which was requested at the Hague

Summit. Davignon submitted the report at the Luxembourg Conference of Foreign Ministers on 27 October 1970 and it was approved. This report was named the Luxembourg Report or Davignon Report and created EPC. According to the Luxembourg Report, the aims of EPC are

> ...To ensure, through regular exchanges of information and consultations, a better mutual understanding on the great international problems and to strengthen their solidarity by promoting the harmonization of their views, the coordination of their positions and where it appears possible or desirable, common actions (Smith 2004: 72).

After the introduction of EPC, the Arab-Israeli conflict became one of the two areas of priorities for EPC besides the Conference on Security and Cooperation in Europe. These two issues were selected as two areas of priority for EPC because, at the time, the preservation of security and stability in Europe's eastern and southern neighbourhood was considered as strategically crucial for Europe's own security and stability (Dieckhoff 1987: 259). Since the first EPC ministerial meeting held in Munich in November 1970, the Arab-Israeli conflict had been a nearly permanent feature of EPC discussions (Musu 2010c: 25), because at the time France, under the leadership of Georges Pompidou, sought to discuss the Middle East conflict under EPC and bring its EC partners closer to the French position and in this way strengthen European support for the Arab cause and assert European independence of the US foreign policy (Nuttall 1992: 56). Pompidou wanted the EC to play the role of a third force alongside the two superpowers. He believed that the EC should develop a third course, beside the imperial logic of the USA and the Soviet Union, and take up its own stance in order to protect its interests in the region, without relying on powers external to the Middle East (Dieckhoff 1987: 259). This was supported by West Germany which wanted to improve its relations with the Arab world without attracting criticism from Israel or the USA (Nuttall 1992: 56).

Since the launch of EPC, EC Member States had gradually developed a joint position towards the Arab-Israeli conflict. EC Member States issued a series of common declarations concerning the Arab-Israeli conflict under the framework of EPC including Schumann Document of

1971, the Brussels Declaration of 1973, the London Declaration of 1977, the Venice Declaration of 1980, which symbolized the culmination of EC Member States' joint position towards the conflict. It can be said that during the 1970s, EC Member States pursued a declaratory policy.

Early Attempts to Develop a Common Position towards the Arab-Israeli Conflict: the Schumann Document of 1971, the Brussels Declaration of 1973 and the London Declaration of 1977

The Schumann Document,[2] which constituted the first common position of EC Member States on the Arab-Israeli conflict, was unanimously approved by the Foreign Ministers on 13 May 1971. The Schumann Document marked the beginning of a distinctive and collective position on the Arab-Israeli conflict (Nuttall 1997: 25). It managed to unite the attitudes of EC Member States towards the Arab-Israeli conflict and served as the basis for the EC's future attitude towards the Middle East (Dosenrode and Stubkjaer 2002: 82). The Schumann Document contained the establishment of demilitarized zones in the 1967 lines, in which international forces would be stationed; an overall Israeli withdrawal from the Occupied Territories with minor border adjustments; the internationalization of Jerusalem; the postponement of any conclusive solution regarding the sovereignty of East Jerusalem; the choice, for the Arab refugees of either returning to their home or being compensated; the approval of the Jarring mission (Greilsammer and Weiler 1984: 133). The Schumann document was consistent with UN Security Council Resolution 242, and, in line with the Resolution, it referred to the Palestinians as Arab refugees (ibid.: 133; Soetendorp 1999: 99).

The Schumann Document was a confidential document; it would not be publicized due to West German and Dutch objections and Italian reservations. However, it was leaked to the German press and the German public opinion and Israel strongly criticized the West German foreign minister Walter Scheel. As a result, Scheel played down the significance of the document, by declaring it only a working document to serve as a basis for further discussions (Ifestos 1987: 421). The Schumann Document led to disarray among EC Member States, especially France. It deteriorated EC Member States' political relations with Israel and marked the start of the Europeans' acquisition of a pro-Arab reputation, one which was to lodge in the minds of the Israeli political establishment. This led to Israeli resistance to any formal European involvement in future attempts at peace-making. It also revealed the challenge of policy harmonization within the EU and the difficulty of maintaining a common position in the event of sustained public criticism (Robin 1997: 72).

Between May 1971 and October 1973, there was no other joint EPC document on the Middle East. EC Member States did not take any initiative on Middle East policy publicly nor make any serious effort to bring their positions closer together after the Schumann Document (Nuttall 1997: 93). At the outbreak of the Yom Kippur Arab-Israeli War in 1973 (6–26 October 1973), just as with the Six-Day Arab-Israeli War, EC Member States adopted divergent positions. The initial reactions of EC Member States to the Yom Kippur War was fragmented and varied considerably (Soetendorp 1999: 101). France and Italy adopted a pro-Arab position. West Germany, Denmark and the Netherlands supported Israel. France and the Netherlands in particular adopted opposite positions. While France expressed some understanding for the Arab attack on Israel, the Netherlands held Egypt and Syria responsible for the beginning of the war (ibid.).

Under pressure from the UK and France, EC Member States issued a joint statement on 13 October 1973 which called for a ceasefire and negotiations on the basis of UN Security Council Resolution 242. On 16 October 1973, the Gulf States announced that until Israel returned to its pre-1967 borders and the Palestinians were able to exercise their right to self-determination, the price of the oil would be raised by 70 per cent. On 17 October 1973, Arab members of OPEC decided on a monthly 5 per cent cutback in oil production. On 20 October 1973, Saudi Arabia declared a total embargo on oil exports to the USA. On 4 November 1973, Arab members of OPEC announced production cutbacks of 25 per cent on September levels with further monthly 5 per cent cuts and created three categories of consumers: friends, enemies and neutrals (Nuttall 1992: 94). Regarding EC Member States, the UK and France were categorized as friends and received normal supplies of oil; however the Netherlands, like the USA, was categorized as an enemy and was completely embargoed. Other EC Member States were accepted as neutrals and were subjected to a monthly 5 per cent reduction in oil exports (Nuttall 1992: 94; 1997: 25).

After the Arabs' selective use of oil embargoes against EC Member states, European political leaders decided to counter this by a common action and issued a joint declaration on 6 November 1973 in Brussels, which was known as the Brussels Declaration. The Brussels Declaration was based on a French-British text and it brought EC Member States' position very close to the French position, which was a pro-Arab one. With this declaration, EC Member States moved away from their previous rather unconditional support to Israel and explicitly broke with the US vision (Aoun 2003: 291).

The Brussels Declaration was a step forward when compared to the Schumann Document. With the Brussels Declaration, EC Member States for the first time referred to the Palestinians rather than 'Arab refugees' and recognized the legitimate rights of the Palestinians (Greilsammer and Weiler 1984: 134–35; Soetendorp 1999: 101). EC Member States also declared the inadmissibility of the acquisition of territory by force rather than emphasizing minor border adjustments mentioned in the Schumann Document and re-emphasized the necessity for Israel to end the territorial occupation which it had maintained since Six-Day War of 1967 (Greilsammer and Weiler 1984; Soetendorp 1999). The Brussels Declaration emphasized the UN rather than the Geneva Conference as the forum for negotiations (Nuttall 1992: 95).

On 14–15 December 1973, the leaders of EC Member States met in Copenhagen. At the Copenhagen Summit, European political leaders confirmed the Brussels Declaration of 6 November. At their meeting on 26–29 November 1973 in Algeria, the Arab States launched an appeal to the EC stating that Europe was linked to the Arab world through the Mediterranean by profound affinities of civilization and by vital interests which can only be developed within the framework of confidence and mutually advantageous cooperation (Nuttall 1992: 96; Dosenrode and Stubkjaer 2002: 86). By relying on the Arab States' appeal to the EC, a delegation of Arab foreign ministers came to Copenhagen to propose to EC Member States to start a dialogue on these lines (Nuttall 1992: 96). EC Member States accepted this offer and called for entry into negotiations with the Arab members of OPEC. At the Copenhagen Summit, European political leaders declared their willingness to enter into negotiations with oil-producing countries on comprehensive arrangements comprising cooperation on a wide scale for economic and industrial development, industrial investments, and stable energy supplies to the member countries at reasonable prices (Ifestos 1987: 431).

On 6 March 1974, EC Member States declared their readiness to launch the Euro-Arab Dialogue and the Arab States agreed to launch the dialogue at the meeting in Tunis on 28 April 1974. The two sides of the dialogue had different motivations for its launch. Europeans' main motive was to secure European oil imports while making a major effort to help Arab economic development (Greilsammer and Weiler 1987: 34). The objective was to promote extensive Euro-Arab cooperation in every economic field: Europe would invest large sums in Arab industrial, agricultural and development, while the Arabs would promise to supply their oil without any interruption and at reasonable prices (ibid.). The main motive of the Arabs was to create a political linkage between the Arab-Israeli conflict and economic issues (Smith 2002: 174). They wanted to politicize the dialogue and use it as an instrument in their war against Israel. They asked Europeans for two major concessions: to give up the free trade agreement signed with Israel in 1975 and to allow an independent representation of the PLO in the dialogue's general commission and the expert committees (Greilsammer and Weiler 1987).

After the conclusion of the Camp David Agreements, Egypt was expelled from the Arab League and a rift emerged among Arab States. This led to the suspension of the Euro-Arab-Dialogue in April 1979 at the request of the Arab League. The main reason behind the Arab states' decision to suspend the dialogue was that they were not satisfied with progress on the political aspects of the Euro-Arab Dialogue and they considered that it was not worth continuing a dialogue which was not making adequate progress on political aspects. During the meetings of the General Committee, the Arab States strove to politicize the Euro-Arab Dialogue by putting the Arab-Israeli conflict on the agenda. However, EC Member States refused to discuss the political issues, including the

Arab-Israeli conflict, in the Euro-Arab Dialogue. EC Member States were determined to exclude from the agenda of the Euro-Arab Dialogue two important issues: the oil problem and the Arab-Israeli conflict (Ifestos 1987: 435). Moreover, the Arab States pressed EC Member States to recognize the PLO, yet EC Member States did not recognize it. After the suspension of the Euro-Arab Dialogue in April 1979, EC Member States attempted to revive the dialogue, but these attempts failed. In 1989 in particular, although the French President François Mitterrand tried to reactivate the dialogue and an agreement was made to pursue new economic, social and cultural projects, the agreed restructured Euro-Arab Dialogue did not materialize (Smith 2002: 175).

The Euro-Arab Dialogue had to some extent played a determining role in the evolution of EC Member States' joint position towards the Arab-Israeli conflict in the second half of the 1970s. During the period between 1973 and 1980, Arab political pressure on EC Member States had been one of the factors in their gradual adoption of a pro-Arab stance in the Arab-Israeli conflict. As can be seen from the London Declaration of 1977, EC Member States located the Palestinian problem at the very core of the Arab-Israeli conflict and recognized the right to a homeland for the Palestinian people which would give effective expression to their national identity. They also called for the participation of the representatives of the Palestinian people in the peace negotiations. EC Member States in their further declarations criticized and condemned Israel's policy of settlement in the Occupied Territories and identified it as the main stumbling block before the achievement of a comprehensive peace settlement in the Middle East. The pressure put by the Arab States at the fourth General Committee meeting held at Damascus on 9–11 December 1978 forced EC Member States to distance themselves from the Camp David Treaty. As will be seen from the Venice Declaration of 1980, EC Member States emphasized the necessity for the Palestinian people to exercise fully their right to self-determination for a comprehensive peace settlement. In addition to that, although EC Member States did not only recognize the PLO as the only representative of the Palestinian people, but also called for its association with the peace negotiations as an important representative of the Palestinian people.

The Euro-Arab Dialogue has provided a sometimes sporadic forum for multilateral political and economic consultation between European and the Arab States (ibid.: 168). It provided the Arab States with an opportunity to negotiate with Europe on an equal basis, to put their collective views on the Arab-Israeli conflict, to create an atmosphere of acceptability around the PLO, whose officials were participating, and to exploit possibilities of future Euro-Arab economic cooperation, given that oil reserves are not finite (Ifestos 1987: 438). Although EC Member States did not recognize the PLO, they allowed the PLO to open information offices supervised by staff operating within the framework of Arab League offices. As a result, the PLO obtained an information presence in Italy, France, the UK, Belgium and Germany and an opportunity to conduct dialogue with the authorities of these countries. (Al-Dajani 1980: 93). The PLO's information offices and the presence of the PLO delegates among the Arab delegation of the Euro-Arab Dialogue enabled the officials of EC Member States to familiarize themselves with the PLO (Ifestos 1987: 450).

Between November 1973 and June 1977 the EC did not carry out any diplomatic activity or issue a declaration on the issue of the Arab-Israeli conflict except starting the Euro-Arab Dialogue. At the European Council meeting in London on 29–30 June 1977, European political leaders issued a joint declaration concerning the Arab-Israeli conflict. This declaration was a restatement of the positions of EC Member States which had been accumulated since the early 1970s.

The London Declaration was a step forward when compared to the 1973 Brussels Declaration concerning the rights of the Palestinian people. By stating that the only solution to the Arab-Israeli conflict would be to recognize the right to a homeland for the Palestinian people, EC Member States located the Palestinian problem at the very core of the Arab-Israeli conflict. Granting Israel secure borders was no longer the essential feature of a peace settlement (Greilsammer and Weiler 1987: 138). Beside the recognition of a right to a homeland for the Palestinian people, the call for the participation of the representatives of the Palestinian people is another new feature of the declaration when compared to the previous one. In addition to the 1973

Brussels Declaration's emphasis on just and lasting peace, the London Declaration emphasized comprehensive settlement of the Arab-Israeli conflict.

The London Declaration demonstrated the fact that the EC came gradually to align itself with the French position, particularly as regards the Palestinian problem (Ifestos 1987: 441). EC Member States as a whole supported the French belief that the recognition of the rights of the Palestinians was the key to the settlement of the Arab-Israeli conflict (Soetendorp 1999: 103). The London Declaration was another crucial step that moved EC Member States towards a pro-Arab position in the Arab-Israeli conflict. EC Member States tried to balance the declaration by emphasizing that the Arab side must be ready to recognize the right of Israel to live in peace within secure and recognized boundaries in response to the Israeli recognition of the legitimate rights of the Palestinian people. Israel strongly rejected the idea of granting a homeland to the Palestinian people, locating the Palestinian problem at the very core of the Arab-Israeli conflict and participation of the representatives of the Palestinian people in a peace settlement on an equal footing with sovereign states (Greilsammer and Weiler 1987: 138). Although the Arab States and the PLO found the London Declaration inadequate, they considered it as a positive development (ibid.). They found it inadequate because, despite their demand from EC Member States to recognize the PLO as the representative of the Palestinian people, in the London Declaration EC Member States did not refer to the PLO as the representative of the Palestinian people (Soetendorp 1999: 102).

Between 1977 and 1980, EC Member States strove to stick to the London Declaration as the main referent document concerning their positions on the Arab-Israeli conflict. A comprehensive settlement of the Arab-Israeli conflict and the need for a homeland for the Palestinian people were emphasized by EC Member States during this period. Moreover, between 1977 and 1980, EC Member States increasingly adopted a more pro-Arab position and increased their criticism towards Israel. For instance, the Belgian Foreign Minister Henri Simonet, while addressing the UN General Assembly in September 1977 on behalf of EC Member States as the President of the EC

Council of Ministers, criticized and condemned the Israeli acts in the Occupied Territories and expressed EC Member States' concerns over the illegal measures taken by Israel in the Occupied Territories and called these measures as an obstacle to the peace process (Ifestos 1987: 442). Between 1977 and 1980, at the UN, EC Member States adopted a pro-Arab stance and increased their criticism towards Israel and supported the texts condemning the Israeli occupation and the methods used by Israel in Jerusalem and the Occupied Territories (Greilsammer and Weiler 1987: 139).

The Camp David Peace Process and the EC

In the Autumn of 1977, an important event happened in the Middle East and consequently, the London Declaration lost its importance and EC Member States were sidelined and marginalized in the region and on the issue of the Arab-Israeli conflict. On 19 November 1977, the Egyptian President Anwar Sadat visited Israel. This visit launched the Egyptian-Israeli peace process which resulted in the Camp David Peace Accords. With the start of the Egyptian-Israeli peace process, the USA became a major player in the Middle East and excluded other external actors. Thus, EC Member States' attempt to play a political role in the quest for peace in the Middle East was sidelined and marginalized by the Camp David peace process culminating in the signing of the Camp David Peace Accords with Israel under the auspices of the US government (Smith 2002: 168).

As a result, the London Declaration lost its importance, because this declaration could only have worked if the EC were to act as a major player in the Middle East. However, in the new context the USA became the major player and excluded the EC from the process. Sadat's visit changed the context in the Middle East and the Arab-Israeli conflict. The London Declaration was issued in a context in which no Arab country had recognized Israel and no one was ready to talk with it. But after Sadat's visit to Jerusalem, not only had Egypt, the most important Arab country, recognized Israel, but it also began negotiating with it about a solution of the Palestinian problem. The solution in the Egyptian and the Israeli mind for the Palestinian problem was not related to the concept of homeland for the Palestinians, but with autonomy for the Palestinians in the West Bank and Gaza Strip (Greilsammer and Weiler 1987: 139). The initiation of the Egyptian-Israeli peace process following Sadat's visit was also contrary to the London Declaration's call for a comprehensive settlement of the Arab-Israeli conflict. It was, rather, based on a step-by-step approach to the settlement of conflict which would lead to separate peace between Israel and Egypt. Sadat's initiative led to a split among Arab countries. All except Sudan and Oman strongly criticized and condemned Sadat's initiative.

France expressed its doubts about Sadat's initiative, because of its unpopularity in the Arab world and its unfavourable implications for French policy (Nuttall 1992: 158). On the other hand, other EC Member States were faced with a dilemma. Although they considered this initiative favourable and did not want to jeopardize this first opportunity given to peace in the Middle East, they also did not want to impair their good relations with the Arabs, which had been developing with difficulty since 1973 (Greilsammer and Weiler 1987: 140). After an EPC ministerial meeting on 22 November 1977, EC Member States agreed on a joint declaration, known as the November 22 *Communiqué*. With this, EC Member States expressed their support for the President Sadat's bold initiative and the unprecedented dialogue started in Jerusalem. EC Member States expressed their hope that the Israeli-Egyptian dialogue would open the way to a comprehensive negotiation leading to a just and lasting overall settlement taking account of the rights and concerns of all parties involved. They pointed out that it was a matter of urgency that genuine peace at last be achieved for all the parties in the region, including the Palestinian people, on the basis of principles recognized by the international community and embodied in the London Declaration of 1977 (Nuttall 1992: 159; Ifestos 1987: 444). They also expressed their hope that it would be possible to convene the Geneva conference in the near future (Nuttall 1992: 159; Ifestos 1987: 444). In the *Communiqué*, although EC Member States declared their support for Sadat's initiative and the subsequent Egyptian-Israeli peace process, they reemphasized their commitment to the need for a comprehensive settlement for the Arab-Israeli conflict and the need for a homeland for the Palestinians. EC

Member States adhered to the London Declaration as the main referent document concerning their positions on the Arab-Israeli conflict.

Until the conclusion of the Camp David Agreements on 17 September
1978, EC Member States did not issue a declaration on the issue of the
Arab-Israeli conflict. During this period, EC Member States had been
subject to pressure from both Egypt and other Arab countries. The
Egyptian president Anwar Sadat exerted pressure upon them to support the Egyptian-Israeli peace process on the contrary; Arab countries pressed them to renounce the process. Despite these pressures EC
Member States adopted a wait and see policy, and issued no other declaration until the conclusion of the Camp David Agreements.

Two days after the conclusion of the Camp David Agreements on
17 September 1978, EC Member States issued a declaration in which
European political leaders congratulated the US President Jimmy
Carter, the Egyptian President Anwar Sadat and the Israeli Prime
Minister Menachem Begin for their successful peace effort. They once
again reemphasized their attachment to a comprehensive and lasting peace settlement and recalled the London Declaration of 1977.
In this declaration, European political leaders expressed their hope
that the outcome of the Camp David conference would be a further
major step on the path to a just, comprehensive and lasting peace, and
that all parties concerned would find it possible to join in the process
to contribute to that end. EC Member States expressed their strong
support to all efforts to achieve such a peace (Ifestos 1987: 445). EC
Member States gave a conditional support to the Camp David Treaty
as they announced that they would support it on the condition that it
would not be a separate peace settlement but instead a first major step
toward a comprehensive peace settlement in which all the parties to
the conflict should be involved. After the Camp David Peace Treaty,
EC Member States firmly adhered to the principles of the London
Declaration and called for a comprehensive settlement for the Arab-
Israeli conflict and a homeland for the Palestinian people. The German
Foreign Minister Hans-Dietrich Genscher, while addressing the UN
General Assembly in 26 September 1978 on behalf of all EC Member
States, once again emphasized EC Member States' call for a compre-
hensive settlement for the conflict. He pointed out that all parties

concerned must be involved in the peace process and that no obstacles should be placed in the way of this peace process which should be kept open and should through further development and wider participation lead to a comprehensive settlement (ibid.). Genscher also emphasized that a peace settlement should take into account the need for a home-land for the Palestinian people (ibid.: 446).

European political leaders' favourable attitude towards the Camp David Treaty began to change after the fourth meeting of the General Commission of the Euro-Arab dialogue held in Damascus on 9–11 December 1978. At this meeting the Arab countries pressed EC Member States to end their support for Camp David and to recognize the PLO as the sole legitimate representative of the Palestinian people. Despite this, EC Member States did not accept these demands and did not recognize the PLO as the sole legitimate representative of the Palestinian people, but they refrained from restating their conditional support for Camp David (Greilsammer and Weiler 1987: 141; Ifestos 1987: 446). In the final *Communiqué* of the meeting, EC Member States agreed that the Palestinian problem was central to the Arab-Israeli conflict and that a peaceful, comprehensive and just settlement of the conflict, including obviously a solution of the Palestinian problem, was not only a matter of vital importance to the Arabs but also of great concern to EC Member States in the view their close relations with the Middle East (ibid.).

On 26 March 1979, EC Member States issued another declaration concerning the Camp David Treaty. In this declaration, EC Member States first of all, expressed their appreciation for the will of the US President Jimmy Carter for peace and efforts of the Egyptian President Sadat and the Israeli Prime Minister Menachem Begin. Then they noted that while a difficult road remained to be trodden before UN Security Council Resolution 242 was implemented in all its aspects and on all fronts, they identified the Camp David Treaty as a cor-rect application of the principles of that resolution, but solely for the Egyptian-Israeli relations (ibid.). In this declaration, EC Member States recalled the London Declaration of 1977 and called for the establish-ment of a comprehensive settlement in the Middle East, which must be based on UN Security Council Resolution 242, translating into fact the right of the Palestinian people to a homeland (Nuttall 1992: 161). The declaration did not approve the Camp David Treaty but instead emphasized the London Declaration of 1977 which called for a comprehensive settlement and right of the Palestinian people to a homeland. The declaration also identified Israel's policy of settlement in the Occupied Territories as the main stumbling block to the achievement of a comprehensive peace settlement. The declaration was a cool and reserved reception of the Camp David Treaty and a polite but frank insistence on the positions of EC Member States as defined in the London Declaration of 1977 (Ifestos 1987: 446).

After 26 March Declaration they once again identified Israel's policy of settlement in the Occupied Territories as the main stumbling block to the achievement of a comprehensive peace settlement and incompatible with UN Security Council Resolutions and a violation of international law (ibid.: 448; Greilsammer and Weiler 1987: 141). EC Member States also condemned the Israeli attacks on South Lebanon (Ifestos 1987: 448; Greilsammer and Weiler 1987: 141).

During the autumn of 1979 and spring of 1980, EC Member States came to the conclusion that the Camp David process had come to a standstill and would not be successful in making progress toward a comprehensive peace settlement for the Arab-Israeli conflict and that it was necessary to launch a European Middle East Peace Initiative. Moreover, during this period the Middle East had become more unstable, due to several important events including the fall of Shah of Iran in 1979, the outbreak of the Iran-Iraq War in 1980, the rise of Islamic fundamentalism, the second energy crisis of 1978–1980 and the Soviet invasion of Afghanistan in 1979. These events increased European concerns over the secure flow of oil to Europe and led them to question the US credibility and ability as a guarantor of security and stability in the Middle East (Ifestos 1987: 452). The EC's doubts about the US ability to maintain security and stability in the Middle East also led EC Member States to believe that there was a need to launch a European Middle East Peace Initiative. At the time, EC Member States believed that the USA, which was preoccupied with the Iranian crisis (seizure of hostages in the US embassy) and with the coming presidential elections, were unable to provide another strategy after Camp David revealed its limits. As a result, there emerged a political vacuum in the region (Dieckhoff 1987: 263). EC Member States believed that the American setback provided a favourable and requisite circumstance for launching a European Middle East Peace Initiative which would fill in the blank spaces in American diplomacy (ibid.).

The Venice Declaration of 1980

Until the Venice Declaration of June 1980, the USA, Israel and Egypt strove to prevent EC Member States to issue a new declaration concerning the Arab-Israeli conflict which might start a process diverging from the Camp David process. The US president Jimmy Carter, who wanted to be re-elected in the coming presidential elections, in particular pressed EC Member States not to take an initiative deviating from the Camp David, because he wanted to use the Camp David as an asset in his election campaign. Carter threatened EC Member States that he would use the US veto right in order to prevent any modification of UN Security Council Resolution 242 (Ifestos 1987: 456; Greilsammer and Weiler 1987: 142). In the early 1980s, EC Member States and the US administration had different approaches to the settlement of the conflict. While the US administration favoured a gradualist or step-by-step approach envisaging separate bilateral peace agreements between Israel and the Arab states as reflected in the Camp David peace process, EC Member States favoured comprehensive settlement of the conflict within the multilateral framework of an international peace conference with the participation of all parties to the conflict. Moreover, while the Camp David granted a marginal place to the Palestinian problem by envisaging autonomy for the Palestinian people in the West Bank and Gaza Strip, EC Member States located the Palestinian problem at the very core of the Arab-Israeli conflict and recognized the legitimate rights of the Palestinian people and the right to a homeland for the Palestinian people (Dieckhoff 1987: 279).

In addition to the US administration, the Israeli government was also against any European initiative deviating from the Camp David. The Israeli Prime Minister Menachem Begin declared that any European initiative based on the right of the Palestinians to self-determination would immediately be rejected by Israel. The Israeli Foreign Minister Yitzhak Shamir visited European capitals to convince EC Member States that the new declaration they were planning to issue would be particularly inopportune and not welcomed by Israel (Ifestos 1987: 456: Greilsammer and Weiler 1987: 142). In addition, the Egyptian President Anwar Sadat warned EC Member States that any European initiative should be complementary to the Camp David Treaty and not against it. He also stated that this initiative should respect that the Camp David is the corner-stone for a comprehensive peace, not just a bilateral Egyptian-Israeli peace; no outside interference should weaken this process and any European initiative must win the US support before it could achieve tangible results (Ifestos 1987: 456). Under this diplomatic pressure, in order to reassure the Americans, Emilio Colombo, the President-in-office of the EC Council, visited Washington and explained to the US Secretary of State Edmund Muskie that EC Member States did not want to oppose the Camp David and that they only wished to be constructive (ibid.; Greilsammer and Weiler 1987: 142). The German Foreign Minister Hans-Dietrich Genscher declared that the EC did not want to propose a change in UN Security Council Resolution 242. After this assurance the USA eased its pressure on the EC. So, as seen from the declaration the US, the Egyptian and the Israeli pressure became effective, because EC Member States issued a much more moderate declaration than had been expected before these pressures (ibid.). It had been expected that the coming declaration of EC Member States would challenge the Camp David process and identify it as inadequate for achieving a comprehensive peace settlement in the Middle East, call for a change in UN Security Council Resolution 242 by replacing the word 'refugees' with the word 'Palestinians', call for recognition of the PLO as the only representative of the Palestinian people and the participation of it in the peace negotiations. As will be seen in the below, the Venice declaration did not meet these expectations.

At the European Council meeting in Venice on 12–13 June 1980, the leaders of EC Member States issued a joint declaration concerning the Arab-Israeli conflict, in which they emphasized that the growing tensions affecting the Middle East constituted a serious danger and made a comprehensive solution to the Arab-Israeli conflict even more necessary and pressing. They also stated that the traditional ties and common interests which link Europe to the Middle East obliged them to play a special role and required them to work in a more concrete way towards peace.

European political leaders declared that their declaration was based on UN Security Council Resolutions 242 and 338, the positions they had expressed in the previous declarations, and the speech delivered by the Irish Foreign Minister Michael O'Kennedy[3] at the UN General Assembly on 26 September 1979 on behalf of all EC Member States. EC Member States proclaimed that there was a need to promote the recognition and implementation of the two principles accepted by the international community: the right to existence and to security of all the states in the Middle East, including Israel, and justice for all the peoples which implied the recognition of the legitimate rights of the Palestinian people (Hartley 2004: 356). By equating the Israeli security needs and the Palestinian rights as parallel objectives of the peace process, EC Member States adopted a balanced and comprehensive approach (Laipson 1990: 11).

European political leaders announced that the necessary guarantees for a secure and peaceful settlement with recognized and guaranteed borders should be provided by the UN. They also declared their preparedness to participate within the framework of a comprehensive settlement in a system of concrete and binding international guarantees, including guarantees on the ground, that is, with troops and observers. EC Member States referred to the Palestinian problem in the declaration and asserted that there is a necessity to find a just solution to the Palestinian problem which is not just a refugee problem. They argued that the Palestinian people must be placed in a position, by an appropriate process defined within the framework of the comprehensive peace settlement, to exercise fully its right to self-determination. EC Member States for the first time collectively pronounced themselves for the Palestinian right of self-determination (Ifestos 1987: 460).

European political leaders proclaimed that the achievement of just, lasting and comprehensive peace settlement required the involvement and support of all the parties concerned including the PLO. Here,

EC Member States distinguished between the Palestinian people and the PLO. The latter was being characterized as an organization which did not necessarily represent all the Palestinians (ibid.). Although EC Member States did not recognize the PLO as the only representative of the Palestinian people, they called for its association with the peace negotiations as an important representative of the Palestinian people. EC Member States emphasized that they would not accept any unilateral initiative designed to change the status of Jerusalem and any agreement on the city's status should guarantee freedom of access for everyone to the holy places. EC Member States asked Israel to end the territorial occupation it had maintained since the 1967 Arab-Israeli War and identified the Israeli settlements in the Occupied Territories as a serious obstacle to the peace process and as illegal under international law. EC Member States called for putting an end to violence and asserted that only renunciation of force or the threatened use of force by all the parties could create a climate of confidence in the region which was the basic element for a comprehensive peace settlement in the Middle East. EC Member States declared their decision to make necessary contacts with all the parties concerned with the objective of ascertaining the position of the various parties with respect to the principles set out in the Venice declaration and in the light of the result of that consultation process to determine the form which such an initiative on their part could take (Hartley 2004: 356).

Israel strongly rejected the Declaration. The Israeli government on 15 June 1980 issued a communiqué stating that nothing would remain out of the Venice Declaration but a bitter memory. The Israeli Prime Minister Menachem Begin likened the declaration to the 'Munich surrender' of 1938.[4] The Venice declaration marked a low point in the Israel-EC relationship from which it has never fully recovered (Peters 1999b: 299). For nearly a decade until the Madrid peace conference of November 1991, Israel strongly opposed any European endeavour to play an important role in the peace process in the Middle East (ibid.).

On the other hand, moderate Arab countries such as Jordan and Saudi Arabia welcomed the declaration although the PLO leadership found it as insufficient and unsatisfactory. The PLO asserted that the Declaration was the product of 'American blackmail' and that it represented a European attempt to save the US-sponsored Camp David Treaty (Greilsammer and Weiler 1987: 145). Apparently, the Venice Declaration did not meet the high expectations of the PLO. In fact, the Palestinians were hoping for a call to change UN Security Council Resolution 242 and a clear assertion that the Camp David framework was insufficient for a comprehensive peace settlement in the Middle East (ibid.). They were also hoping that the PLO would be recognized as the only representative of the Palestinian people (ibid.: 146). Still, the Egyptian Minister of State for Foreign Affairs Butros Ghali identified the declaration as a positive contribution to the peace process. He found it compatible with the goals of the Camp David, because both were based on UN Security Council Resolutions 242 and 338 (Ifestos 1987: 466). The USA was also satisfied with the Declaration and showed a moderate reaction to it. The US Secretary of State Edmund Muskie declared that the text did not seem to directly challenge the Camp David process or divert efforts of the parties to the Camp David process from their work (ibid.: 467).

The major aim of the Venice Declaration was to promote an active role for the EC in the Arab-Israeli conflict, instead of a purely declarative one: the term 'European initiative' was used to define the process set into operation by the Declaration (Greilsammer 1987: 286). The Venice Declaration marked the emergence of a distinct and common European stance towards the Arab-Israeli conflict and outlined a collective position on the steps to be taken for its peaceful resolution (Peters 1999b: 298). The Venice Declaration outlined the basic principles of the EC's policy towards the Arab-Israeli conflict and these principles still constitutes the basis of the EC's policy (Peters 2000: 154).

To sum up, as discussed previously, throughout the 1970s, EC Member States gradually developed a joint position towards the Arab-Israeli conflict. The Venice Declaration of 1980 marked the peak point of this development. During the 1970s, EC Member States had gradually developed a pro-Arab position towards the Arab-Israeli conflict. The EC's pro-Arab position can be observed in the EC's declarations concerning the Arab-Israeli conflict, the speeches of the representatives of the EC at the UN General Assembly and their voting behaviour in the UN General Assembly. During the 1970s, EC Member

States' dependence on oil produced by the Arab states in the Middle East and the Arab political pressure on them were the most important factors in their gradual adoption of a pro-Arab position in the Arab-Israeli conflict. EC Member States located the Palestinian problem at the very core of the Arab-Israeli conflict and recognized the legitimate rights of the Palestinian people. They called for a comprehensive peace settlement in which the Palestinian people would be located in a position to exercise fully their right to self-determination. They also called for the association of the PLO with the peace negotiations as an important representative of the Palestinian people. EC Member States in their declarations criticized and condemned Israel's policy of settlement in the Occupied Territories and identified it as the main stumbling block before the achievement of a comprehensive peace settlement in the Middle East.

During the 1970s EC Member States pursued a 'declaratory policy'. The Brussels Declaration of 1973, the London Declaration of 1977 and the Venice Declaration of 1980 were three important declarations in the development of the EC's position towards the Arab-Israeli conflict.

The Quest for a European Peace Initiative in the Middle East in the 1980s

After the Venice Declaration, in the early 1980s, EC Member States attempted to launch their own Middle East peace initiative. In accordance with the Venice Declaration, in order to know the position of the various parties toward the principles outlined in the Venice declaration and to determine the form of the European peace initiative in the light of the results of consultations with the parties, EC Member States sent two fact-finding missions to the Middle East (the Thorn mission and the Van der Klaauw mission) to make necessary contacts with all the parties concerned.[5]

Israel adopted a negative attitude towards these two missions and any European peace initiatives. The Israeli denial of any European peace initiative as one of the parties of the Arab-Israeli conflict made it impossible to start any European peace initiative. After the failure of these missions, EC Member States did not launch any European peace initiative in the Middle East.

During the second half of 1981 and first half of 1982 several important developments prevented the launch of a European peace initiative in the Middle East. The first development was the assassination of the Egyptian President Anwar Sadat on 6 October 1981. EC Member States decided to wait for Sadat's successor and his attitudes toward European peace efforts. The second development was the change of the Presidency in France and a change in French Middle East policy. In spring 1981, François Mitterrand became the French President and after his election the French attitude towards a European peace initiative changed. Mitterrand's France stopped supporting a European peace initiative. Another important development was the publication of the Fahd Plan in August 1981. In August 1981, Prince Fahd of Saudi Arabia launched a peace plan for the Middle East and this led to hesitation on the part of Europeans about how to respond to this plan and to reconcile the Fahd[6] and Venice plans (Greilsammer and Weiler 1987: 155). After their political cooperation meeting of 13 October 1981, the EC foreign ministers decided to support the Fahd plan. However, the plan was rejected by both the Arab States, at the Arab Summit at Fez, and Israel.

During this period, some EC Member States, such as the UK[7] and France, started to pursue their own national initiatives in the Middle East rather than supporting a European initiative. This further prevented the emergence of a European peace initiative in the Middle East. Especially, France under the Presidency of Mitterrand started to carry out its own national diplomatic initiatives.

During this period four EC Member States, France, the UK, Italy and the Netherlands, decided to participate in the Multinational Sinai Force and Observers which was based on the Egyptian-Israeli Camp David Peace Treaty. On 26 October 1981, the French Foreign Minister Claude Cheysson declared the French determination to participate in the international peace-keeping force to be established in the Sinai in April 1982. On 23 November 1981 the UK, Italy and the Netherlands also declared their decision to participate. On 24 November 1981 other EC Member States approved these four countries' decision on the condition that their participation would facilitate any progress in the direction of a comprehensive peace settlement in the Middle East on the basis of the mutual acceptance of the right to existence and security of all states in the region and the need for the Palestinian people to exercise fully their right to self-determination (Ifestos 1987: 494). These conditions confirmed that these four EC Member States wanted to participate in the MFO on the basis of the principles set out in the Venice Declaration. These four states informed the Israeli Prime Minister Menachem Begin about the conditions for their participation. However, Israel rejected the participation of Europeans on the basis of the principles which contradicted Camp David and asserted that their participation should be based on the Camp David Treaty (ibid.: 496). EC Member States accepted Israel's demand and assured the Israelis that their participation in the MFO would not depend on any political condition, whether stated previously in Venice or elsewhere. After this assurance, Israel approved their participation. As a result of these developments during the early years of the 1980s any possibility of launching a European peace initiative faded away (ibid.).

Israel invaded Lebanon on 5 June 1982 as part of Peace in Galilee operation. On 9 June 1982 the EC foreign ministers met in Bonn and issued a declaration condemning the Israeli invasion of Lebanon. They identified the Israeli invasion as obvious violation of international law and they called for Israel's immediate and unconditional withdrawal from Lebanon with all its forces (ibid.: 505). EC Member States also warned Israel that if Israel continued not to comply with UN Security Council Resolutions which called for the Israeli armed forces' immediate and unconditional withdrawal from Lebanon, they would examine possibilities for future action (ibid.). This phrase implied sanctions against Israel. On 14 June 1982 the EC sent a document to Israel which asked for assurances on 10 points: the recognition of Lebanese sovereignty; a commitment not to occupy or annex any part of Lebanese territory; non-interference in the internal affairs of Lebanon; cooperation with the UN Secretary General; commitment to non-hostility towards the Palestinian people; commitment to non-aggression against neighbouring countries including Syria; observance of the cease-fire established in the territory; the application of the Geneva Convention particularly in respect of the Palestinian and Lebanese prisoners; commitment to grant normal facilities to the press; and commitment to allowing humanitarian organizations to carry out their work without hindrance (Khader 1984: 177). Israel found this list of demands to be unacceptable and rejected them.

At the European Council meeting in Brussels on 28–29 June 1982 European political leaders issued a joint declaration concerning the Arab-Israeli conflict. They repeated their strong condemnation of the Israeli invasion of Lebanon and called for a simultaneous withdrawal of the Israeli and the Palestinian forces from Beirut and the rapid withdrawal of the Israeli forces from the whole of Lebanon (Ifestos 1987: 508). They declared that the return of Lebanon to lasting peace required the total and rapid withdrawal of the Israeli forces from Lebanon, as well as the departure of all foreign forces, excepting those authorized by a legitimate and widely representative Lebanese government, whose authority had been entirely reestablished over the whole of its national territory (Khader 1984: 178). They also reemphasized that peace negotiations should be based on the principles of security for all states and justice for all peoples. Moreover, Israel could achieve this security by satisfying the legitimate aspirations of the Palestinian people, which must be able to exercise its right to self-determination with all that this implied (ibid.). They also stated that Israel could not achieve the security to which it was entitled through the use of force and by presenting other parties with a *fait accompli* (ibid.). They noted that in order for negotiations to be possible, the Palestinian people must be involved and represented (ibid.). EC Member States wanted the Palestinian people to be able to promote their claims and demand by political means. The satisfaction of these claims must take account of the need to recognize and respect the existence and security of all parties involved (ibid.). The Brussels Declaration of 1982, unlike the Venice declaration, used the phrase 'the right to self-determination with all that implies for the Palestinian people' rather than emphasizing the principle of the need for a homeland for the Palestinian people.

Concerning the sanctions against Israel, European political leaders decided to adopt sanctions which could not have any practical
effect on Israel (Greilsammer 1987: 291). They decided to freeze
any high level contact between EC officials and the Israeli government, not to convene the Council of Cooperation provided by the
1975 Cooperation Agreement and also to freeze the two 1977 protocols. They also decided to put off the signing of the second Financial
Protocol (48 million ECU) (ibid.). Nevertheless, throughout the freeze
the contacts between EC officials and the Israeli diplomats continued.
As the two 1977 protocols had a very limited scope, the freeze of these
protocols did not have a significant effect on Israel. Since the amount
of EC funds promised to Israel with the second Financial Protocol was
very small, its postponement did not have a practical effect on Israel
(ibid.: 292).

During the summer of 1982, EC Member States did not take any
collective initiative. France and Egypt carried out a diplomatic initiative during the summer of 1982. On 1 September 1982 the US
President Ronald Reagan announced his peace plan for the Middle
East. The Reagan Plan envisaged total autonomy for the West Bank
and Gaza population, but in association with Jordan, free elections for
the Palestinian authorities in the Occupied Territories, an immediate
freeze of the Israeli settlement policies in the Occupied Territories,
gradual transfer of authority over five years to the elected authorities
(Ifestos 1987: 511). This plan was an extension of the Camp David and
diverged from EC Member States' position on three points: first of all,
it did not envisage self-determination for the Palestinian people; secondly, it did not envisage association of the PLO in the negotiations;
and thirdly, it put forward that the Palestinians in the West Bank and
Gaza would be associated with Jordan, but EC Member States emphasized that this should be decided by the Palestinians depending on the
principle of self-determination (ibid.). Nonetheless, in September 1982
EC Member States issued a declaration and welcomed the Reagan
Plan. They declared that this plan offered an important opportunity
for peaceful progress on the Palestinian question and a step towards the
reconciliation of the parties' conflicting aspirations (ibid.). However,
the Reagan Plan was rejected by both the PLO and Israel.

On 9 September 1982, Arab leaders met at the Fez summit and adopted their own peace plan for the Middle East. This plan included eight points:

1. the Israeli withdrawal from all Arab territories occupied in 1967 including East Jerusalem;
2. the dismantling of the Israeli settlements on the Arab territories after 1967;
3. the guarantee of freedom of worship and practice of religious ceremonies for all religions in the holy places;
4. the reaffirmation of the Palestinian people's right to self-determination and the exercise of its imprescriptible and inalienable national rights under the leadership of the PLO, its sole and legitimate representative, and indemnification of all those who do not desire to return;
5. placing the Gaza Strip and the West Bank under the auspices of the UN for a transitory period not exceeding a few months;
6. the establishment of an independent Palestinian state with Jerusalem as its capital;
7. the guarantee of the UN Security Council for the peace among all states of the region including the independent Palestinian state;
8. the guarantee of the UN Security Council for the respect of the above-mentioned principles.

EC Member States welcomed the Fez Plan and called all the parties to seize the present opportunity to initiate a process of mutual rapprochement leading towards a comprehensive peace settlement. EC Member States highlighted the significance of the Fez Plan. EC Member States identified it as an expression of the common will of the participants of the Fez summit, including the PLO, to work for the achievement of a just peace in the Middle East encompassing all states in the region including Israel (ibid.: 512). However, the Fez Plan was strongly rejected by Israel.

In the later part of the 1980s EC Member States did not attempt to launch their own collective Middle East peace initiative. They began to pursue a common policy of supporting the Reagan Plan, the Fez Plan and the Franco-Egyptian diplomatic initiatives while relegating the Venice Declaration to the background (Greilsammer and Weiler

1987: 91). They continued to emphasize their commitment to a comprehensive, just and lasting settlement of the Arab-Israeli conflict in accordance with UN Security Council Resolutions 242 and 338, the right to existence and security of all states in the Middle East, the right of the Palestinian people to self-determination, with all that implies, the association of the PLO with peace negotiations. They called on Israel to end its territorial occupation which it has maintained since the 1967 war.

Toward the end of the 1980s, especially after the outbreak of the First Palestinian Intifada in 1987, European political leaders called for the convening of an international peace conference under the auspices of the UN for the solution of the conflict, which would represent a suitable framework for the necessary negotiations between the parties directly concerned. They pronounced their preparedness to play an active role in bringing the positions of the parties concerned closer to one another with a view to such a Conference being convened (Ifestos 1987: 528). They affirmed their readiness to contribute to the search for a comprehensive, just and lasting settlement of the Arab-Israeli conflict, including the Palestinian problem, in accordance with the 1980 Venice Declaration. They announced their preparedness to cooperate fully in the economic and social development of the people of the Middle East. With these statements, EC Member States emphasized their willingness to move from common declarations to common diplomatic action. In December 1988 EC Member States appointed a contact group of foreign ministers assigned with the task to promote the principle of a peace conference (Aoun 2003: 292).

In summary, after the Venice Declaration of 1980, in the early 1980s, although EC Member States had attempted to launch their own collective Middle East peace initiative and set their own path, independently of the USA, they had failed. During this period, individual EC Member States, mainly the UK and France, carried out their individual peace initiatives. Still, EC Member States collectively issued common declarations recalling the EC's previously agreed principles and rhetorically supporting other peace initiatives or condemning the Israeli acts in the Occupied Territories and the Israeli invasion of Lebanon. During the 1980s, EC Member States continued pursuing a declaratory policy. During the 1980s, the EC's policy was based on 'declarations rather than action' or 'declarations and call to action'. As a result, EC Member States remained bystanders at successive peace initiatives (Robin 1997: 74) while the USA became the major player in finding peaceful solutions to the Arab-Israeli conflict. Especially after Camp David, the USA became the main mediator in the MEPP as the EU just played a supplementary and subordinate role to the US diplomatic efforts (Ifestos 1987: 515). EC Member States supported the US diplomatic initiatives, such as the Reagan Plan. Ellen Laipson (1990: 7) argued that during the 1980s the EC had not played a major role in the Middle East either as a crisis mediator or peacemaker. In addition to Laipson, Hazel Smith also correctly put forward that during the 1980s, the EC failed to play a significant part in securing the amelioration of the Arab-Israeli conflict or in making any noteworthy contribution to peace (Smith 2002: 169).

During the 1980s the EC was sidelined and marginalized; this was mainly due to the Israeli and the US denial of the EC to play an active role in the quest for a peaceful solution to the Arab-Israeli conflict. As Ilan Greilsammer and Joseph Weiler (1987: 103) argued, in spite of various declarations, visits, participations in multinational forces and all the rest, the EC did not have a visible impact on the Arab-Israeli conflict (ibid.). They added that the USA directly, and the Soviet Union indirectly, acted as the major actors, with Venice and its aftermath not really producing a real European presence (ibid.). As Joel Peters (1999b: 300) argued, the positions and diplomacy adopted by the EC throughout the 1980s did little to advance its ambitions of playing an important role in bringing about a peaceful resolution to the Arab-Israeli conflict.

During the 1980s there were three reasons which prevented EC Member States from playing an effective and active role in the mediation efforts in the MEPP. First of all, the EC's pro-Arab stance reflected in its declarations made it an unacceptable honest mediator in the eyes of Israel. Secondly, the EC had neither the capacity nor any decisive influence over the parties to bring them to the negotiating table (ibid.). Especially, EPC's institutional deficiency prevented the EC to play an effective and active role in the mediation efforts in the MEPP. EPC did not possess a permanent and central institution like the General Secretariat of the Council for the EC, which would enable the EC to swiftly respond to and intervene in international crises like the Middle East conflict (Dieckhoff 1987). The lack of an administrative secretariat, which would have enabled the Presidency to organize meetings, prepare the topics debated and ensure the political tasks are following up, prevented European political leaders from agreeing on a joint position in times of crisis (ibid.: 275–76). For instance, it took one month to agree on the Brussels Declaration of 1973. The institutional weakness of EPC made it highly reactive process with declaratory outputs lacking operational capacity (ibid.: 277). Although European political leaders made joint statements, they were unable to concretize these statements due to their lack of tools for that purpose (ibid.). For example, the Venice Declaration of 1980 emphasized the Palestinians' right to self-determination and the need to involve the PLO in any negotiations, but the Declaration could not provide concrete proposals to put these ideas into action (ibid.). Hence, EPC's limited potential for crisis management acted as a considerable impediment and prevented the EC to play an effective and active role in the mediation efforts in the MEPP (ibid.: 278). Thirdly, the USA did not want to share the driving seat in the MEPP (Musu 2007: 16) and reserved for itself the role of a major player.

The Quest for a Pro-Active European Role in the MEPP in the 1990s

During the 1990s, EU Member States went beyond just issuing common declarations on the Arab-Israeli conflict. They began to emerge from the sidelines and play an active role in the MEPP. As put forward by an EU official, the EU became a player in the MEPP in the 1990s. He noted that since the early 1990s, the EU has got involved in the game.[8] The EU participated in the multilateral track of the Madrid Peace Process. The EU acted as the chair or gavel-holder of the Regional Economic Development Working Group, one of the working groups of multilateral track of the Madrid Peace Process. In the 1990s the EU became the largest donor of financial and technical aid to the Palestinian Authority and the MEPP. In the political dimension of the peace process and in bilateral negotiations, the USA continued to play the role of the sole mediator of the peace process and although the EU played a significant role in the economic dimension of the peace process, it was still sidelined and excluded from the political dimension of the peace process. The Israeli rejection of any country except the USA to play the role of the sole mediator of the peace process and the EU's lack of military capabilities and sufficient political instruments forced the EU to focus on the economic dimension of the peace process (Özcan 2005). The EU played a key role in the construction of the peace process between the Palestinians and the Israelis (ibid.). In 1995 the EU launched the EMP, which was seen by many as complementary to the MEPP. The EMP provided a multilateral forum for the conflicting parties, the Arabs and the Israelis to sit on the same table and discuss. During the second half of the 1990s, the EU appointed its special representative for the MEPP in 1996. In 1999, Javier Solana was appointed as the High Representative for the CFSP. These two appointments enhanced the EU's presence and visibility in the MEPP in the late 1990s.

The Maastricht Treaty and the Launch of the CFSP

During the early 1990s the Cold War, which had shaped international politics since the early 1950s, ended and the security environment in Europe changed. The Soviet Union no longer posed a threat to Europe and the bipolar character of international politics faded away. The new security challenges for Europe can be listed as political and economic instability in Central and Eastern Europe, ethnic and nationalist conflict, cross-border terrorism, massive immigration, destruction of environment, organized crime, spread of nuclear weapons and massive violation of human rights. (Sjursen n.d.; Sakellariou and Keating 2003: 84). In the post-Cold War period, two important events convinced EU Member States to further their cooperation in areas of foreign and security policy and to launch the CFSP by the Maastricht Treaty. These events were the Gulf War in 1991 and the Yugoslav Conflicts in the early 1990s.

During the Gulf Crisis and War, EU Member States failed to maintain a common position on the crisis due to the diverging domestic political considerations and varying national interests of EU Member

States. On the issue of European hostages in Iraq and Kuwait in particular, unilateral initiatives[9] by France, Britain and Germany undermined the coherence of EU Member States. The Gulf Crisis and War significantly affected the negotiations over the EU's CFSP. The Gulf Crisis and War changed the course of discussion on a common foreign and security policy. Before the war, the EU's foreign policy laid on peaceful lines. The trend of history laid in disarmament and dismantling of military alliances and it was accepted that the EU's contribution to the new security environment in Europe was through non-military means as a civilian power (Nuttall 2000: 147). However, the Gulf War obliged Member States to confront their global responsibilities in the post-Cold War world, and the security and defence dimensions of the CFSP gained more importance (ibid.: 129).

During the breakdown of the former Yugoslavia, EU Member States also lacked a coherent approach especially on issues of the recognition of Croatia and Slovenia and military intervention. Therefore, EU Member States were not able to stop the conflict and bloodshed in the region. Their lack of coherence during the crisis undermined the EU's effectiveness and international credibility, because EU Member States were not able to stop civil war in Yugoslavia and bloodshed continued until the UN became involved in the conflict, and although in the early days of the conflict, Jacques Poos declared it was the hour of Europe not of the Americans, and that the Yugoslav conflict could only be solved by the Europeans, it could not turn into reality and the hour of Europe had lasted 14 months (ibid.: 223).

These two events demonstrated to EU Member States that they needed to adopt and maintain a coherent position in order for the EU to become an effective international actor and have an impact on international events. The recognition crisis[10] during the Yugoslav Conflict and the hostage crisis during the Gulf War demonstrated the limits of EPC's ability in coordinating the foreign policies of Member States and motivated them to form a common foreign policy rather than a coordination of foreign policies of Member States. Furthermore, the Gulf War and the Yugoslav Conflict broke the deadlock on security and defence issues in the ongoing Maastricht negotiations. EU Member States realized the risk of serious security and defence problems in the Post-Cold

War era and the deficiencies in the ability of EPC to influence the foreign policies of most powerful Member States like Germany. Moreover, the reluctance of the USA to be involved in the conflict led Europeans to believe that they should take more responsibility for their own security in the Post-Cold War era (Smith 2004: 179).

The Maastricht Treaty, or Treaty on European Union, was signed by EU Member States on 7 February 1992 and entered into force on 1 November 1993 following its ratification by all Member States. With the Maastricht Treaty, the European Community took the name of the European Union and it was constructed on three pillars: the European Community, the CFSP and Cooperation in Justice and Home Affairs. With the Maastricht Treaty, a single institutional framework was established and all three pillars were put under a single institutional framework. With the introduction of the CFSP, cooperation in areas of foreign and security policy was replaced by a common policy. With the Maastricht Treaty, all questions related to the security of the EU were put under the CFSP. In order to ensure concerted and convergent action of Member States, two new instruments of action were introduced: common positions and joint actions. With the Maastricht Treaty, the old Ministerial Meetings of EPC was replaced by the General Affairs Council (Foreign Ministers) as the only decision-making body at the ministerial level for all matters concerning foreign affairs. EPC Secretariat merged with the General Secretariat of the Council. The EU Presidency was tasked with representation of the EU in matters related to the CFSP, implementation of common measures and expressing the position of the EU in international organizations and international conferences.

The main reason behind EU Member States' launch of the CFSP was to achieve a CFSP which would enable the EU to project onto the international arena the combined power of EU Member States. It was hoped that in this way the EU would carry more weight and influence in international affairs than the power exercised by each member state independently (Musu 2010c: 52). The creation of the CFSP symbolized acceleration in the process of European political integration and in the transformation of the EU into a global actor, increasing its aspirations of playing a more relevant role in the Middle East (Musu 2007a: 17).

The Madrid Peace Process and the EU

In the autumn of 1991, the USA took another Middle East peace initiative. In the autumn of 1990, the US administration promised a peace process for the Middle East in order to get the Arab countries to join the international coalition against Iraq or persuade them to stay on the sidelines (Bilgin 2005). After its success in the Gulf War in early 1991, the US administration decided to establish a framework for negotiations, which could lead to a comprehensive peace settlement in the Arab-Israeli conflict (Dosenrode and Stubkjaer 2002: 120). After the US success in the Gulf War US President George Bush declared that the campaign to contain Iraqi aggression and force Iraq to withdraw from Kuwait should be understood in the context of a 'New World Order', in which international disputes would be settled through peaceful means (Tessler 1994: 749). In March 1991, President Bush declared the achievement of the Arab-Israeli peace on the basis of UN Security Council Resolution 242 and through an exchange of land for peace as one of the four objectives of the US Middle East policy (ibid.: 750). After this speech, US Secretary of State James Baker visited the Middle East and stated that the USA would propose a series of confidence-building measures as a prologue to the Arab-Israeli peace talks to be held under the co-sponsorship of the USA and the Soviet Union (ibid.). On 19 October 1991, the USA with the Soviet Union sent a letter of invitation to the parties of the Arab-Israeli conflict, including Israel, Syria, Lebanon, Jordan and the Palestinians, which invited them to come together and hold a peace conference in Madrid. The invited parties accepted the invitation and the Madrid Peace Conference was convened in Madrid on 30 October 1991. The USSR was the co-sponsor of the conference with the USA. Delegations from Lebanon, Syria, Jordan, Egypt and Israel participated in the conference; the Palestinian representatives participated as a part of the Jordanian delegation, because Israel rejected their participation as a separate entity. The EU with the UN and the Gulf Cooperation Council attended to the conference as observer.

At the European Council meeting in Luxembourg on 28–29 June 1991, the leaders of EU Member States declared their firm support for the US peace initiative. As a participant, they declared that they

aimed to make their full contribution to the success of the peace conference and to the negotiations between parties. They also declared their
determination to contribute to the economic and social development
of all peoples in the region once the prospect of peace was clear. On 10
October 1991 the leaders of EU Member States issued a declaration on
the MEPP which reiterated their full support for the US and the Soviet
Union's Middle East peace initiative. They welcomed the agreement
in principle of all parties of the conflict to the approach proposed by
US Secretary of State James Baker. They declared their determination
to give all possible support to efforts to convene a Middle East Peace
Conference and to play an active role as a full participant in such a
Conference alongside the USA and the Soviet Union.

At the European Council meeting in Maastricht on 9–10 December
1991, the leaders of EU Member States reiterated their commitment
to make an active contribution to progress in the multilateral track of
negotiations on regional cooperation. They emphasized that multilateral and bilateral negotiations should run in parallel and be complementary with each other. They also reemphasized their commitment
to do all they could to promote significant steps towards a comprehensive, just and lasting peace settlement for the Middle East.

The Madrid Peace Conference launched the Peace Process which
was composed of two tracks: bilateral and multilateral. The EU was
sidelined and excluded from bilateral political talks between Israel and
the Arab states, but was given a more prominent role within the multilateral track of the Madrid Peace Process by the USA, because the
US policymakers expected the EU to contribute a substantial share to
the funding of the peace process (Soetendorp 2002: 286). A Palestinian
diplomat suggested that the Europeans were 'sitting in the last seat of
the conference' and did not play a political role in the Madrid Peace
Process. He maintained that there was an absence of the EU as a political actor in the Madrid Peace Process.[11]

Bilateral talks took place under the auspices of the USA in
Washington, but the EU was not invited to participate. The talks concentrated on the political issues of territorial control and sovereignty,
border demarcations, security arrangements and the political rights of
the Palestinians (Peters 1999b: 300). The USA took the monopoly of

high politics, the bilateral political talks between Israel and the Arab states (Dieckhoff 2005: 54).

The EU participated in the multilateral track of the Madrid Peace Process, which was opened in Moscow in January 1992. The first purpose of the multilateral talks was to facilitate progress at the bilateral talks of the peace process by creating a separate forum in which Israel and the Arab states could discuss technical issues of reciprocal concern, which in turn would serve as confidence-building measures between the parties (Peters 1996: 5). The second purpose of the multilateral talks was addressing region-wide problems at a regional level (ibid.). Multilateral talks concentrated on a range of primarily non-political issues which extend across national boundaries, and the resolution of which is essential for the promotion of long-term regional development of security (ibid.). Multilateral talks mainly focused on low politics issues, such as water resources, environment, regional economic development and refugees.

The multilateral talks were different from bilateral talks. They provided Israel and the Arab states with an alternative diplomatic area to engage in low-risk communication and exchange, to develop new forms of cooperation and to generate creative solutions and plans for the future on a regional level (Peters 1999a: 4).

The idea of a multilateral track was grounded in a functionalist and liberalist approach to international cooperation and peace: the entangling of the states in the Middle East in an ever-widening web of economic, technical and welfare interdependencies would drive them to leave behind their political and/or ideological rivalries (Peters 1999b: 302). The process of continuing cooperation in areas of reciprocal concern would blur long-held hostilities and would create a new perception of shared needs. Continuous interaction would be accompanied by a learning process which would promote a fundamental change in attitudes and lead to a convergence of expectations and the institutionalization of norms of behaviour (ibid.). Out of progress in the multilateral domain would emerge a vision of what real peace might entail and the benefits that would accrue to all parties, thereby facilitating progress in bilateral talks. Drawing parallels from the experience of European integration process, it was believed that functional cooperation would eventually spill over into regional peace (Peters 1996: 6). Moreover, the multilateral talks indicated the emerging concept of cooperative security in the post-Cold War era, with a greater emphasis on dealing with the root causes of conflict and promoting confidence, rather than relying primarily on deterrence and containment (Peters 1999a: 1).

Multilateral talks encompassed five working groups, on water resources, environment, refugees, arms control and regional security, and regional economic development (Peters 1996: 10). The EU acted as the gavel-holder (chair) for one of five working groups, the Regional Economic Development Working Group. The EU as a gavel-holder has the responsibility to ensure the smooth functioning of the meeting and exert authority only if discussions become too disorderly (ibid.: 11). As the gavel-holder, the EU actively promoted ideas and ventures for future economic cooperation among the parties of the region (Peters 1999b: 303). REDWG was the largest and most active of the five working groups both in terms of the number of participants and in terms of the number of projects and intersessional activities (Peters 1996: 46; Miller 2006: 643). The purpose of the REDWG was to bring together the regional parties and to draw the international community into the peace process (Peters 1999b: 303). The REDWG was for the creation of a new set of mutually beneficial relations between the parties and the building of a new era of economic prosperity for the Middle East as a whole (Peters 1996: 46). It was believed that sustainable peace in the Middle East could only be achieved if bilateral agreements, once concluded, were accompanied by a long-term process of economic cooperation among all the parties of the region.

The first three rounds of talks of the REDWG took place in Brussels from May 1992 to May 1993. During these rounds a list of 10 areas of activity was determined and 'shepherds' were assigned to take responsibility for the running in each of these areas. Most of these areas of activity focused on infrastructural development or on sectoral coordination. The areas included communications and transport led by France, energy led by the EU, tourism led by Japan, agriculture led by Spain, financial markets led by the UK, trade led by Germany, training led by the USA, networks led by the EU, institutions, sectors and principles led by the Egypt and bibliography led by Canada. At the fourth round of talks that took place in Copenhagen in November 1993, the Copenhagen Action Plan was adopted. This plan formed the working basis of the activities of the REDWG. At the plenary meetings held in Rabat in June 1994 and Bonn in January 1994, the participating countries responsible reported on the various activities undertaken and announced new initiatives within their respective areas of activity. In order to finance these activities the EU declared that it would allocate $6 million for the preparation of feasibility studies and a further $9.2 million for the preparation of studies and the running of intersessional activities for the rapid implementation of the Copenhagen Action Plan (ibid.: 47).

The EU encouraged the regional parties to explore ideas about the future long-term nature of their economic relations and to develop a vision of potential institutional mechanisms and frameworks to support and sustain their efforts towards regional cooperation. At the plenary meeting at Rabat in June 1994 regional parties agreed on a number of guidelines and principles; they recognized that there was a need for the pooling of common capacities and joint tackling of common problems through coordinated efforts; the removal of obstacles to private sector's ability to play a more prominent role; the promotion of regional trade; the facilitating of investment and the development of infrastructure; and the encouragement of the free flow of people, goods, services, capital and information within the region.

At Rabat it was also decided to establish a Monitoring Group composed of Egypt, Israel, Jordan and the Palestinians which would take a more direct role in implementing the Copenhagen Action Plan, in organizing the various sectoral activities and in developing a set of priorities and identifying future projects for the working group. The Monitoring Group was composed of Egypt, Israel, Jordan, the Palestinians, the EU, the USA, Russia, Japan, Canada, Saudi Arabia, Tunisia and Norway and co-chaired by the EU and four core regional participants including Egypt, Israel, Jordan and the Palestinians. In order to effectively coordinate extensive range of activities of the working group, at the Amman Economic Summit in November 1995, it was decided that a permanent Secretariat would be established in Amman. After its establishment, the Secretariat organized several regional meetings and workshops focusing on practical programmes, often of a technical nature, aimed at promoting regional economic cooperation. The establishment of the Secretariat was an important, qualitative step in the institutionalization of the multilateral process, and in leaving responsibility for directing process of regional cooperation in the hands of the regional parties themselves (Peters 1999a: 5). At the time the REDWG Secretariat was the first and only functioning regional institution, produced by the MEPP and headed by the EU, in which the Egyptian, the Israeli, the Jordanian and the Palestinian officials could work together on a daily basis (Peters 1999b: 306).

Bilateral talks came to a halt after the change of government in Israel and the election of Benjamin Netanyahu as the Prime Minister of Israel in 1996. Both talks and the activities of the REDWG came to a halt. There were three main reasons behind the halt of both bilateral and multilateral talks. First, Arab policy-makers thought that there had not been enough progress in the bilateral talks. Second, Arab policymakers were concerned about the Israeli domination in the economic and technological fields if they agreed to strengthen Middle Eastern regionalism. Third, Arab policy-makers were frustrated with the US double standards. They thought that while ignoring the Israeli failure to implement UN resolutions on Palestine, the USA used threat of air attacks against Iraq which failed to cooperate with the UN inspection team (Bilgin 2005: 155).

Multilateral talks played a complementary role to the bilateral talks and mainly provided a forum for the discussion of areas which were primarily technical in nature (Peters 1998: 68). The multilateral talks allowed the states in the region to attend to long-term issues that should be dealt with if and when a settlement was reached (ibid.). The multilateral talks also enabled the states in the region to begin to develop a set of principles, norms, rules and decision-making procedures to govern the nature of their future regional economic, social and cultural relations (ibid.). The multilateral talks also enabled active participation of the international community in securing a comprehensive and lasting peace settlement of the Arab-Israeli conflict. The multilateral talks in general, REDWG in particular, enabled the states in the region and international community to promote a unique partnership among them in promoting the conditions for a new era of regional cooperation in the Middle East (Peters 1996: 60). REDWG facilitated political ties and cooperation between the Arabs and the Israelis (Soetendorp 2002: 287).

The EU, as the gavel-holder of the largest and most active one of five working groups, played an important role in the multilateral and economic dimension of the Madrid Peace Process which was a process complementary to the bilateral talks. The EU with its historical experience in solving interstate conflicts and achieving peace through economic cooperation helped the states in the region to establish a dialogue on the future regional and multilateral economic cooperation among them.

The Madrid Peace Process was the confirmation of a position long defended by the EU that it was necessary to convene an international peace conference for finding a comprehensive, just and lasting settlement for the Arab-Israeli conflict, which would represent a suitable forum for the direct negotiations between the parties concerned. The EU's other long-defended position, the necessity of the participation of the PLO as the only representative of the Palestinian people in the peace negotiations, was realized by the Oslo Process in which Israel and the PLO recognized each other and carried out direct negotiations.

The Oslo Peace Process and the EU

During 1993 the officials of Israel and the PLO carried out secret direct negotiations in Oslo, Norway under the sponsorship of the Norwegian government, which culminated in the Oslo Peace Process. This process led to a breakthrough in the Arab-Israeli Conflict when Israel and the PLO reached an agreement on 20 August 1993 and signed the Oslo Accords, the so-called Declaration of Principles on Interim Self-Government Arrangements in Washington on 13 September 1993. The EU was excluded from these direct negotiations. Although the EU was represented at the signing ceremony in Washington by the Belgian Foreign Minister Willy Claes for the EU Presidency and the President of the European Commission Jacques Delors, their role was limited to issuing of statements of support (Martin-Diaz 1999: 32). The Oslo Peace Process represented the mutual recognition of Israel and the PLO which had been one of the long-defended positions of the EU since the late 1970s and early 1980s. It confirmed the EU's basic assumption that negotiations could not proceed without prior mutual recognition by the two parties to the conflict (Salamé 1994: 231). The Israeli Prime Minister Yitzhak Rabin and the PLO's chairman Yasser Arafat signed a series of mutual recognition letters on 9 September 1993 by which Israel recognized the PLO as the legitimate representative of the Palestinian people and the PLO recognized Israel's right to exist and also renounced terrorism, violence and its desire for the destruction of Israel. The Oslo Accords were the materialization of the EU's long-standing call for association of the PLO with the peace negotiations as the sole and legitimate representative of the Palestinian people.

The Oslo Accords provided a framework for a future peace settlement. It envisaged the withdrawal of the Israeli forces from parts of the Gaza Strip and West Bank and the establishment of a Palestinian Interim Self-Government Authority,[12] an elected Council, for the Palestinian people in the West Bank and the Gaza Strip, for a interim period not exceeding five years, leading to a permanent settlement based on the UN Security Council Resolution 242 and the UN Security Council Resolution 338, an integral part of the whole peace process.

In order that the Palestinian people in the Gaza Strip and the West Bank would govern themselves according to democratic principles, the Oslo Accords envisaged direct, free and general elections to be held for the Council. According to the Oslo Accords, the five-year interim period would begin with the withdrawal of the Israeli forces from the Gaza Strip and Jericho area. Permanent status negotiations would begin as soon as possible between Israel and the Palestinians, but not later than the beginning of the third year of the interim period. Permanent status negotiations, which would start as soon as possible, would cover the remaining issues, including Jerusalem, refugees, settlements, security arrangements, borders, relations and cooperation with other neighbours, and other issues of common interest. The Oslo Accords envisaged the transfer of authority from the Israeli military government and its Civil Administration to the authorized Palestinians in areas of education and culture, health, social welfare, direct taxation and tourism. In order to guarantee public order and internal security for the Palestinians in the Gaza Strip and West Bank, the Palestinian Council would establish a strong police force, while Israel would continue to carry the responsibility for defending against external threats as well as the responsibility for overall security of the Israelis to protect their internal security and public order. The Oslo Accords envisaged the establishment of an Israeli-Palestinian Economic Cooperation Committee in order to develop and implement in a cooperative manner the programmes identified in the protocols. The Oslo Accords also envisaged the redeployment of the Israeli military forces in the West Bank and the Gaza Strip.

After the signing of the Oslo Accords the EU started to become the largest external donor of financial and technical aid to the Palestinian Authority. The EU invested €3.47 billion in the Palestinian Authority during the period between 1994 and 2001 (Miller 2006: 644). This aid has been mainly directed toward projects in the field of housing, micro-credit and the assistance of small-scale businesses and education, the Palestinian economic and social infrastructure building and the Palestinian institution building (Peters 2000: 163). The logic behind this aid was that it was expected that it would trigger sufficient private sector investment flows to bring the living conditions of the Palestinians living in the West Bank and the Gaza Strip up to acceptable levels (Martin-Diaz 1999: 32).

On 13 September 1993, the leaders of EC Member States issued a declaration on the MEPP. They appreciated the vision and courage of the Israeli and the Palestinian leaders who signed the Oslo Accords. They also declared their political support and readiness to participate in further international arrangements arising in connection with the implementation of the agreement. They also declared their intention to continue to be the largest financial contributor to the Occupied Territories. They reiterated their commitment to a comprehensive peace. They declared their hope that progress would be accomplished in other bilateral negotiations and in multilateral talks of future cooperation. Finally, as the gavel-holder of REDWG, they declared their preparedness to contribute to all forms of regional economic cooperation.

On 19 April 1994, the EU Council adopted the Joint Action[13] in support of the MEPP. In the Joint Action it was stated that in order to work for the achievement of a comprehensive peace settlement in the Middle East based on the relevant UN Security Council Resolutions, the EU would participate in international arrangements agreed by the parties to guarantee peace in the context of the Madrid Peace Process. It was also stated that the EU would use its influence to encourage all the parties to support the peace process unconditionally on the basis of the invitations to the Madrid Conference and work for the strengthening of democracy and respect for human rights and make its contribution to defining the future shape of relations between the regional parties in the context of the Arms Control and Regional Security Working Group. The EU would also develop its role in the Ad Hoc Liaison Committee responsible for the coordination of international aid to the Occupied Territories, maintain its leading role in the REDWG and develop its participation in other multilateral groups and consider additional ways in which it might contribute towards the development of the region.

The EU would pursue confidence-building measures, which it had submitted to the parties, pursue *démarches* to the Arab States with the aim of securing an end to the boycott of Israel and closely follow the future of the Israeli settlements throughout the Occupied Territories and pursue *démarches* to Israel about this issue. It was emphasized in the Joint Action that in order to contribute actively and urgently to the creation of a Palestinian Police Force, the EU would provide assistance; the EU Presidency, in close cooperation with the Commission, would facilitate coordination through an exchange of information between Member States on their bilateral assistance. The EU would allocate a maximum amount of 10 million ECUs for the provision of assistance for the creation of a Palestinian Police Force. The EU would, at the request of the parties, participate in the protection of the Palestinian people through a temporary international presence in the Occupied Territories, as called for in UN Security Council Resolution 904. The EU, at the request of the parties, would implement a coordinated programme of assistance in preparing for and observing the elections in the Occupied Territories prefigured by the Oslo Accords.

Israel and the PLO continued their negotiations after the signing of the Oslo Accords and these negotiations resulted in the signing of Cairo Agreement on 4 May 1994. Cairo Agreement marked the beginning of the self-government interim period for the Palestinians, and can be identified as the first application of the Oslo Accords (Martin-Diaz 1999: 33). The EU only attended the signing ceremony of Cairo Agreement, represented by the Vice-President of the European Commission Manuel Marin, who informed Yasser Arafat that the European Commission would be contributing €10 million to help finance the Palestinian police force (ibid.). At the Corfu European Council on 24–25 June 1994, EU Member States welcomed the Cairo agreement and identified it as an important step towards the full implementation of the Oslo Accords. EU Member States also welcomed the creation of a Palestinian police force and reiterated the EU's willingness to provide further assistance to move the peace process towards a successful conclusion.

On 26 October 1994, Israel and Jordan signed a peace treaty near Aqaba and the EU was represented at the signing ceremony by the German Foreign Minister Klaus Kinkel for the EU Presidency and Hans Van den Broek for the European Commission (ibid.). Following the Israeli-Jordan Treaty of Peace, the Israeli-Palestinian Interim Agreement on the West Bank and the Gaza Strip (Oslo II Agreement) was signed in Washington on 28 September 1995. The agreement envisaged the expansion of the geographic borders of the Palestinian self-government on the West Bank and the election, the transition period, of a Palestinian Council which would be vested with legislative and executive powers (ibid.: 35). The EU was represented at the signing ceremony by the Spanish Prime Minister Felipe Gonzales for the EU Presidency, who signed the Treaty as a witness (ibid.).

The EU welcomed both the Israeli-Jordan Treaty of Peace and the Israeli-Palestinian Interim Agreement on the West Bank and the Gaza Strip. During the post-Oslo period, the EU has continued its financial contribution to the peace process, but was still sidelined from bilateral political negotiations. The USA had continued to play the role of main mediator in the bilateral talks among the parties of the conflict. The EU had continued to play a supplementary and subordinate role to the US diplomatic efforts. The EU had provided the basic economic foundation of the peace process (Musu 2007a: 19).

The EU Foreign Ministers at the General Affairs Council meeting on 2 October 1995 emphasized the historic importance of the Interim Agreement. They declared that they considered it necessary to contribute towards the success of that agreement and that economic and social development was a key factor for achieving just and lasting peace. They pronounced their determination to strengthen cooperation by the EU with the Territories covered by the peace agreement. They invited the European Commission to start explanatory talks with the Palestinian Authority with a view to the conclusion of a Euro-Mediterranean Association Agreement as soon as circumstances permitted. They called upon the Commission to take necessary measures to enable the Territories covered by the peace agreement to benefit from increased aid. They called upon the European Investment Bank to allocate 250 million ECUs in the form of appropriation for projects for developing the Territories covered by the peace agreement. They announced that for the observation of the election for the Palestinian Legislative Council, the Council and the Commission had set up the European Electoral Unit and 10 million ECUs had been allocated for it. This declaration demonstrated the EU's determination to financially contribute to both the Oslo Peace Process and the Palestinian Authority.

In accordance with the Oslo Accords, the election for the Palestinian Legislative Council was held on 20 January 1996 in the West Bank, Gaza Strip and East Jerusalem. The EU had financially and politically contributed to the elections. The EU donated 17 million ECUs via CFSP, 7 million ECUs were allocated for the preparation of the technical aspects of the elections, such as the establishment of polling stations, funding a voter education campaign and setting up a press centre, and 10 million ECUs were spent on ensuring international monitoring of elections (Dosenrode and Stubkjaer 2002: 136–37). The EU deployed the EU Electoral Unit, composed of 300 observers under the chairmanship of the former Swedish Minister of Justice, Carl Lidbom to observe elections to the Palestinian Legislative Council, scheduled for 20 January 1996. After the elections Lidbom issued a press release which stated that although not perfect the elections were reasonably free (Martin-Diaz 1999: 38). After the elections the EU Presidency issued a declaration on 22 January 1996 on behalf of EU Member States in which it congratulated the candidates elected and the Palestinian people for the political maturity they had shown in their approach to democracy (ibid.).

The Euro-Mediterranean Partnership

The progress in both the multilateral and bilateral tracks of the Madrid Peace Process and the signing of the above-mentioned treaties and agreements provided a favourable environment for the EU to launch the EMP. The EMP, or the so-called Barcelona Process, was launched at the Euro-Mediterranean Conference of Ministers of Foreign Affairs, held in Barcelona on 27–28 November 1995. Along with 15 Member States of the EU, 12 Mediterranean countries including Algeria, Cyprus, Egypt, Israel, Jordan, Lebanon, Malta, Morocco, Syria, Tunisia, Turkey and the Palestinian Authority were the members of the EMP. The EMP was the successor of the GMP,[14] which was launched by EC Member States at the Paris Summit on 19–20 October 1972. The GMP reflected the EC's regional and economic approach to the Mediterranean region. With the GMP, the EC for the first time addressed the Mediterranean non-member countries as a region, within a single policy framework (Bicchi 2007: 63).

In the mid-1990s the main motivation behind the EU policy-makers' launch of the EMP was to help maintain security in its southern periphery by the way of encouraging inter-state cooperation and increasing regional interdependence as a means of maintaining stability in the Mediterranean (Bilgin 2005: 271). The EMP aimed to establish a wide framework of political, economic and social relations between Member States of the EU and Partners of the Southern Mediterranean. It was designed to build a comprehensive political, economic and social partnership between EU Member States and the Southern Mediterranean countries. The EMP was designed to develop regional cooperative frameworks in the region (Peters 1998). The EMP has three main objectives: to establish a comprehensive political and security partnership, which refers to the establishment of a common area of peace and stability through the reinforcement of political and security dialogue on a regular basis; to establish a comprehensive economic and financial partnership, which refers to the construction of a zone of shared prosperity through an economic and financial partnership and the gradual establishment of a free trade area by the year 2010; and to establish a comprehensive partnership in social, cultural and human affairs, which refers to the development of human resources, the promotion of understanding between different cultures and exchanges between civil societies. The EMP was the EU-only initiative in which the USA did not take part; this enhanced the EU's profile, presence and visibility in the region.

Although the EMP was not designed as an instrument for the MEPP and was supposed to be independent from it, it made significant contributions to it. The EMP provided a complementary diplomatic multilateral forum in which tensions could be reduced between Israel and the Arab states (ibid.: 71). The EMP, to a certain extent, imitated and expanded the model of the multilateral track of the Madrid Peace Process (Dannreuther 2004: 158). Most of the issues discussed in the multilateral talks, such as water resources, industry and energy policy, tourism and environment, found resonance in the follow-up meetings to the EMP. Most of the security issues discussed at the EMP were built upon the ideas developed within the Arms Control and Regional Security Working Group (Peters 1999a: 71).

The EMP provided a framework in which, among other processes, the parties to the Middle East conflict would be able to build trust and institutionalize their relations in the political, economic and societal spheres as well as in the security field (Asseburg 2004: 179). It served the aim of peace-building and long-term regional stabilization by laying the foundations for economic development and regional integration (ibid.).

The EMP provided a multilateral regional forum for dialogue between the parties of the Arab-Israeli Conflict, notably Israel, Lebanon and Syria. Until the Barcelona Process, Syria and Lebanon refused to participate in both bilateral and multilateral tracks of the Madrid Peace Process, because they considered it as a cover for the normalization of relations with Israel before a comprehensive political settlement of the

Arab-Israeli conflict had been reached. Syria and Lebanon argued that the Arab world should not discuss regional cooperation with Israel until a comprehensive political settlement of the Arab-Israeli conflict had been reached at the bilateral level (Robin 1997: 81; Peters 1999a: 69). However, Lebanon and Syria participated in the EMP and signed the Barcelona Declaration along with Israel. The EU managed to bring Syria and Lebanon to the negotiating table with Israel in a multilateral forum, which the multilateral track of peace process had failed to do (ibid.: 70). Moreover, the EMP enabled the Palestinian Authority to participate as an equal Mediterranean partner and thus a quasi-national actor, which was a fact of high symbolic value with regard to the Palestinian self-determination. Also, with the EMP, the Arab States accepted Israel as a partner in the process, thus allowing Israel to begin to break out of its regional isolation (Asseburg 2003: 179).

The EMP reflected the EU's regional, multilateral and economic approach for promoting peace, security and stability in the Mediterranean region. The EU's prominent role in the multilateral track of the MEPP in the 1990s was complemented by the EMP. Although the EU intended the two processes to be independent of each other, the Barcelona Process and the MEPP followed a parallel development. Progress in both the bilateral and the multilateral track of the MEPP facilitated a progress in the Barcelona Process and the stalemate in the peace process had a negative spill over effect on the Barcelona Process in the second half of the 1990s. The stalemate emerged in the peace process between 1996 and 1999 hindered progress in the Barcelona Process. Moreover, after the outbreak of the Al-Aqsa Intifada in September 2000 and the escalation of violence between the Israelis and the Palestinians, the Barcelona Process was deadlocked. The Marseilles meeting of Euro-Mediterranean foreign ministers in November 2000 was cancelled, because Syria and Lebanon refused to sit around the same table with Israel in protest at the Israeli military reaction to the Al-Aqsa Intifada (ibid.: 174). The 'Mediterranean Charter for Peace and Stability' which was expected to be signed at the Marseilles meeting had to be cancelled (ibid.).

The Barcelona Process was the EU-only initiative in the region. Previous extra-regional initiatives in the region were launched by the

USA, however, the EMP initiative was launched by the EU, and the USA was excluded from this process. Its main contribution to the peace process was that it provided a multilateral regional forum for the parties involved in the MEPP to meet in a different context from that of the difficult and comprehensive negotiations on political and security issues (Musu 2006). The EU's launch of the EMP was both an important indicator of its multilateral approach for promoting peace, security and stability in the Mediterranean region and a consistent act with its commitments and responsibilities as a promoter of effective multilateralism.

The Years of Stalemate in the Peace Process and the EU (1996–2001)

During the late 1995 and early 1996 period, Arab-Israeli relations deteriorated and the Oslo Peace Process came to a halt, due to several important events including the assassination of the Israeli Prime Minister Yitzhak Rabin on 4 November 1995 by an Orthodox far-right student who was against the Oslo Peace Process; an increase in Palestinian terror attacks against Israeli targets in early 1996; the launch of the Operation Grapes of Wrath by the Israeli Military Forces in April 1996 against Lebanon; the election of Benjamin Netanyahu, who was critical about the Oslo Peace Process, as the Israeli Prime Minister in May 1996; the opening of an entrance to an ancient tunnel (Hasmonean Tunnel) running under part of the Temple Mount in Jerusalem in November 1996.

In the second half of 1996, EU Member States were determined to revive the stalemated Oslo Process and to increase the EU's political involvement in the MEPP in order to match their economic and financial role. They intended to play not only the role of the payer but also that of a player. In order to contribute to the revival of stalemated peace process, enhance the EU's political involvement and presence in the MEPP and make the EU's political role more visible in the MEPP, the EU Foreign Ministers decided to appoint a special European envoy to the peace process at the General Affairs Council meeting in Luxembourg on 28 October 1996. The Council of Ministers appointed Miguel Angel Moratinos, the former ambassador of Spain to Israel, as the EU Special Envoy for the MEPP[15] on 25 November 1996. As Joel Peters (2000: 160) argued

> the presence of a European special envoy has enhanced Europe's political standing, has afforded it a more prominent profile in the peace process and has allowed European Middle East policy to become more visible to regional and extra-regional actors, to become more flexible and responsive to developments in the peace process and to identify specific areas where Europe can undertake practical measures to help build confidence between the parties and support agreements reached.

The EU Special Envoy for the MEPP allowed the EU to play a more active political role in the peace process. Moratinos became a valuable partner to the US Special Envoy Dennis Ross in helping to mediate political agreements between the Palestinians and the Israelis, using the leverage the EU had with the Palestinians (Soetendorp 2002: 289). During the Israeli-Palestinian negotiations which led to the Hebron agreement envisaging the withdrawal of the Israeli troops from Hebron, Dennis Ross acted as the mediator and Moratinos worked behind the scenes and complemented his mediation efforts. During these negotiations, while the USA had sent letters of assurances to both sides, the EU sent Arafat another letter of assurance stating that the EU would use all its political and moral weight to ensure that the agreement would be fully implemented (Peters 1999b: 312). It was the first time that the EU had been actively involved in the US peace diplomacy and was able to show its value to the peace process (Soetendorp 2002: 290). Moreover, in 1997, Moratinos carried out efforts to revive negotiations between Syria and Israel and he pursued a shuttle diplomacy between Damascus and Jerusalem to this end (Peters 1999b: 312). The EU started to play a supportive and complementary role to the USA in bilateral political negotiations between Israel and the Palestinian Authority in late 1996 and early 1997, and this role has increased over the course of time.

In addition to its mediation efforts, Moratinos also launched a number of practical, small-scale initiatives aiming at building confidence between parties and has identified several areas, namely water

and refugees, in which the EU might contribute to final status negotiations. The EU, under the auspices of Moratinos, set up an EU-Israeli Joint Dialogue in which European and Israeli experts met regularly in five separate working groups (passage of goods and peoples, labour issues, financial and fiscal issues, Gaza Port, long-term economic development) to discuss ways of overcoming obstacles to the Palestinian economic development. Furthermore, the EU, under the auspices of Moratinos, developed an assistance programme which aimed to train the Palestinian security forces to support the Palestinian Authority in helping prevent terrorist activities in the territories under its control, and set up a forum in which representatives of the Palestinian security forces meet regularly with their counterparts from the EU with the aim of developing joint cooperation on security issues (Peters 2000: 161).

At the European Council meeting in Amsterdam on 16–17 June 1997, the leaders of EU Member States issued the 'Call for Peace in the Middle East'. They called on the peoples and governments of the region to revive the spirit of mutual confidence established in Madrid and in Oslo in order to raise hopes for achievement of a just, lasting and comprehensive peace. The EU identified peace as necessary and urgent in the Middle East. They declared stagnation on the Palestinian, the Syrian and the Lebanese tracks as a permanent threat to security of all in the region. They reemphasized that the peace settlement should be based on the right of all States and peoples in the region to live in peace within safe, recognized borders; respect for the legitimate aspiration of the Palestinian people to decide their own future; the exchange of land for peace; the non-acceptability of the annexation of territory by force; respect for human rights; the rejection of terrorism of all kinds; good relations between neighbours; and compliance with existing agreements and the rejection of counterproductive unilateral initiatives. They called upon the Israeli and Palestinian leaders to continue the negotiations to foster the implementation of the Oslo Accords and Hebron Agreements and to carry on permanent status negotiations. In this declaration, they reiterated their call for mutual recognition of Israel's legitimate right to exist within safe and recognized borders by the Palestinian people and the Palestinians' right to exercise self-determination, without excluding the option of a state.

They also emphasized their commitment to human rights, democracy and the promotion of civil society in the Arab-Israeli context and condemned violations of those rights. They declared their determination to continue their efforts for the continuation of the peace process through the efforts of the EU's Special Envoy for the MEPP, through the EU's diplomatic relations and economic involvement, and through the EU's relations of friendship and trust with the various parties, to work together with the USA, Russia and the relevant parties in the region.

During 1998, the USA continued its diplomatic efforts to resume the peace process and the EU continued to play its complementary role to the US efforts. As a result, Israel and the Palestinian Authority signed the Wye River Memorandum on 23 October 1998 in Maryland, the USA. The Memorandum envisaged a further withdrawal of the Israeli forces from the West Bank. According to the Memorandum, both the Israeli and the Palestinian sides promised to take measures to prevent any acts of terrorism, crime and hostilities against the other side. The US President Bill Clinton played the role of the main mediator between the parties in Wye talks and the EU was not invited to Wye talks. The EU was once again excluded from the bilateral political talks.

On 26 October 1998, the EU issued a statement which welcomed the signing of Wye River Memorandum. The EU called on the parties to complete negotiations on remaining issues under the Interim Agreement which were not settled as soon as possible. The EU also asked the parties to begin final status negotiations without delay and meanwhile to avoid all the unilateral acts which could prejudice the final outcome, thus building confidence which is essential for a lasting peace in the region. The EU also declared its determination to continue to play its full part in the success of peace process and to continue its economic and technical assistance to the Palestinian people.

On 20 December 1999 the Israeli government suspended the implementation of the Wye River Memorandum. After its suspension the opposition Labour party withdrew the 'safety net' for the government in Knesset, which it had been providing pending implementation of Wye, and this led to the passing of a vote of no confidence

(Martin-Diaz 1999: 48). The Netanyahu government was forced to hold general and prime ministerial elections on 17 May 1999. On the other hand, in early 1999, the President of the Palestinian Authority Yasser Arafat contemplated the proclamation of the Palestinian State on 4 May 1999, the formal deadline for the Oslo Accords' five-year interim period if there was no progress in the peace process (ibid.). The EU and the USA were against any unilateral proclamation of the Palestinian state at that time, because they wanted a change of Israeli government which would facilitate the continuation of the peace process. However, they believed that any unilateral declaration of statehood would lead to an outbreak of violence and a formal annexation of the Occupied Territories which would increase Netanyahu's chance of re-election. The EU and the USA strove to dissuade Arafat from proclaiming the Palestinian state before the Israeli elections (Peters 1999b: 312). They were eventually able to convince Arafat to postpone the unilateral proclamation of the Palestinian state. On 29 April 1999, the PLO Central Council decided to postpone the proclamation of statehood.

At the Berlin European Council held on 24–25 March 1999, the EU leaders issued a declaration concerning the MEPP. They reiterated their support for a negotiated settlement of the Middle East conflict which would be based on the principles of 'land for peace' and ensure both collective and individual security of the Israeli and the Palestinian peoples. They called upon the parties to implement the Wye River Memorandum fully and immediately. They also called upon the parties to resume final status negotiations as soon as possible and on an accelerated basis. The EU leaders reemphasized the continuing and unqualified Palestinian right to self-determination including the option of a state and declared that they looked forward to the early fulfilment of this right. They declared that this right appealed to the parties to strive in good faith for a negotiated solution on the basis of the existing agreements, without prejudice to this right, which is not subject to any veto. The EU leaders declared that the creation of a democratic, viable and peaceful sovereign Palestinian state on the basis of the existing agreements and through negotiations would be the best guarantee of Israel's security and Israel's acceptance as an equal partner in the region. The EU leaders also declared their readiness to consider the recognition of a Palestinian state in due course in accordance with the basic principles referred to above. With this declaration, EU Member States for the first time declared their readiness to recognize the Palestinian state which would be established on the basis of existing agreements and through negotiations. EU Member States also denied any veto against the Palestinian proclamation of state.

Javier Solana, the former Secretary General of NATO was appointed as the High Representative for the CFSP for five years by European Council on 18 October 1999 and started his new occupation in November 1999.[16] Solana was chosen because he was a high profile, respected, competent diplomat and administrator. The appointment of Solana further fostered the EU's visibility and presence in the MEPP. His appointment clearly improved the external performance of the EU and thus increased the political impact of the EU in the MEPP (Soetendorp 2002: 294). Since his appointment, Solana together with the EU Special Envoy of MEPP acted as the voice and face of the EU in the MEPP. As argued by EU officials, since his appointment, Solana became a recognizable figure in the MEPP.[17] The Israelis identified Solana as a visible and important figure and argued that he had increased the EU's visibility in the Middle East and acted in a way as the face and voice of the EU.[18] In addition to its major financial and economic role in the peace process, the EU increasingly sought to get involved in the political dimension of the peace process.

Ehud Barak from the Labour Party was elected as the Prime Minister of Israel in the May 1999 elections and he strove to resume the peace process which had been stalemated during the Netanyahu government. Israel withdrew from southern Lebanon security zone on 22 May 2000. On 11–25 July 2000, the Israeli Prime Minister Ehud Barak and the President of the Palestinian Authority Yasser Arafat met at Camp David under the sponsorship of the US President Bill Clinton to negotiate final status negotiations. The Camp David Summit did not lead to an agreement between the parties. After the failure of the Summit, Likud leader Ariel Sharon visited Haram al-Sharif/Temple Mount on 28 September 2000 and this increased the tension between the Israelis and the Palestinians. This visit resulted in the outbreak of the Second Intifada or the so-called Al Aqsa Intifada. The wave of the Palestinian violence and the Israeli counter attacks resulted in the suspension of negotiations and security cooperation. In order to stop the escalation of violence and put the peace process back on track, the US President Bill Clinton invited the parties to hold a summit meeting. The summit meeting was held at Sharm al-Sheikh in Egypt on 17 October 2000 with the participation of the representatives of the Americans, the Israelis, the Egyptians, the Jordanians, the Palestinian Authority, the UN and the EU. The EU was represented by Javier Solana at the Summit. Solana's participation in the summit increased the EU's political involvement, visibility and presence in the MEPP.

At the Sharm al-Sheikh Summit, it was decided to establish an international fact-finding commission with the task of proposing recommendations to stop violence, to prevent its recurrence and to find a way back to the peace process. (Dosenrode and Stubkjaer 2002: 149). An international fact-finding commission was established under the chairmanship of former US Senator George Mitchell and was named as the Mitchell Commission. The Mitchell Commission was composed of the Former President of Turkish Republic Süleyman Demirel, the Norwegian Foreign Minister Thorbjoern Jagland, the former US Senator Warren B. Rudman and the High Representative for the CFSP, Javier Solana.

In his last days in office the US President Bill Clinton strove to revive the final status negotiations between Israel and the Palestinian Authority. He offered a 'bridging proposal' to the parties to carry out further talks in Washington and Cairo and then in Taba, Egypt in order to stop the Al Aqsa Intifada on 23 December 2000. The parties accepted this offer and they first met at Washington and then Cairo. After these two meetings, on 21–27 January 2001, the Israeli and the Palestinian delegations met at Taba. Although the Taba talks did not yield an agreement between parties, it was crucial for the EU's political involvement, visibility and presence in the MEPP. The EU Special Envoy of MEPP, at the time Miguel Moratinos, participated in the Taba talks as the only third party. Moratinos was assigned by both parties to keep accurate record of what took place. Moratinos and his team, after consultations with the Israeli and the Palestinian sides, prepared an unofficial report about the Taba talks and presented it to the parties. This unofficial report was accepted by the parties as being a relatively fair description of the outcome of the negotiations on the permanent status issues at Taba. In order to find ways to come to joint positions, the report drew attention to the extensive work which had been undertaken on all permanent status issues like territory, Jerusalem, refugees and security (EU description of the outcome of permanent status talks at Taba). Furthermore, it demonstrated that there were serious gaps and differences between the two sides, which would have to be overcome in future negotiations (ibid.). From that point of view, the paper uncovered the challenging task ahead in terms of policy determination and legal work, but it also demonstrated that both sides have travelled a long way to accommodate the views of the other side and that solutions were possible (ibid.). At the Sharm al-Sheikh Summit and the Taba talks, the High Representative for the CFSP, Javier Solana and the EU Special Envoy of MEPP Miguel Moratinos through their personal intervention and good offices, played an important role in bringing the sides close to a definitive agreement (Benli Altunışık 2008: 110: Batt et al. 2003: 95).

After the Taba talks on 6 February 2001, the Likud party, under the leadership of Ariel Sharon, who refused to meet the President of the Palestinian Authority Yasser Arafat, won the elections and became the new prime minister of Israel. On 30 April 2001, the Mitchell Commission delivered its report and recommended three steps to be taken: ending the violence, rebuilding confidence and resuming negotiations. The Bush Administration, which was committed to selective engagement in global diplomacy at the time, showed relatively little interest in involving in Middle East Affairs and did not attach importance to the Mitchell Report.

Following the failure to implement the Mitchell Report, in order to end the Israeli-Palestinian violence and resume negotiations, the Director of US CIA George Tenet proposed a Israeli-Palestinian Ceasefire and Security Plan (Tenet Plan) which would have been taken effect on 13 June 2001. At the European Council meeting in Goteborg on 15–16 June 2001, EU Member States welcomed the Tenet Plan and declared that there was a need for an effective commitment to bring about sustainable progress in security situation and the lifting of closures. Although the Tenet Plan proposed that a period of seven days free of violence was a condition for resuming negotiations, the mutual violence did not end. Thus, the Tenet Plan was not implemented. After the failure to implement the Mitchell Report recommendations and the Tenet Plan, until the 9/11 Terrorist Attacks, there were no significant initiatives to stop mutual violence and put stalemated peace process back on the track.

Conclusion

Since the introduction of the EPC in the early 1970s, EU Member States began to develop a common position towards the MEPP. Within EPC, the EU has brought out an *acquis politique* with regard to the MEPP (Dieckhoff 1987: 275). Throughout the 1970s, 1980s and 1990s, EU Member States collectively pursued a declaratory policy towards the MEPP. During these years, EU Member States issued a series of common declarations concerning the MEPP first under the framework of EPC until 1993 and then under the framework of the CFSP since 1993, including the Brussels Declaration of 1973, the London Declaration of 1977, the Venice Declaration of 1980 and the Berlin Declaration of 1999. These declarations were milestones in the evolution of the EU's position towards the MEPP.

The EU's position towards the MEPP has demonstrated continuity and consistency. All throughout, the EU has defended a comprehensive, just and lasting solution to the Arab-Israeli conflict with the participation of all parties including the PLO in the peace process as the representative of the Palestinian people. As noted by EU officials, the EU has a regional approach concerning the MEPP. The EU considered it as a regional issue rather than a process between the Israelis and the Palestinians. Therefore the EU defended the involvement of all regional actors in the MEPP.[19] The EU also maintained that the peace settlement in the Middle East should be based on the principles of exchange of land for peace; the non-acceptability of the annexation of territory by force; respect for human rights; the rejection of terrorism of all kinds; good relations between neighbours; and compliance with existing agreements and the rejection of counterproductive unilateral initiatives. The EU defended that the solution to the Arab-Israeli conflict should be based on UN Security Council Resolutions and international law. The EU also emphasized the mutual recognition of Israel's legitimate right to exist within safe and recognized borders by the Palestinian people, and the Palestinians' right to exercise self-determination, without excluding the option of a state by Israel. The EU had persistently criticized and condemned Israel's policy of settlement in the Occupied Territories and identified it as the main stumbling block to the achievement of a comprehensive peace settlement in the Middle East. The EU emphasized that they would not accept any unilateral initiative designed to change the status of Jerusalem. The EU identified the creation of a democratic, viable and peaceful sovereign Palestinian State on the basis of existing agreements and through negotiations as the best guarantee of Israel's security.

The EU played a complementary role to the USA in the MEPP while the USA played the role of the sole mediator. The EU supported the US peace initiatives in the Middle East. However, the EU was sidelined and excluded from the political dimension of the peace process and bilateral negotiations in which the USA has been dominant. While the USA reserved for itself the leading role, the EU confined itself to a supporting role. The reason behind the EU's exclusion was the Israeli and the American objection against the EU's participation in the bilateral peace negotiations as an active mediator. On the one hand, Israel considered the EU as pro-Arab and rejected its participation; on the other hand, the USA wanted to be the only mediator in the peace process and excluded the EU from the bilateral peace negotiations. The EU mainly played a significant and active role in the economic and multilateral dimension of the peace process through its participation in the multilateral track of the Madrid Peace Process and its status of being the largest donor of financial and technical aid to the Palestinian Authority and the MEPP. The EU also launched the EMP in 1995 which was a complementary multilateral initiative to the MEPP and provided a multilateral forum for the conflicting parties, the Arabs and the Israelis to sit at the same table and discuss. Although with the significant and active role it played in the economic and multilateral dimension of the peace process, the EU gained a higher profile and significant stake in the peace process in the 1990s than before, it was still not at the heart of the peace process. The main negotiations over the peace process were conducted between Israel, the Palestinian Authority and the USA (Stavridis and Hutchene 2000).

In the second half of the 1990s, the appointment of Miguel Angel Moratinos as the EU Special Envoy of the MEPP and the appointment of Javier Solana as the High Representative for the CFSP enhanced the EU's presence, visibility and political involvement in the MEPP. These two figures acted as the voice and face of the EU in the MEPP. In addition to its major financial and economic role in the peace process; the EU was increasingly involved in the political dimension of the peace process. For instance, Javier Solana participated in the Sharm al-Sheikh Summit as the representative of the EU and he was also one of the members of the Mitchell Commission which was established at the Sharm al-Sheikh Summit. The EU's political involvement and presence on the ground in the MEPP would continue to increase in the post-9/11 era with the EU's membership of the Quartet on the Middle East, which was designed for mediating the peace process in the Middle East and composed of the EU, the USA, the UN and Russia. The High Representative for the CFSP of the EU/Secretary General of the Council of the EU, the EU Commissioner for External Relations and European Neighbourhood Policy and the foreign minister of the member state holding the Council Presidency represented the EU in the Quartet.

As Alain Dieckhoff (2005: 53) and Stephan Stetter (2007: 109) rightly argued, the EU played a modest role in the MEPP in the 1970s and 1980s. The EU had developed guidelines for a just and lasting peace settlement in the Middle East and supported peace initiatives, mostly through its financial and technical aid to the Palestinian Authority (Dieckhoff 2005: 53). However, in the 1990s, the EU's role, visibility and presence in the MEPP increased and the EU began to play a more assertive and active role. As Joel Peters argued (1999b; 2000), the EU emerged from the sidelines and carved out a role and presence in nearly every dimensions of the peace process. The EU has promoted the development of the Palestinian institutions, supported agreements and promoted regional economic development (ibid.: 167).

CHAPTER 5

LEVELS OF CONGRUITY: THE EU'S ROLE CONCEPTIONS AND ROLE PERFORMANCE IN THE MEPP IN THE POST-9/11 ERA

In the post-9/11 era, the EU's political role and presence in the MEPP increased with its membership of the Quartet on the Middle East, which was designed for mediating the peace process in the Middle East and was composed of the EU, the USA, the UN and Russia. The EU continued to be the largest donor of financial aid to the Palestinian Authority. The Palestinian Authority is the world's largest recipient of the EU's financial aid. The EU supported the reform process of the Palestinian Authority towards the creation of an independent, economically and politically viable, sovereign and democratic Palestinian State. The EU supported the Palestinian reform process in the promotion of judicial independence, the promotion of accountability and transparency in the fiscal system, security sector reform, reform of administration and the executive, holding of free and fair elections, developing a modern education system and media based on peace, tolerance and mutual understanding and the promotion of pro-peace civil society. The EU also increased its role in the security dimension of the MEPP with the launch of two ESDP operations: EUPOL COPPS and EUBAM Rafah. In the post-9/11 era, the EU remained to be committed to a negotiated settlement resulting in two states, Israel and an independent, viable, sovereign and democratic Palestinian State, living side-by-side in peace and security on the basis of the 1967 borders and in the framework of a just, lasting and comprehensive peace in the Middle East, based on UN Security Council Resolutions 242, 338 and 1515, as well as the terms of reference of Madrid Conference of 2002 and the principle of 'land for peace'. This chapter starts with a general overview of the EU's involvement in the MEPP before analyzing the level of congruity between EU's role conceptions and role performance in the MEPP in the post-9/11 era.

The EU and the MEPP in the Post-9/11 Era: A General Overview

Peace Efforts in the Immediate Post-9/11 Era and the EU

After 9/11, the US administration concentrated on the MEPP in order to secure the 'coalition against terrorism' (Musu 2009: 2). After 9/11, the USA initiated a 'global war on terrorism' and within this framework it was preparing for an operation against al-Qaida bases in Afghanistan. The Bush administration wanted to secure Arab countries' support for its operation in Afghanistan, so it focused its attention on the MEPP. Within this context, the US President George Bush declared his support for a Palestinian State and sent retired Marine Corps General Anthony Zinni to broker a cease-fire between the Israelis and the Palestinians and implement the Mitchell Report recommendations and the Tenet Plan. EU Member States welcomed the US decision to send Zinni to the Middle East and declared their readiness to support his efforts through the EU Special Envoy of MEPP, Miguel Moratinos. However, Zinni's mission failed due to the escalation of mutual violence between the Israelis and the Palestinians. On 17 October 2001, the Israeli Minister for Tourism, Rehavam Zeevi was assassinated by Palestinian militants in Jerusalem. Israel initiated a military operation against the cities of West Bank.

In February 2002, France took the initiative to revive the stale-mated peace process and offered a 'Non-paper on the Revival of a Dynamics of a Peace in the Middle East'. This Non-paper envisaged the holding of elections in the Palestinian Territories based on the theme of peace and the recognition of the Palestinian State as a start-ing point of a negotiation process. The French proposal called for the creation of a Palestinian State first and discussions on refugees, the capital of State and settlements at a later stage (Islam 2002a: 10). However, Germany and the UK did not support French proposal. The German Foreign Minister Joschka Fischer noted that before focusing on reinjecting political momentum into the MEPP, it was necessary to deal with security issues in the region. He said that 'terrorism and violence have to end, that is the precondition for eve-rything. We have to find a durable ceasefire' (Islam 2002b: 6). The British Foreign Minister Jack Straw did not want to take an initia-tive independent from the USA and he advocated that the EU could not break ranks with US policy in the Middle East (ibid.). Italy and Belgium offered the organization of an international economic recov-ery conference for the region (Islam 2002a: 10). The Spanish Foreign Minister Josep Pique, as the foreign minister of the country holding the EU Presidency, tried to regroup different ideas into a coherent EU approach. He offered a guideline for EU policy in the Middle East which called for an urgent need to restore an approach based on political action and an urgent implementation of security measures, including peace formulas proposed by the Mitchell Report and the Tenet Plan (Islam 2002b: 6). Spain presented this guideline to the EU governments and asked them to support 'contacts and dialogue going in the direction of the early establishment of a Palestinian State' including a joint peace drive by the Israeli Foreign Minister Shimon Peres and Ahmad Quray, the speaker of the Palestinian Legislative Council (ibid.). The Spanish proposal envisaged the establishment of a Palestinian State before the start of permanent status negotiations (ibid.). Josep Pique also called for a joint peace effort by the USA, the EU, the UN, Russia and the Arab League (Islam 2002a: 10). However, EU Member States did not agree on a common strategy for the peace process.

While EU Member States tried to develop a common EU position towards the MEPP, mutual violence continued in the region. In retaliation against increasing suicide bomb attacks against the Israelis, on 29 March 2002, the Israeli Defence Force initiated a large-scale military operation against cities on the West Bank, which was called as 'Operation Defensive Shield'. The Israel Defence Forces invaded Palestinian cities including Tulkarm, Qalqilya, Betlehem, Jenin and Nablus. The Israeli Defence Forces surrounded the headquarters of the President of the Palestinian Authority Yasser Arafat in Ramallah and confined him to his headquarters, the Muqata. At the Barcelona European Council held on 15–16 March 2002, the EU leaders issued a declaration concerning the MEPP. The EU leaders called on parties to take action to stop the bloodshed in the region. They called on Israel to lift immediately all restrictions on Arafat's freedom of movement. They declared their determination to play the EU's role together with the countries in the region, the USA, the UN and Russia in the pursuit of a solution, based on UN Security Council Resolutions 242, 338 and 1397 and on the principles of the Madrid Conference, Oslo and subsequent agreements, which would allow the two states, Israel and Palestine, to live in peace and security and play their full part in the Middle East. They declared their objective on the MEPP: the creation of a democratic, viable and independent Palestinian State, bringing an end to the occupation of 1967 and the right of Israel to live within safe and secure boundaries, guaranteed by the commitment of the international community, and in particular Arab countries.

During the 'Operation Defensive Shield', the EU carried out a crisis management activity aimed at the settlement of a micro-security crisis, the Siege of the Church of the Nativity in Bethlehem (Youngs 2006: 152). The EU, through Miguel Moratinos, Javier Solana and the Spanish Foreign Minister Josep Pique, as the foreign minister of the country holding the EU Presidency, brokered an agreement on the release of the Palestinians holed up in the Church of Nativity in Bethlehem in April 2002. On 2 April 2002, the Israeli Defence Forces surrounded the Church of Nativity in order to capture the Palestinian militants, and the siege of the Nativity Church lasted until 10 May 2002. The siege ended with the agreement reached between the

Israelis and the Palestinians when the EU offered asylum to 13 of the Palestinians who were wanted by Israel for allegedly organizing terror operations (Christian Century Foundation 2002). The men designated for expulsion were to be sent to six European countries: Spain, Italy, Greece, Ireland, Portugal, Finland and Cyprus. For the EU circles, the resolution of the Bethlehem siege has been seen as a diplomatic coup for the EU, whose interventions in the Middle East have tended to be overshadowed by the USA.

In April 2002, Javier Solana and the Spanish Foreign Minister Josep Pique visited the region in order to broker a ceasefire between the Israelis and the Palestinians. They met with the Israeli Foreign Minister Shimon Peres, but they were not allowed by the Israelis to meet with Arafat, who was besieged in his headquarter in Ramallah. Javier Solana and Moratinos were able to meet with Arafat at Muqata on 24 April 2002. After EU Member States' failure to agree on a common strategy for the peace process and a failed diplomatic mission of Solana and Pique, EU Member States decided not to take a peace initiative independently from the USA and stepped back from earlier plans to play a more active role in seeking to end mutual violence between the Israelis and the Palestinians (Islam 2002c: 13; Musu 2010b). EU Member States decided to support US Secretary of State Colin Powell's Middle East peace mission. Miguel Moratinos, Javier Solana and the Spanish Foreign Minister Josep Pique's involvement in the security dialogue and humanitarian action during the worst stage of conflict in spring 2002 increased the EU's visibility and presence (Batt et al. 2003: 97).

The Creation of the Quartet and the Launch of the Roadmap for the Middle East

On the diplomatic side of the MEPP another important development occurred in April 2002. On 10 April 2002, the US Secretary of State Colin Powell, the UN Secretary General Kofi Annan, the Russian Foreign Minister Igor Ivanov, the Spanish Foreign Minister Josep Pique and the High Representative for the CFSP of the EU Javier Solana met in Madrid to discuss the situation in the Middle East.

The Madrid Quartet on the Middle East[1] which was composed of the EU, the USA, the UN and Russia, emerged from this meeting. The Quartet was established with two main aims: to help to broker a solution to the Middle East conflict and in the intermediate term to allow the Quartet members to take collective actions in response to events on the ground (Khaliq 2008: 282). After the first meeting held, on 10 April 2002, the Quartet members issued a common statement which expressed their great concern about the prevailing situation, including the mounting humanitarian crisis and the growing risk to regional security. They called on the parties to move towards a political resolution of their disputes based on UN Security Council Resolutions 242 and 338, and the principle of land for peace – which formed the basis for the Madrid Conference of 1991. They emphasized that there was a need to find a peaceful solution to the dispute which should be based on two states, Israel and Palestine, living side-by-side within secure and recognized borders. They called on Israel to halt its military operations immediately. They called for an immediate, meaningful ceasefire and an immediate Israeli withdrawal from the Palestinian cities, including Ramallah, specifically including Chairman Arafat's headquarters. They asked Israel to fully comply with international humanitarian principles and to allow full and unimpeded access to humanitarian organizations and services. They asked Israel to refrain from the excessive use of force and undertake all possible efforts to ensure protection of civilians. They called on Chairman Arafat to undertake immediately the maximum possible effort to stop terror attacks against innocent Israelis including suicide bombs which were illegal and immoral and had caused severe harm to the legitimate aspirations of the Palestinian people.

With the creation of the Quartet, the EU and US approaches to the peace process formally converged (Musu 2003: 69). In the view of an EU official, due to the Quartet, Europeans and Americans began to adopt similar positions concerning the peace process.[2] In the view of another EU official, the Quartet is a formal tool for bringing European and American positions together.[3]

On 24 June 2002, the US President George Bush made a speech on the situation in the Middle East and declared his vision concerning the peace process: two states, living side-by-side in peace and security. He declared that in order to achieve the peace, there was a need for a new and different Palestinian leadership. He demanded the removal of Arafat from the Palestinian leadership. He stated that when the Palestinian people had new leaders, new institutions and new security arrangements with their neighbours, the USA would support the creation of a Palestinian State, whose borders and certain aspects of its sovereignty would be provisional until resolved as part of a final settlement in the Middle East. He emphasized that there was a need for Palestinian reform. For him, new political and economic institutions based on democracy, market economics and action against terrorism were necessity for peace in the region. He criticized the concentration of power in the hands of few in Palestine and called for the preparation of a new constitution which would separate the powers of government. According to this constitution, the Palestinian parliament should have the full authority of a legislative body. Local officials and government ministers need authority of their own and the independence to govern effectively. Bush declared that the USA, along with the EU and the Arab states, would help the Palestinian leaders to create a new constitutional framework and a working democracy for the Palestinian people, for instance through helping them organize and monitor fair, multi-party local elections by the end of the year with national elections to follow.

Bush stated that the USA, the international donor community and the World Bank were ready to work with the Palestinians on a major project of economic reform and development. The USA, the EU, the World Bank and the International Monetary Fund would oversee reforms in the Palestinian finances, encouraging transparency and independent auditing. The USA and members of the international community were ready to work with the Palestinian leaders to establish, finance and monitor a truly independent judiciary. He also called for the rebuilding and reform of the Palestinian security services in order to enable the Palestinian leaders to engage in a sustained fight against the terrorists and dismantle their infrastructure. This reform would aim to create a security system which must have clear lines of authority and accountability, and a unified chain of command. He stated that if Palestine fulfilled these conditions successfully, final status negotiations including the final borders, the capital and other aspects of this state's sovereignty would be negotiated between the parties. He declared that before the start of final status negotiation, there was need for a political, administrative, economic, financial and security reform in Palestine. Bush went on by stating that a stable, viable, democratic and peaceful Palestinian State was necessary for the security of Israel. He called on Israel to withdraw to the positions held before 28 September 2000. He called on Israel to stop settlement activities in the Occupied Territories in accordance with the Mitchell Report recommendations and take concrete steps to support the emergence of a stable, viable, democratic and peaceful Palestinian State. He noted that in order to achieve a real peace there was a need to end the Israeli occupation that began in 1967 through a settlement negotiated between the parties, based on UN Security Council Resolutions 242 and 338, with the Israeli withdrawal to secure and recognized borders. This speech formed the basis of the 'Performance-Based Roadmap to a Permanent Two-State Solution to the Israeli-Palestinian Conflict'.

At the Seville European Council, held on 21–22 June 2002, EU Member States issued a declaration on the Middle East which ran parallel with Bush's vision concerning the peace process. They declared that settlement to the dispute should be achieved through negotiations. According to them, the aim of negotiations should be an end to the Israeli occupation and the early establishment of a democratic, viable, peaceful and sovereign Palestinian State, on the basis of the 1967 borders, if necessary with minor adjustments agreed by the parties. The end result of the negotiations should be two states living side-by-side within secure and recognized borders enjoying normal relations with their neighbours. Just like Bush, they identified the political, administrative, economic, financial and security reform of the Palestinian Authority as a necessity and they declared their willingness to support these reforms.

At their meeting in New York on 16 July 2002, the Quartet members welcomed President Bush's speech of 24 June 2002 and declared their strong support for the principles and objectives outlined in the speech. In their next meeting in New York on 17 September 2002, the Quartet Members released a statement outlining a three-phase plan toward a final peaceful settlement of the Middle East Conflict. This plan formed the first draft of the Roadmap for peace in the Middle East. EU Member States played a crucial role in the preparation of the Roadmap. As noted by EU officials, Europeans wrote the Roadmap and it was a European document.[4] Based on the German Foreign Minister Fischer's 'Idea Paper for the Middle East',[5] the Danish EU presidency proposed a three-phase roadmap to the EU foreign ministers at the Helsingor meeting and they agreed upon it at this meeting (Asseburg 2003: 185). This had a great influence on the Quartet statement of 17 September 2002. Moreover, the EU played a key role in keeping the USA working on finding a common approach despite the fact that at the time had different priorities such as continuing 'Operation Enduring Freedom' in Afghanistan and forthcoming war against Iraq (ibid.).

At their meeting in New York on 16 July 2002, the Quartet members agreed to intensify their efforts in support of their shared goal of achieving a final Israeli-Palestinian settlement based on their common vision, as expressed by the US President Bush in his speech of 24 June 2002. They declared that they would continue to encourage all parties to step up to their responsibilities to seek a just and comprehensive settlement to the conflict based on UN Security Council Resolutions 242, 338 and 1397, the Madrid terms of reference, the principle of land for peace, and implementation of all existing agreements between the parties. The Quartet declared that they would work closely with the parties and consult key regional actors on a concrete, three-phase implementation Roadmap that could achieve a final settlement within three years. The Quartet members emphasized that for the success of the plan, comprehensive security performance was essential. In order to be successful; the plan should address political, economic, humanitarian and institutional dimensions and should spell out reciprocal steps to be taken by the parties in each of its phases. In this approach, progress between the three phases would be strictly based on the parties' compliance with specific performance benchmarks to be monitored and assessed by the Quartet.

The Roadmap was published and presented to the Israeli and Palestinian Prime Ministers on 30 April 2003 along the lines of

President Bush's speech of 24 June 2002 and the Quartet's 16 July and 17 September 2002 statements. It offered a performance-based and goal-driven Roadmap, with clear phases, timelines, target dates and benchmarks aimed at progress through mutual steps by the two parties in the political, security, economic, humanitarian and institution-building fields, under the auspices of the Quartet. The objective was to achieve a final and comprehensive settlement of the Israel-Palestinian conflict by 2005 in three phases as outlined in the Quartet Statement of 17 September 2002.

The first phase of the Roadmap (Ending Terror and Violence, Normalizing Palestinian Life, and Building Palestinian Institutions), which extended until May 2003, contained performance-based criteria for comprehensive political reform in the Palestinian Authority including drafting a Palestinian constitution, and holding of free, fair and open elections. It called for the Israeli withdrawal to the positions held before 28 September 2000, freezing of settlement activity in the Occupied Territories and the restoration of the status quo that existed on 28 September 2000 by two sides, as security performance and cooperation progress. It also called on Israel to help the Palestinians normalize their life and build their institutions. The second phase (Transition), which would extend between June 2003 and December 2003, envisaged the creation of an independent and democratic Palestinian State with provisional borders and attributes of sovereignty, based on a new constitution, as a way station to a permanent status settlement. The final phase (Permanent Status Agreement and End of Israeli-Palestinian Conflict), which extended between January 2004 and December 2005, envisaged consolidation of reform and stabilization of the Palestinian institutions, sustained, effective Palestinian security performance, and the Israeli-Palestinian negotiations aimed at a permanent status solution in 2005, which would signify the end of the Israeli occupation that began in 1967 through a settlement negotiated between the parties based on UN Security Council resolutions 242, 338 and 1397.

Permanent Status Agreement would also include an agreed, just, fair and realistic solution to the refugee issue, and a negotiated resolution on the status of Jerusalem that would take into account the political and religious concerns of both sides, and would protect the religious interests of Jews, Christians, and Muslims worldwide, and would fulfil the vision of two states, Israel and sovereign, independent, democratic and viable Palestine, living side-by-side in peace and security.

Although the Palestinians had some reservations concerning the Roadmap, they judged that in the prevailing geopolitical climate they had no option other than accepting it.[6] Thus, the Palestinians accepted the Roadmap without reservations. The Israelis also had some reservations concerning the Roadmap.[7] Only after the US Administration guaranteed that they would 'fully and seriously' address the Israeli government's reservations concerning the Roadmap did the Israelis accept it with reservations.

The USA had taken the lead in launching the Roadmap. In June 2003, the US President Bush met with the Israeli Prime Minister Ariel Sharon and the Palestinian Authority Prime Minister Mahmoud Abbas at Aqaba, Jordan in order to persuade them to commit to the Roadmap. At this meeting, Bush was able to achieve their commitment to the Roadmap. The Palestinian Prime Minister Abbas denounced any kind of terrorism against the Israelis and promised to end the armed intifada. Ariel Sharon, promised to resume direct negotiations in accordance with the steps outlined in the Roadmap and dismantle unauthorized settler outposts (Hartley 2004: 302).

Although it was included in the Roadmap, the EU did not take part in these negotiations. The EU was once again sidelined and excluded from bilateral political talks by the USA (Beitler 2006: 125). Nevertheless, at the Thessaloniki European Council held on 19–20 June 2003, the EU leaders welcomed the Israeli and the Palestinian decision to accept the Roadmap and reiterated their commitment to contribute in all aspects of the implementation of the Roadmap. Moreover, on 21 July 2003, the Council adopted a Joint Action which appointed Marc Otte, the former ambassador of Belgium to Israel, as the EU Special Envoy of MEPP replacing Miguel Angel Moratinos.

On 29 June 2003, radical Islamic Groups in Palestine including Hamas, Islamic Jihad and al-Aqsa Martyrs Brigades announced a three-month cease-fire (*Hudna*) which included suspension of all attacks on the Israeli targets within Israel and in the Occupied Territories in return for a halt to acts of aggression against the Palestinians and the freeing of the Palestinians held in Israeli prisons (Hartley 2004: 303). Although the mutual violence decreased significantly, it did not halt. The Israeli assassination against leaders of radical Islamic Groups and radical Islamic Groups' retaliation through suicide bomb attacks against the Israeli targets continued.

The EU Election Observer Mission for the Presidential Elections in the West Bank and Gaza Strip

On 11 November 2004, the President of the Palestinian Authority Yasser Arafat died. On 14 November 2004, the Palestinian officials scheduled presidential elections for 9 January 2005. On 22 November 2004, the Commissioner for External Relations and the European Neighbourhood Policy Benita Ferrero-Waldner decided to deploy an EU Election Observer Mission to observe the Presidential Elections in the West Bank and Gaza scheduled for 9 January 2005. The European Commission identified the decision as a concrete expression of the EU's effort to support the development of democratic institutions and stability in the Palestinian Territories. They emphasized that the presence of the EOM and the reporting of its observers would help increase transparency and build confidence in the election process. The EOM for the Presidential elections in the West Bank and Gaza Strip began work on 10 December 2004. The EU sent the largest ever observation mission with 260 observers to monitor the Presidential elections. The main objective of the mission was to give Palestinian society a chance to hold meaningful and credible elections to provide democratic legitimacy for the institutions on the road to statehood. According to European Commission, some €14 million had been allocated since 2003 to prepare the elections and €2.5 million of this was allocated to the EOM (http://ec.europa.eu/external_relations/human_rights/eu_election_ass_observ/westbank/ip04_1462. htm.). Mahmoud Abbas won the elections and became the new president of the Palestinian Authority. On 10 January 2005, the EOM, headed by Member of the European Parliament and former French Prime Minister Michel Rocard reported that the Palestinian presidential elections had proceeded in a satisfactory manner despite the difficult circumstances. The President of European Commission José Manuel Barroso identified the presidential elections as an important step towards the creation of a democratic and viable Palestinian State.

The Israeli 'Security Fence' and 'Disengagement Plan' and the EU

In summer 2002, on the basis of its right to self-defence and security concerns – in order to prevent intrusion of suicide bombers and illegal immigrants and car thieves into the Israeli cities – the Israeli government decided to construct a separation barrier, called by the Israelis as the 'security fence',[8] partly along the 'Green Line' which demarcated the border between Israel and the West Bank.[9] After the approval of the construction by the Israeli Cabinet in August 2002, the construction of the security fence started.

EU Member States opposed the construction of the 'security fence' and identified it as an obstacle before the implementation of the Roadmap, a threat which would make the implementation of a two-state solution physically impossible and a source of misery to thousands of Palestinians (Islam 2003b: 10). They called on Israel to stop the construction of the security fence along with the settlement activities and land confiscations in the Occupied Territories. Javier Solana identified the construction of the security fence as a threat to the creation of a viable Palestinian State (Islam 2003c: 16).

At the Brussels European Council held on 16–17 October 2003 EU Member States declared that although they recognized the Israeli right to protect its citizens from terrorist attacks, the envisaged departure of the route of the security fence from the 'Green Line' would prejudge future negotiations and make the two-state solution physically impossible to implement. It would also cause humanitarian and economic difficulties for the Palestinians. Thousands of Palestinians living on the west side of the fence were being cut off from essential services in the West Bank, while Palestinians living on the east side of the fence would lose access to land and water resources. For the EU, the major problem is that it was unilaterally establishing a permanent border, which illegally annexes the Palestinian Territories, denies the Palestinian right to self-determination and makes the creation of a politically and economically viable Palestinian State far more difficult to achieve (Khaliq 2008: 336). In their later declarations, although EU Member States called on Israel to end the construction of the security fence, its construction still continues at the time of writing.

In addition to the 'security fence', in order to reduce terrorism as much as possible and grant the Israeli citizens the maximum level of security, on 18 December 2003 the Israeli Prime Minister Ariel Sharon announced his unilateral 'disengagement plan'[10] which envisaged the Israeli withdrawal from 21 settlements in the Gaza Strip and from four settlements in the northern West Bank, including Ganim, Kadim, Sa-Nur and Homesh by the end of 2005. Sharon, in his address to the Herzliya Conference on 18 December 2003, argued that the process of disengagement would lead to an improvement in the quality of life, and would help strengthen the Israeli economy. The US Administration approved and supported the Disengagement Plan. The EU identified disengagement plan as a significant step, offering the best chance of sustained peace in the region for many years (Commission of the European Communities 5 October 2005: 2). The EU's support for the Disengagement Plan was conditional. The EU declared that it could support it on the condition that it coincided with the Roadmap. At the Brussels European Council, held on 25–26 March 2004, EU Member States declared that the Israeli unilateral withdrawal in the framework of the Disengagement Plan should represent a significant step towards the implementation of the Roadmap. They set out five conditions which the Disengagement Plan should carry. First, withdrawal should take place in the context of the Roadmap; second, it should be a step towards a two-state solution; third, it should not involve a transfer of settlement activity to the West Bank; fourth, there should be an organized and negotiated handover of responsibility to the Palestinian Authority; fifth, Israel should facilitate the rehabilitation and reconstruction of Gaza. The EU added that it would not recognize any change to the pre-1967 borders other than those arrived at by agreement between the parties. It began to be implemented on 15 August 2005 and was completed on 12 September 2005 with the end of the Israeli military presence in Gaza.

The EU Presidency issued a declaration on 25 August 2005 which emphasized that disengagement should be a significant step towards implementing the Quartet Roadmap. They called on two parties to continue their cooperation on the remaining steps to complete disengagement. At the GAERC meeting on 3 October 2005, European foreign ministers once again welcomed the Israeli withdrawal as a significant step towards implementing the Roadmap. They declared their readiness to help the Quartet Special Envoy for disengagement, James Wolfensohn for resolving the outstanding issues on disengagement, especially concerning the economic viability of Gaza and confidence-building at Gaza's southern border. They emphasized the importance of reaching an agreement on access to Gaza for people and goods through land borders, a port and an airport.

The European Commission adopted a Communication entitled 'EU-Palestinian Cooperation Beyond Disengagement – Towards a Two-state Solution' on 5 October 2005 in order to define the priorities for EU engagement after the Israeli disengagement from the Gaza Strip and parts of the Northern West Bank, *inter alia* in support of the reform and institution-building efforts of the Palestinian Authority. The European Commission proposed that in the post-disengagement period, the EU's financial assistance should focus on the promotion of institution-building by the Palestinian Authority. The institution-building should contain establishing a functioning judiciary, effective enforcement of legislation and strengthening the rule of law; strengthening institutions and reinforcing administrative capacity and building on the progress already made in establishing an accountable system of public finances.

The European Commission set out actions and priorities required to pave the way for the creation of a politically and economically viable Palestinian State. In order to achieve the political viability of the future Palestinian State, the Commission set out the following priorities:

• reinforcing legitimacy and accountability through supporting electoral process;

- strengthening the rule of law through assisting the Palestinian reform efforts in the judiciary and developing a short-term strategy for consolidating the rule of law, including the fight against corruption and organized crime;
- promoting respect for human rights and fundamental freedoms through continuing to address the issue of incitement in political dialogue with the Palestinian Authority and supporting civil society initiatives for human rights;
- improving security through complementing EUSR's work on the transformation of civil police;
- engaging civil society through promoting civil society initiatives in support of the MEPP;
- making public administration more effective through supporting the Palestinian public administration reform efforts;
- developing a strategy of assistance for East Jerusalem;
- addressing the refugee issue beyond immediate humanitarian needs through contributing discussions on future role of the UNRWA.

In order to achieve economic viability of the future Palestinian State, the Commission set out the following priorities:

- developing bilateral and regional trade relations through improving market access for the Palestinian products, providing technical assistance, facilitating dialogue to overcome administrative and regulatory obstacles, developing scenarios for economic arrangements with Israel and encouraging integration of the Palestinian economy in the region;
- building up a customs administration through providing support, considering seconding experts and offering to provide third party presence;
- reconstructing and rehabilitating the West Bank and Gaza Strip through providing funds for quick-start infrastructure projects and promoting a renewed inflow of investment;
- creating the enabling environment for private sector investment through assisting the Palestinian efforts to review the legal framework;

- supporting the private sector through working with the European Investment Bank to combine loan and grant resources for private sector investment and providing assistance and training to SMEs to improve management capacity and performance;
- improving the management of public finances through supporting Palestinian efforts to modernize revenue administration and providing assistance for further development of financial control;
- developing a knowledge-based economy through examining options for support to roll-out of broadband applications;
- addressing the social dimension through contributing to social welfare programmes, in particular the World Bank's Social Safety net reform programme.

These political and economic priorities provided a roadmap for the EU's engagement with the Palestinian Authority in the latter's effort to build a politically and economically viable state.

In November 2005, the US Secretary of State, Condoleezza Rice, the High Representative for the CFSP, Javier Solana, and the Special Envoy of the Quartet on the Middle East, James Wolfensohn, brokered the negotiations on 'Agreement on Movement and Access from and to Gaza' between the Israelis and the Palestinians. On 15 November 2005, the agreement was signed by the Israelis and the Palestinians. The main objective of the agreement was to promote peaceful economic development and improve the humanitarian situation in Gaza. The details of the agreement were outlined in two documents: 'Agreement on Movement and Access' and 'Agreed Principles for Rafah Crossing'. The latter document envisaged the presence of a third party on the ground which would have the authority to ensure the compliance of the Palestinian Authority with all applicable rules and regulations concerning the Rafah crossing point and the terms of this agreement. In case of non-compliance the third party would have the authority to order the re-examination and reassessment of any passenger, luggage, vehicle or goods. The third party would assist the Palestinian Authority to build capacity, including training, equipment and technical assistance, on border management and customs. With the agreement of the two parties, the EU was assigned to the task of the third party on the ground which would carry out these tasks.

The EU welcomed the agreement and accepted the third party monitoring role at the Rafah Crossing Point on the Gaza-Egypt border. The EU High Representative for the CFSP Javier Solana and the British Foreign Minister Jack Straw, representing the EU Presidency, issued a joint statement on 15 November 2005 welcoming the agreement. They stated that the issues addressed in the agreement were fundamental to improving the humanitarian situation on the ground in Gaza as well as essential for promoting peaceful economic development and they expressed their hope that both sides would now make every effort to ensure that the commitments made were translated into reality. They also expressed the EU's willingness in principle to provide assistance with the operation of crossing at Gaza/Egypt border at Rafah. They noted that they were undertaking the necessary preparations and planning.

Moreover, the EU Commissioner for External Relations and European Neighbourhood Policy, Benita Ferrero-Waldner, issued a statement welcoming the agreement. She stated that this agreement would open the way to much needed greater mobility for the Palestinians and with the EU presence they would be able to manage the border between Gaza and Egypt. She added that the European Commission was already active in capacity building on border issues, and in supporting the modernization of the Palestinian customs services. She noted that a €40 million infrastructure facility had been launched during her last visit to the region. She expressed her hope that it would also be possible to release €25 million which she had earmarked for building a new cargo terminal for the Gaza airport. At the GAERC meeting on 21–22 November 2005, the foreign ministers of EU Member States decided to launch a civilian crisis management mission, called the European Union Border Assistance Mission for the Rafah Crossing Point (EUBAM Rafah) within the framework of the ESDP to monitor the operations at the Rafah crossing point.

European Union Border Assistance Mission for the Rafah Crossing Point (EUBAM Rafah)

The Palestinian Authority on 20 November 2005 and the Israeli government on 23 November 2005 sent letters of invitation to the EU to establish EUBAM Rafah. The Council adopted the Joint Action of 12 December 2005 which established EUBAM Rafah. The aim of the mission was to provide a third party presence at the Rafah Crossing Point in order to contribute, in cooperation with the Community's institution-building efforts, to the opening of the Rafah Crossing Point and to build up confidence between the Israeli government and the Palestinian Authority. The mandate of the mission included actively monitoring, verifying and evaluating the Palestinian Authority's performance with regard to the implementation of the Agreed Principles for Rafah Crossing and ensuring the Palestinian Authority's compliance with all applicable rules and regulations concerning the Rafah crossing point and the terms of the Agreed Principles for Rafah Crossing. The mandate of the mission was determined as one year. The operational phase of the mission started on 25 November 2005. Between 26 June 2005 and 25 June 2006, 279,436 people crossed through the Rafah Crossing Point with EU monitoring (Bulut 2009: 302). After an Israeli soldier, Gilad Shalit, was captured by Hamas militants on 25 June 2006, the Rafah Crossing Point was closed for normal operations and opened on an exceptional basis only. As a result of EUBAM Rafah's efforts to keep it open it remained open for 83 days between 25 June 2006 and 13 June 2007, allowing nearly 163,632 people to cross (ibid.). Immediately after Hamas took over Gaza forcefully on 13 June 2007, the Rafah Crossing Point was closed and the operations of EUBAM Rafah mission were temporarily suspended. Despite this, the mandate of the mission has been extended several times and on 10 November 2008, its mandate was extended until 24 November 2009. Since June 2007, EUBAM has continued its presence on the ground in Ashkelon, Israel and remained on standby; ready to engage at short notice in the case of the reopening of the Rafah Crossing Point. It is noted by the EU officials that following the re-establishment of the Palestinian Authority's control over Gaza, the EU expects it to be reopened.[11]

European Union Police Mission for the Palestinian Territories (EUPOL COPPS)

In addition to EUBAM Rafah, at the GAERC meeting on 7 October 2005 foreign ministers of EU Member States decided to launch, within the framework of the ESDP, a Police Mission in the Palestinian Territories to build on the work of 'the EU Coordinating Office for Palestinian Police Support',[12] which would have a long-term reform focus and would provide enhanced support to the Palestinian Authority in establishing sustainable and effective policing arrangements (Euromed Synopsis 2005: 1).

There were two main reasons behind the launch of EUPOL COPPS. The first one was to help the Palestinian Authority in rebuilding institutions and capacities that were largely destroyed during the Israeli 'Operation Defensive Shield' in 2002 (Asseburg 2009a: 84). These included the increase in security chaos following the destruction of the Palestinian security infrastructure, the inability of the Palestinian justice and prison systems to cope with this chaos and the lack of rule of law necessitated the launch of EUPOL COPPS. The second reason was to enhance the effectiveness of the security organs by reforming the highly fragmented and opaque structures inherited from the Arafat era that did not have transparent hierarchies, clear competencies and political oversight (ibid.). EUPOL COPPS has been a significant element of the EU's efforts to assist and facilitate the Palestinian Authority to live up to its Roadmap obligations in terms of restoring law and order in the Palestinian Territories and fight terrorism effectively (ibid.).

The Council adopted the Joint Action of 14 November 2005 which established the European Union Police Mission for the Palestinian Territories. The aim of the mission was defined as contributing to the establishment of sustainable and effective policing arrangements under the Palestinian ownership in accordance with best international standards, in cooperation with the Community's institution building programmes as well as Security Sector reform including Criminal Justice Reform. The mandate of the mission included assisting the Palestinian Civil Police in the implementation of the Palestinian Civil Police Development Plan by advising and closely mentoring senior members of the Palestinian Civil Police and criminal justice system, coordinating and facilitating EU and Member State assistance, and where requested, international assistance to the Palestinian Civil Police, and advising on police-related Criminal Justice elements. The mandate of the mission was determined as three years. The operational phase of the mission started on 1 January 2006. The mandate of the mission was extended until 31 December 2010 with the Joint Action of 16 December 2008. Since Hamas takeover of Gaza forcefully on 13 June 2007, EUPOL COPSS has been operational only in the West Bank, because the EU refused to work with Hamas.

The EU Election Observer Mission for the Palestinian Legislative Council Election of 2006

On 21 November 2005, the European Commission decided to deploy in mid-December 2005 an EU Election Observation Mission for elections to the Palestinian Legislative Council, scheduled for 25 January 2006. The Commissioner for External Relations and the European Neighbourhood Policy Benita Ferrero-Waldner emphasized the importance of the mission and stated that

> free and fair elections are essential steps on the way to a viable Palestinian State as foreseen in the Roadmap. Impartial observation can help create confidence in the democratic process and highlight areas where further improvements are necessary. By working with the Palestinians, the EU is helping to lay the foundations for a modern accountable administration and a more peaceful future for the Palestinian people (http://ec.europa.eu/external_relations/human_rights/eu_election_ass_observ/west-bank/legislative/index.htm).

The mandate of the EOM was determined as assessing whether the electoral process was conducted in accordance with international standards. The mission would assess the whole election process, including the legal framework, the political environment and campaign, electoral preparations, voting and counting as well as the post-election period. It issued a preliminary statement shortly after election day. The EOM for the Palestinian Legislative Council elections in the West Bank and Gaza Strip began to work on 12 December 2005. The EU sent 240 observers to monitor the elections. The main objective of the mission was to give Palestinian society a chance to hold meaningful and credible elections to provide democratic legitimacy to the Palestinian Parliament on the road to statehood. According to the Commission, some €17 million had been allocated since 2003 to prepare the elections and €3 million of this was allocated to the EOM (http://ec.europa.eu/external_relations/human_rights/eu_election_ass_observ/westbank/legislative/index.htm). Hamas won the elections with a decisive majority, winning 74 seats of the 132-seat legislative council. The ruling Fatah only won 45 seats. This provided Hamas the ability to form a majority government on their own.

On 25 January 2006, the EOM, headed by Member of the European Parliament Foreign Affairs Committee and the European Parliament Delegation for Relations with the Mashreq Countries Véronique de Keyser, reported that the elections for the Palestinian Legislative Council had been successfully conducted. This reflected an open and fairly-contested electoral process that was efficiently administered by a professional and independent Palestinian Central Elections Commission. According to the report, these elections marked another important milestone in the building of the Palestinian democratic institutions, which is a fundamental component in the peace process foreseen in the 2002 Roadmap. The EU High Representative for the CFSP Solana issued a statement on 26 January 2006 which welcomed the peaceful running of the Palestinian elections. At the GAERC meeting on 30 January 2006, the foreign ministers of EU Member States welcomed the holding of elections to the Palestinian Legislative Council and congratulated the President Abbas and the Palestinian people for a free and fair electoral process. They emphasized that violence and terror are incompatible with democratic processes and called on the victorious Hamas and all other factions to renounce violence, to recognize Israel's right to exist and to disarm. They also called on the new Palestinian government to commit to a peaceful and negotiated solution of the conflict with Israel based on existing agreements and the Roadmap as well as to the rule of law, reform and sound fiscal management. At their meeting in New York on 30 January 2006, the Quartet members issued a statement which once again called on the new Palestinian government to commit to nonviolence, recognition of Israel and acceptance of previous agreements and obligations, including the Roadmap. They called on both parties to respect their existing agreements, including 'Agreement on Movement and Access'.

After the establishment of the Hamas-led Palestinian government in March 2006, the EU continued to call on the government to meet and implement the three principles of non-violence including the laying down of arms, recognition of Israel's right to exist and acceptance and fulfilment of existing agreements and obligations, including the Roadmap. The EU made its future financial aid to the Hamas-led Palestinian government conditional on the recognition of the above-mentioned principles. At the GAERC meeting on 10–11 April 2006, foreign ministers of EU Member States concluded that the Hamas-led Palestinian government did not commit itself to the above-mentioned principles and decided to suspend direct aid to the Hamas-led government. Although they decided to suspend direct aid to the government, they underlined their determination to continue to provide necessary assistance to meet the basic needs of the Palestinian people.

On 9 May 2006 the Quartet on the Middle East addressed the humanitarian situation in the Palestinian Territory and asked the EU to propose a 'Temporary International Mechanism' which would be limited in scope and duration and operate with full transparency and accountability and enable direct delivery of assistance to the Palestinian people while bypassing the Hamas-led Palestinian government. The mechanism was developed under the patronage of the Commissioner for External Relations and the European Neighbourhood Policy Benita Ferrero-Waldner. At the European Council in Brussels on 15–16 June 2006, the EU leaders approved the proposal for the establishment of TIM. On 17 June 2006, the Quartet on the Middle

East approved the EU's proposal for the establishment of TIM. The objective of TIM was to relieve the current socio-economic crisis in the West Bank and the Gaza Strip, to ensure continued delivery of essential social public services to the Palestinian people and to facilitate the maximum level of support by international donors and the resumption of the Palestinian revenue transfers by Israel. Between June 2006 and March 2008, the EU provided €455.5 million through TIM to the Palestinian people. In March 2008, TIM was replaced by a new mechanism called the European Mechanism of Support to the Palestinians (PEGASE[13]).

EU Member States' Contribution to UNIFIL

On 12 July 2006 Hezbollah militants located in the Southern Lebanon crossed the Israeli border and killed eight Israeli soldiers and captured two. The Israeli Defence Forces then started a military operation against Hezbollah strongholds in Southern Lebanon and targets in Beirut, including Beirut International Airport. In retaliation, Hezbollah launched rocket attacks against Israeli cities and towns. The military conflict between Hezbollah militants and the Israeli Defence Forces ended on 14 August 2006 after both parties to the conflict accepted UN Security Council Resolution 1701.

From the outset of the war, the EU called on both parties to calm down and refrain from any action which would lead to the escalation of already tense situation in the region. The EU called for an immediate cessation of the conflict. On 13 July 2006, the Finnish EU Presidency issued a statement on behalf of the EU and expressed the EU's concern about the disproportionate use of force by Israel in Lebanon in response to attacks by Hezbollah on Israel. The Presidency condemned the loss of civilian lives and the destruction of civilian infrastructure. They noted that the imposition of an air and sea blockade on Lebanon could not be justified. They emphasized that actions which were contrary to international humanitarian law could only exacerbate the vicious circle of violence and retribution could not serve anyone's legitimate interest. The Presidency called on Hezbollah to release the captured the Israeli soldiers immediately and unconditionally, and to cease all attacks on

Israel. The Presidency also called on the government of Lebanon to do its utmost to prevent such attacks.

During the war, the EU representatives carried out diplomatic efforts. The Finnish Foreign Minister Erkki Tuomioja, the Commissioner for External Relations and the European Neighbourhood Policy Benita Ferrero-Waldner and the High Representative for the CFSP Javier Solana visited the region in July 2006 and met with the Israeli, Palestinian and Lebanese senior figures. They called on Hezbollah to release the Israeli soldiers held hostage immediately and unconditionally and to end rocket attacks against the Israeli towns and cities. While recognizing Israel's right to self-defence, they called on Israel to use its force in response to Hezbollah attacks in a way which is proportionate and measured and fully respect its obligations under international humanitarian law.

During the war, in order to relieve the worsening humanitarian situation in Lebanon, the EU provided humanitarian aid for the victims of the conflict in Lebanon. During the conflict, the EU had provided over €108 million humanitarian aid in monetary terms. In addition, the EU had also provided substantial amount of aid in kind in the form of food, medicine and shelter. The EU also provided €11 million from the Rapid Reaction Mechanism for helping the evacuation and repatriation of around 10,000 citizens of developing countries. With consular cooperation between EU Member States and EU institutions in Beirut, around 40,000 EU citizens were evacuated and repatriated.

After the end of the war, EU Member States made the most significant military contribution to the expanded UN Interim Force in Lebanon. The expansion of UNIFIL was requested by UN Security Council Resolution 1701, adopted on 11 August 2006. In order to implement expanded mandate of UNIFIL, the UN Security Council called for an increase in the force strength of UNIFIL to a maximum 15,000 troops. At the Extraordinary GAERC meeting on 25 August 2006, foreign ministers of EU Member States gave their full support to the swift implementation of UN Security Council Resolution 1701 and committed to providing half of the expanded force. Although the political decision to contribute to UNIFIL was adopted by Member

States, this would not be an operation under the framework of the ESDP (Keukeleire and MacNaughtan 2008: 185). EU Member States did not assign EU Council General Secretariat the role of a clearing house for the management of the national contributions directly to UNIFIL; Member States would make their individual contributions to the force (Pirozzi 2006: 3). Since it was not an EU operation, EU institutions did not take the political responsibility of the operation. The political responsibility of the operation was in the hands of the UN Security Council.

EU Member States provided the backbone of the force by providing 7,000 troops, crucial military components and the operational command for UNIFIL (Dembinski 2007).[14] France, Italy and Spain took the lead in taking the responsibility of the operational command of the force. Until February 2007, French General Alain Pellegrini had been in charge of the Force Commander of UNIFIL. Between February 2007 and January 2010 Italian General Claudio Graziano had served as the Force Commander of UNIFIL. On 28 January 2010 Spanish General Alberto Asarta Cuevas took over the command of UNIFIL from General Graziano. The strategic and operational command of the force had been in the hands of EU Member States.

EU Member States' presence in Lebanon enabled them to be more pro-active in the Middle East peace efforts. In November 2006 the Israeli Defence Force started 'Operation Autumn Clouds' and entered into the Gaza Strip in order to stop rocket attacks against the Israeli cities and towns from the Gaza Strip. Following the operation, three EU Member States, France, Italy and Spain (the three largest contributors to UNIFIL), launched a new Middle East Peace Initiative. In the words of the Italian Prime Minister, these three countries took their presence in Lebanon as a starting point to develop the operational and concrete aspects of a wider initiative in the Middle East in order to give a real contribution to the pacification of the whole Middle East region (Musu 2007a: 28). Their five-point peace proposal called for an immediate ceasefire; formation of a national unity government by the Palestinians that could gain international recognition; an exchange of prisoners, including the Israeli soldiers whose seizure sparked the war in Lebanon and fighting in Gaza in summer 2006; talks between the

Israeli prime minister and the Palestinian president; and an international mission in Gaza to monitor a ceasefire (Brian Whitaker and Agencies 2006). Israel and the USA did not endorse the proposal. The Palestinians declared that they would welcome any initiative, but they did not endorse it warmly. As the other EU Member States did not back the plan, the peace initiative failed.

Analyzing the Level of Congruity between EU's Role Conceptions and Role Performance in the MEPP in the Post-9/11 Era

The EU's Role Performance as Force for Good

On the issue of the MEPP, EU Member States discursively constructed the EU as force for good or positive force. At the Brussels European Council held on 20–21 March 2003 EU Member States declared their intention to act as a force for good by emphasizing that the EU would work to achieve peace in the Middle East to the benefit of both the peoples of the region and international peace and stability. In this statement, EU Member States did not emphasize the importance of settlement of the conflict for their self-interest in terms of European energy security and settlement of a conflict which has the potential of a negative spill-over effect on European security and stability. Rather, they emphasized the importance of the settlement of the conflict for the global common good, which is the benefit of the peoples in the region and international peace and stability.

In order to evaluate the performance of the EU's role as a force for good in the MEPP, there is a need to test whether the EU measures up to its self-image as a force for good. We should assess whether the EU has pursued ethically balanced policy. It is necessary to evaluate whether there exists a balance between the EU's interests and ethical considerations, whether there exists a balance between member and non-member concerns and whether the EU's actions satisfy the preferences of all the actors involved. Thus, in order to evaluate the EU's role performance as a force for good, we should evaluate whether the EU's actions and decisions advance the global common good or not.

The EU has adopted a balanced and comprehensive approach towards the Arab-Israeli Conflict. The EU's equating of the Israeli security needs and the Palestinian rights as parallel objectives of the peace process since the 1970s reflected its balanced and even-handed approach. The EU emphasized the right to existence and to security of all the states in the Middle East, including Israel, and justice for all the peoples, which implied the recognition of the legitimate rights of the Palestinian people. Another indicator of the EU's even-handed approach is the EU's continuous criticism and condemnation of the Palestinian terrorist attacks against the Israeli targets and the Israeli policy of settlement in the Occupied Territories, the Israeli military incursions, excessive use of force and the extrajudicial killings, forms of collective punishment and the construction of the Israeli 'Security Fence' and restrictions on movement that Israel has imposed on the Palestinians. The EU regarded them as the main stumbling blocks to the achievement of a negotiated settlement of the conflict resulting in two states, Israel and an independent, viable, sovereign and democratic Palestinian state, living side-by-side in peace and security on the basis of the 1967 borders and in the framework of a just, lasting and com-prehensive peace in the Middle East. The EU's emphasis on achiev-ing a comprehensive peace settlement of the Arab-Israeli Conflict in which all the parties to the conflict can be involved reflected its com-prehensive approach. The EU's balanced and even-handed approach to the Arab-Israeli conflict matched its rhetoric as a force for good.

Since the Berlin European Council of 1999, EU Member States have emphasized that the creation of a democratic, viable and peaceful sov-ereign Palestinian State on the basis of the existing agreements and through negotiations would be the best guarantee of Israel's security. Later on in the post-9/11, the US administration agreed on this term and identified a stable, viable, democratic and peaceful Palestinian State as necessary for the security of Israel. With the launch of the Roadmap, this became the official position of the international community. In order to contribute to the creation of an independent, economically and politically viable, sovereign and democratic Palestinian State, the EU provided financial and technical aid to the Palestinian Authority and supported the Palestinian reform process in areas of the promotion of judicial independence, promotion of accountability and transparency in the fiscal system, the security sector reform, reform of administration and the executive, holding of free and fair elections, developing a modern education system and media based on peace, tolerance and mutual understanding, the promotion of pro-peace civil society. Moreover, the EU has continued its status of being the largest external donor of financial and technical aid to the Palestinian Authority and the MEPP in the post-9/11 era. This aid prevented the Palestinian economy from collapse; without it the Palestinian Authority would not have been able to finance even the basic functions of governance (Pace 2008: 213). The collapse of the Palestinian Authority might have resulted in the escalation of conflict (ibid.). The EU's contribution to the creation of a democratic, viable and peaceful sovereign Palestinian State through its aid to the Palestinian Authority and support to the Palestinian reform process clearly matched its rhetoric as a force for good. Since the creation of such a Palestinian State is the best guarantee for the Israeli security, the EU's contribution to it serves to the benefit of both parties to the conflict and international community.

The EU's third party presence at the Rafah Crossing Point through EUBAM Rafah is consistent with the EU's rhetoric as a force for good. Through its third-party monitoring role at the Rafah Crossing Point on the Gaza-Egypt border, the EU facilitated the implementation of 'Agreement on Movement and Access' and 'Agreed Principles for Rafah Crossing'. Furthermore, the EU contributed to the opening of the Rafah Crossing Point and to building up confidence between the Israeli and the Palestinian Authority. Through its presence the EU contributed to the reconciliation of the Israeli security concerns with both the Palestinian demand for an autonomous border management and the requirements of Gaza's economic recovery, which predisposes open borders (Del Sarto 2007: 70). By meeting both parties' concerns, EUBAM Rafah enhanced the EU's standing of a force for good in the conflict.

During the Israel-Lebanon War of 2006, in order to stop the conflict, the EU representatives including the Foreign Minister Erkki Tuomioja, the Commissioner for External Relations and the European Neighbourhood Policy Benita Ferrero-Waldner and the

High Representative for the CFSP Javier Solana carried out diplomatic efforts. They visited the region in July 2006 and met with Israeli, Palestinian and Lebanese senior figures. They acted as facilitators for the cessation of the conflict. Moreover, in order to relieve the worsening humanitarian situation in Lebanon, the EU provided humanitarian aid in monetary terms and in kind in the form of food, medicine and shelter for the victims of the conflict in Lebanon. The EU also provided €11 million from the Rapid Reaction Mechanism for helping the evacuation and repatriation of citizens of developing countries. After the end of the war, EU Member States made the most significant military contribution to the expanded UNIFIL. EU Member States provided the backbone of the force by providing 7,000 troops, crucial military components and the operational command for UNIFIL. The EU's diplomatic efforts, provision of humanitarian assistance and military contributions enhance its standing as a force for good in the Middle East. Through its efforts the EU acted for the benefit of the peoples in the region and international peace and stability.

In its relations with the two sides of the conflict the EU also refrained from resorting to negative conditionality or coercion, except in the case of Hamas. The EU generally prefers political dialogue and engagement rather than confrontation and coercion in its relations with the parties to the conflict. The EU refrained from using sanctions against Israel, which would be harmful for both sides. Israel has been the one of the largest EU trading partners in the Euromed area ranking as the EU's 25th major trade partner (http://ec.europa.eu/trade/issues/bilateral/countries/israel/index_en.htm). The EU's total trade with Israel was more than €25 billion in 2007. The EU has a trade surplus with Israel; while EU imports from Israel were at €11.3 billion, EU exports to Israel totalled €14 billion in 2007. Thus, any trade and economic sanctions against Israel would be detrimental to both sides. It would mean some kind of self-imposed punishment for the EU (Dieckhoff 2005: 60).

Moreover, the EU's use of economic and trade sanctions would undermine its political credibility in Israel and would result in the loss of its status as legitimate interlocutor (ibid.: 61). The EU's imposition of sanctions against Israel would result in raising the Israeli perception that the European states were biased against it. The EU thus refrained from using sanctions against Israel which would have detrimental effects on both its material interest and contradict its rhetoric as force for good. The EU refrained from using sanctions even when Israel systematically violated human rights and international humanitarian law through its conduct in the Occupied Territories, such as excessive use of force and extrajudicial killings, forms of collective punishment, the construction of the Israeli 'Security Fence' and restrictions on movement that Israel imposed on the Palestinians through closures, checkpoints and curfews. Here, the EU tried to strike a balance between European and the Israeli concerns. However, this resulted in an intra-role conflict for the EU. The EU's role as force for good holds conflicting expectations for the performance of this role. This effectively means, that on the one hand, the EU's role as a force for good urged it to refrain from using sanctions against Israel; but on the other hand, it simultaneously urged it to promote human rights and international humanitarian law including the use of sanctions against the violators.

A clear example of intra-role conflict for the EU was 'the rules of origin' issue in which the EU refrained from using sanctions against Israel even in the case of the Israeli breach of international humanitarian law and the EU-Israeli Association Agreement. The EU-Israeli Association Agreement applied only to industrial and agricultural goods produced in the EU and Israel (Douma 2006: 446). The territorial scope of the agreement was limited to 'the territory of the State of Israel', thus excluding, on the basis of the international humanitarian law, the territories under Israeli occupation since 1967, including the West Bank, the Gaza Strip, East Jerusalem and the Golan Heights (Tocci 2007: 117). As the agreement did not specify any detailed definition of territorial scope of the agreement, Israel considered some of these territories as a part of the State of Israel and issued certificates of origin accordingly (Douma 2006: 446). In determining the origin of its exports, Israel did not distinguish between goods produced in Israel and in the Occupied Territories (Tocci 2007: 117–18). This led to the preferential treatment of goods produced in the Israeli settlements in the Occupied Territories and made these products eligible for the customs reduction that the Israeli goods enjoyed under the

Association Agreement (ibid.: 118). This was a material breach of both EU-Israeli Association Agreement and the Fourth Geneva Convention Relative to the Protection of Civilian Persons in Time of War.

The EU asked Israel to stop labelling any goods produced in the Occupied Territories as 'made in Israel', since the Occupied Territories are not part of Israel on the basis of the Fourth Geneva Convention and are not entitled to be subject to customs reductions that the Israeli goods have enjoyed under the Association Agreement (Schmid et al. 2006: 15). However, until November 2003, Israel, by relying on the argument that the EU recognition of the Paris Agreement created a customs union between Israel and the Palestinian Authority, refused to distinguish between goods produced in Israel and in the Occupied Territories and to accept the treatment of goods produced in the Occupied Territories differently from goods produced in Israel (ibid.).

During the course of time, despite the Israeli breach of EU law and international humanitarian law, the EU did not use any sanctions or legal mechanisms of passive enforcement against Israel. Thus, the EU put itself in the position of facilitating the infringement of the Fourth Geneva Convention, which was prohibited by the Article 1 of the Fourth Geneva Convention.[15] The EU tried to solve the issue through dialogue and negotiations with Israel. As a result of negotiations, the 'rules of origin' issue was settled with an agreement between the EU and Israel on a technical arrangement in 2004 which entered into force on 1 February 2005. With this agreement Israel agreed to specify the place of production by naming localities of production on the proofs of origin of its exports to the EU (Tocci 2007: 118).

This arrangement provided satisfactory solutions for both Israel and the EU. With this arrangement the EU was able to strike a balance between its own and the Israeli concerns. First of all, by enabling the EU customs authorities to identify which exported goods originated from the Israeli settlements in Occupied Territories and which from Israel and treat them accordingly (Douma 2006: 449) the arrangement enabled the EU to prevent a breach of EU and international humanitarian law. Secondly, this arrangement enabled Israel to continue to use the word 'Israel' to describe the location of settlements in the Occupied Territories (ibid.: 448) and represent all localities as situated within the State of Israel, including settlements in the Occupied Territories, and to issue proofs of origin for products produced in the settlements (Tocci 2007: 118). However, the arrangement's entitlement of Israel to represent all localities as situated within the State of Israel resulted in the EU's recognition of the Occupied Territories within Israel's territorial scope (Emerson et al. 2005: 26). As a result of this, Israel's occupation would become enshrined in the EU law, which in turn, would constitute an infringement of EU Member States' duties under international law (ibid.). In the rules of origin issue, the EU's refraining from using sanctions against Israel and its ability to find a satisfactory solution for both Israel and itself matched the EU's rhetoric as a force for good; however, its inability to promote international humanitarian law even with the use of sanctions against the Israeli infringement of the Fourth Geneva Convention was incongruent with this rhetoric.

The EU has been the largest external donor of financial and technical aid to the Palestinian Authority. This aid prevented the Palestinian economy from collapse; without this aid the Palestinian Authority would not have been able to finance even the basic functions of governance. The EU, aware of the detrimental effects of sanctions on the Palestinian Authority, refrained from using sanctions even when the Palestinian Authority failed to progress in areas of political and economic reform. However, in March 2006 when the Hamas-led Palestinian government failed to meet and implement the three principles of non-violence including the laying down of arms, recognition of Israel's right to exist and acceptance and fulfilment of existing agreements and obligations, including the Roadmap, the EU decided to boycott Hamas and impose sanctions on the Hamas-led Palestinian government. In Palestine and in the wider Arab world, the EU's imposition of sanctions on the Palestinian Authority was interpreted as an imposition of a severe and inhumane regime of sanctions against the Palestinian people under occupation (Pace 2008: 214). The EU's imposition of sanctions on a democratically elected Hamas-led government with free and fair elections is incongruent with the EU's rhetoric of a force for good.

By imposing sanctions on the Hamas-led Palestinian government, the EU did not serve the good of either the Palestinian people or itself.

The sanctions resulted in a grave economic crisis which threatened the collapse of the Palestinian Authority without necessarily harming Hamas, in terms of either finance provision or of public support (Tocci 2007: 121). Although deteriorating economic and social conditions in the Palestinian Territories forced the members of the Quartet to launch TIM, which enabled direct delivery of assistance to the Palestinian people while bypassing the Hamas-led Palestinian government, it represented a drop in the ocean[16] compared to the scale of challenges facing the Palestinian Territories and did not prevent a significant increase in poverty levels amongst the Palestinians (Youngs 2007). TIM's support was small in scale and it only covered a small part of medical needs and salaries (ibid.). This situation increased the Palestinian people's dependence on Hamas for basic services. With the introduction of TIM, EU aid to Palestine began to shift from development projects and institutional reform to humanitarian and emergency aid (Kolarska-Bobinska and Mughrabi 2008: 13).

The EU's imposition of sanctions on the Hamas-led government did not serve the interests and good of the EU either. The EU lost much popularity and good will amongst the Palestinian people and the wider Arab world (Youngs 2007). The EU's imposition of sanctions on a democratically elected government undermined its credibility as a promoter of democracy. Sanctions increased suspicions about the EU's commitment to supporting the democratization of the Palestinian Authority. The EU's imposition of sanctions negatively affected the trust of the Palestinian people and the wider Arab world's belief in the EU's good will as well as in the whole process of reform, transformation and the belief in principle of democracy (Kolarska-Bobinska and Mughrabi 2008: 13). The Palestinians and the wider Arab world regarded the EU's refusal to deal with the democratically elected Hamas government as a clear demonstration of political insincerity (Barbé and Johansson-Nogués 2008: 94). The EU's imposition of sanctions on a government which was elected with a fair, free and transparent election was regarded by the Palestinians as the EU's ignorance of the democratic expression of the Palestinian people (although the EU had made democracy one of the conditions for its financial aid to the Palestinian Authority) and the deprival of many

Palestinians of their livelihood: in effect a contradiction – although Hamas had a legal mandate to govern through a fair, free and transparent vote, it was considered as a terrorist organization by the EU and the USA (Pace 2009a: 46). Furthermore, imposition of sanctions interrupted the long process of confidence building between the officials of the Palestinian Authority and the EU (Kolarska-Bobinska and Mughrabi 2008: 13). Although the Palestinian people took an important step towards democratization, the EU's reaction to the Hamas victory stood in stark contrast to its discursive practices regarding the importance of fair, free and transparent elections as crucial dimensions of much needed democratization momentum on the Palestinian side for a possible resolution to the Israeli-Palestinian conflict (Pace 2008: 214).

Moreover, by imposing sanctions and cutting off relations with Hamas and preferring a policy of isolation rather than engagement, the EU has lost the chance of strengthening the more moderate wing of Hamas, which preferred the domestic governance of Palestine to confrontation with Israel and was therefore interested in continued EU support (Biscop 2007: 15). By undermining moderates, who were willing to continue peace negotiations with Israel, this policy only strengthened those groups who believed in violence as the only effective tactic. The EU's policy of isolation against Hamas prevented it from positively influencing the divisions within Hamas leadership between moderates and hard-liners (Emerson, Tocci and Youngs 2009). The EU's lack of engagement with Hamas strengthened the radical wing of Hamas (ibid.). The strengthening of Hamas's radical wing, which favoured confrontation with Israel, resulted in the aggravation of the Arab-Israeli conflict. Thus, the EU's imposition of sanctions also had a detrimental effect on the MEPP. It acted to the disadvantage of the peoples in the region and of international peace and stability. In the meantime, the internal conflict between Hamas and Fatah and the separation of Palestine between Hamas-controlled Gaza and Fatah-controlled West Bank and the Israeli conflict with Hamas-controlled Gaza demonstrated the detrimental effect of strengthening the radical wing of Hamas. Moreover, the EU's continuing financial aid to the unelected Fatah administration in the West Bank, while isolating the elected Hamas administration in Gaza, further aggravated the situation. In doing so EU aid did not act as an encouraging tool for the Palestinian internal reconciliation between Fatah and Hamas or for Palestinian democracy (ibid.). This did not positively induce moderation within Hamas and aggravated polarization between the internationally supported Fatah and the boycotted Hamas (Tocci 2007: 125). Although the EU, with good intentions, tried to strengthen a moderate Palestinian leadership through its support to the unelected Fatah administration in the West Bank, its policy of isolation towards the elected Hamas administration in Gaza contributed to the deepening of the Palestinian internal divisions and actually to the further weakening of Fatah (Möller 2009).

Muriel Asseburg (2009b: 35) also put forward the suggestion that the EU's policy of isolation not only sought to isolate Hamas but also backed the Israeli embargo on the Gaza Strip and put the Gazans under massive pressure to change their political preferences by imposing measures of collective punishment. This policy was both contrary to the EU's norms and aims of state- and institution-building, and cost European taxpayers immensely, because more funds were required to alleviate the humanitarian consequences of embargo.

The EU's imposition of sanctions on the Hamas-led government diminished the EU's image amongst Middle Eastern countries. Some Middle Eastern countries began to perceive that the 'rules of the game' were biased against the Arab world. As a result, those who would have liked to drive a permanent wedge between the West and the Arab world exploited this situation. As an example of this, Jordan's active pro-Islamist movement turned the unresolved Palestine question and the perceived bias of the USA and the EU against the Hamas government into an argument against Jordanian civil society accepting EU funds for projects in the country. The EU started to face difficulty in finding receivers for its funds for value promotion in Jordan (Barbé and Johansson-Nogués 2008: 94). Moreover, the EU's stance also reinforced the Middle Eastern countries' belief that the EU's lack of understanding/misreading of Middle Eastern affairs rather than its normative stance dominated its foreign policy agenda (Pace 2009b). The EU was considered as a timid spectator in the unfolding of the

Middle Eastern events, awaiting the USA to give the green light for any move in the Middle East (ibid.).

In the Hamas case, the EU faced a difficult political dilemma to handle. On the one hand, there was democratically elected Hamas government. On the other hand, democratically elected Hamas was on the EU's list of terrorist organizations[17] and refused to meet and implement the three principles put forward by the Quartet on the Middle East, including non-violence, comprising the laying down of arms, recognition of Israel's right to exist and acceptance, and fulfilment of existing agreements and obligations, including the Roadmap. EU Member States faced a hard choice between upholding the principle of democracy and safeguarding the EU's credibility and standing as an actor in the MEPP by maintaining its commitment not to deal with organizations that had been labelled as 'terrorist' by the international community (Barbé and Johansson-Nogués 2008: 94). Faced with a hard choice, the EU preferred to impose sanctions on the Hamas government in order to force it to meet and implement three principles. The EU's failure to find a satisfactory solution for both the Palestinian people and itself in respect of the Hamas electoral victory compromised what the EU claimed to stand for – acting as a force for good in the conflict.

To conclude, the EU can be identified as a limited force for good in the case of the MEPP. The EU's balanced and comprehensive approach to the conflict, its contribution to the creation of an independent, economically and politically viable, sovereign and democratic Palestinian State, its provision of financial and technical aid to the Palestinian Authority and support for the Palestinian reform process and its contribution to the mediation efforts all demonstrated that the EU to some extent struck a balance between its and conflicting parties' concerns. The EU's actions and decisions in some measure can be said to have been satisfactory for the preferences of all actors involved in the conflict. The EU's actions served the benefit of the peoples in the region and international peace and stability. However, the EU's decision to impose sanctions on the democratically elected Hamas-led Palestinian government was incongruent with the EU's role conception as force for good. As discussed above, the EU's decision to impose sanctions on Hamas acted to the detriment of all actors involved in the conflict.

The paradox that the EU faced between its policy of promotion of democracy – refraining from using coercion against parties to the conflict and its security considerations in terms of refraining from dealing with a terrorist organization, which refused to renounce violence – prevented the EU from acting in a satisfactory manner for both the Palestinians and itself. The Hamas case put a limit on the EU's role performance as a force for good which claims to act for the global common good. Furthermore, intra-role conflict, which the EU faced on the issue of employing sanctions against Israel, put a further limit on the performance of the EU's role as a force for good.

The EU's Role Performance as Force for International Peace, Security and Stability

The Arab-Israeli conflict, settlement of which was perceived by the EU as crucial for European energy security and its potential to adversely affect the EU's internal social and political stability and security due to spill over effect, was a good case for the evaluation of the performance of the EU's role as a force for international peace, security and stability. The settlement of the conflict can be identified as some form of self-defence for the EU as identified in the ESS document. Bringing peace, security and stability to the region, which is geographically very proximate to Europe, by contributing to the settlement of the Arab-Israeli conflict was in the enlightened self-interest of the EU. First of all, the settlement of the conflict would bring security, stability and peace to the region and would be beneficial for the countries in the region. Secondly, settlement of the conflict would relieve the above-mentioned security concerns of the EU. Thus, while the EU was acting to further the interests of the countries in the region and promote international peace, security and stability, ultimately it served its own self-interests. Settlement of the Arab-Israeli conflict can be therefore identified as a positive-sum situation for the EU, Israel, the Palestinian Authority and other countries in the region.

The EU's role performance as a force for international, peace, security and stability in the MEPP in the post-9/11 era can be evaluated by examining to what extent the EU measures up to its self-image. I focus on the EU's actions and decisions towards the negotiated settlement of the conflict resulting in two states, Israel and an independent, viable, sovereign and democratic Palestinian State, living side-by-side in peace and security on the basis of the 1967 borders and in the framework of a just, lasting and comprehensive peace in the Middle East, basing on UN Security Council Resolutions 242, 338 and 1515, the terms of reference of Madrid Conference of 2002 and the principle of 'land for peace'.

The EU used various foreign policy instruments – including political, diplomatic, military and civilian and development – towards the peaceful settlement of the Arab-Israeli conflict. Through its diplomatic efforts the EU contributed to the settlement of the conflict, carried out two ESDP operations and militarily contributed to UNIFIL, used ENP (two parties to the conflict are partners of the EU under the framework of ENP), provided financial and technical aid to the Palestinian Authority and supported its reform process towards the creation of an independent, economically and politically viable, sovereign and democratic Palestinian State.

In the immediate post-9/11 era, in order to stop mutual violence between the Israelis and the Palestinians, EU representatives and representatives of EU Member States played an active role in the mediation efforts and carried out several diplomatic missions. Although they attempted to broker a ceasefire between the Israelis and the Palestinians, their mediation had limited success and did not succeed in bringing an end to the mutual violence of the two sides. In this period the EU could only play a complementary role to the US mediation efforts: the EU representatives played a crucial role in the settlement of a micro-security crisis such as the issue of the Siege of the Church of the Nativity in Bethlehem. On this issue, during the Israeli 'Operation Defensive Shield' in 2002, the mediation efforts of Miguel Moratinos, Javier Solana and the Spanish Foreign Minister Josep Pique contributed to the peaceful settlement of the conflict. As the Spanish Foreign Minister Josep Pique noted, without the EU efforts, the Church of the Nativity would have remained under siege and the Israeli troops would have remained on the streets of Bethlehem. Moreover, during the Israel-Lebanon War of 2006, EU representatives carried out diplomatic efforts in order to stop conflict. The Finnish Foreign Minister Erkki Tuomioja as the foreign minister of the country holding the EU Presidency, the Commissioner for External Relations and the European Neighbourhood Policy Benita Ferrero-Waldner and the High Representative for the CFSP Javier Solana visited the region in July 2006 and met with Israeli, Palestinian and Lebanese senior figures. Their mediation efforts contributed to the settlement of the conflict. As EU officials emphasized, the EU was able to calm the atmosphere in the Middle East. It was able to contain the conflict and situation in the region.[18] Diplomatic efforts by EU representatives demonstrated the EU's willingness to play an active role in promoting and preserving peace, security and stability in the Middle East.

The EU has been one of the members of the Quartet on the Middle East since April 2002. The Quartet provided the EU with a formal framework to participate in the diplomatic and political dimension of the peace process, alongside the USA, Russian Federation and the UN. The EU played an active role in the preparation and the implementation of the Roadmap. German and Danish proposals formed the basis of the Roadmap agreed by the Quartet on the Middle East in September 2002. The EU played the role of facilitator for the Palestinian Authority to fulfil its obligations under the Roadmap. It contributed to the normalization of Palestinian life and Palestinian institution-building. The EU supported the reform process of the Palestinian Authority toward the creation of an independent, economically and politically viable, sovereign and democratic Palestinian State which was identified by the Quartet members as a precondition for the start of the negotiations for the final settlement of the conflict. The EU supported the Palestinian reform process in the areas of drafting a new constitution, the promotion of judicial independence, promotion of accountability and transparency in the fiscal system, the security sector reform, reform of administration and the executive, holding of free, fair and open elections, developing a modern education system and media based on peace, tolerance and mutual understanding, the promotion of pro-peace civil society. The EU facilitated the Palestinian Authority's preparations for the permanent status negotiations with Israel which would lead to the settlement of the Israeli-Palestinian Conflict. As noted by a British diplomat, helping the Palestinians in building an independent, economically and politically viable, sovereign and democratic Palestinian State was the EU's part in the implementation of the Roadmap.[19] Despite the EU's efforts, the Israeli unilateral actions, including construction of the Security Fence and the Disengagement Plan, and continuing mutual violence between the Israelis and the Palestinians decreased the prospect of the successful implementation of the Roadmap and led it into a dead end.

The ENP

Although the EU's use of the ENP as a foreign policy tool for the promotion of peace, security and stability in the Middle East is not directly related to the EU's efforts towards the peaceful settlement of the Arab-Israeli conflict, it indirectly contributed to the promotion of peace, security and stability in the region. Both actors in the conflict – Israel and the Palestinian Authority – are partners of the EU under the framework of the ENP. Both actors signed Action Plans with the EU. The government of Israel and the Palestinian Authority signed Action Plans with the EU in 2004. These Action Plans included a political dialogue and agreed governance reforms and measures preparing both partners for gradually integrating in the EU's internal market (Schmid et al. 2006: 15). In this section, rather than going into details of the ENP partnership of these two actors with the EU, I prefer to focus on the relevance of the ENP with the EU's contribution to the peaceful settlement of the conflict.

In the Action Plan for Israel, the EU and Israel agreed on several priorities for action which were directly related to the peaceful settlement of the Arab-Israeli conflict. One of these priorities was to enhance political dialogue and cooperation, based on shared values, including facilitating efforts to resolve the Middle East conflict. In order to fulfil this priority, under the heading of situation in the Middle East, the EU and Israel agreed on several actions. These actions include strengthening political dialogue and identifying areas for further cooperation on

progress towards a comprehensive settlement of the Middle East conflict; bilateral cooperation between the EU and Israel towards the comprehensive settlement of the Middle East conflict in accordance with
the Roadmap; supporting the Palestinian Authority's efforts to stop
terrorist activities and violence; facilitating the secure and safe movement of civilians and goods, safeguarding, to the maximum possible,
property, institutions and infrastructure while recognizing the Israeli
right of self-defence, the importance of adherence to international law
and the need to preserve the perspective of a viable comprehensive
settlement, minimizing the impact of security and counter-terrorism
measures on the civilian population; improving economic and social
conditions for all populations; further improving access and coordination to facilitate the implementation and delivery of humanitarian and
other forms of assistance and facilitate the reconstruction and rehabilitation of infrastructure; pursuing efforts to support and facilitate
reforms, transparency, accountability and democratic governance in
the Palestinian Authority, and the consolidation of all security services; promote a climate conducive to the resumption of cooperation in
all areas; and taking concrete actions against incitement to hatred and
the use of violence from all sources.

This Action Plan envisaged a bilateral political cooperation between
the EU and Israel for the peaceful settlement of the conflict. In addition to its efforts within the multilateral framework of the Quartet, the
EU also tried to utilize the ENP's bilateral framework for the peaceful
settlement of the Arab-Israeli conflict. However, some features of the
Action Plan prevented the EU from using it effectively to facilitate the
settlement of the conflict in accordance with the Roadmap. First of
all, the Action Plan was largely a declaration of mutual objectives and
commitments. Actions are little more than declarations and intentions
and they lack concreteness (Douma 2006: 457). Secondly, the political
commitments demanded from Israel in return for its participation in
the EU's internal market were vague (Del Sarto 2007: 70). The reason
behind the vagueness was to enable both parties to agree on a document which they could present as a clear achievement for themselves,
while understating the concessions which were granted (ibid.). Due to
this vagueness, the EU and Israel maintained different interpretations

of the Action Plan. For the EU, it represented Israel's official acceptance of the EU's involvement in the Middle East peacemaking, along with the principles of the Roadmap (Del Sarto 2007: 70). The EU granted as much importance to the political dimension of the partnership as the economic one. However, Israel tried to separate bilateral economic relations with the EU from political ones and focused on the economic dimension. For Israel, the Action Plan represented the upgrading of bilateral economic relations and gradual economic integration of Israel in the EU's internal market, but not an instrument for the settlement of the conflict (ibid.).

Israel was successful in excluding issues related to the Arab-Israeli conflict and the Palestinian issue from its bilateral talks with the EU. For instance, although there was an official political dimension to the institutional EU-Israel framework, there has never been such political discussions within the daily dialogue between Israel and the European Commission concerning the Palestinian dimension (Schmid et al. 2006: 15). Although both sides reiterated their commitment to the trilateral EU-Israel-Palestinian trade group, which aimed to examine ways to improve trade flows and cross-border movements of the Palestinian goods between Gaza, the West Bank, Israel and the EU, most of the bilateral talks concerned how Israel could be integrated better in the internal market (ibid.). On only one occasion, in 2005, did the EU, Israel and the Palestinian Authority attempt to cooperate in energy and transport, but the Hamas victory prevented the application of the joint initiative. In this case, although the European Commission backed joint activities between Israel and the Palestinian Authority in the form of financial and political support for joint Israel-Palestinian Energy Offices to improve coordination in electricity and gas networks, after the Hamas victory in the Palestinian legislative elections of 2006 all activities were halted (ibid.).

The declaratory character of the Action Plan, the contracting parties' different interpretations of the Action Plan, the Israeli success in excluding issues related to the Arab-Israeli conflict and the Palestinian issue from its bilateral talks with the EU, the EU's reluctance to exert any form of conditionality toward Israel even when Israel failed to fulfil its commitments within the framework of the

Action Plan prevented the EU from using the ENP as an effective tool for the peaceful settlement of the conflict in accordance with the Roadmap. While the ENP strengthened the economic partnership between the EU and Israel, this did not lead to a bilateral political partnership for the settlement of the Arab-Israeli conflict in accordance with the Roadmap.

The EU utilized the ENP as a tool for assisting and facilitating the Palestinian Authority to fulfil its obligations under the Roadmap, especially with regard to the creation of an independent, economically and politically viable, sovereign and democratic Palestinian State. Unlike Israel, the EU used the ENP as an effective tool for the achievement of the objectives set by the Roadmap in the Palestinian case.

In the Action Plan for the Palestinian Authority, the ENP was identified as part of the EU's response to the Palestinian Authority's political and economic reform process towards the consolidation of democracy, accountability, transparency and justice in the Palestinian Territories. In the Action Plan, the EU and the Palestinian Authority agreed on several priorities for action which were directly or indirectly related to the peaceful settlement of the Arab-Israeli conflict. The first priority directly referred to the settlement of the Arab-Israeli Conflict. The first priority of the Action Plan was to facilitate efforts to resolve the Middle East Conflict and alleviate the humanitarian situation in Palestine. Other priorities were indirectly related to the peaceful settlement of the Arab-Israeli conflict; they were related to the EU's support of the political and economic reform process of the Palestinian Authority towards the creation of an independent, economically and politically viable, sovereign and democratic Palestinian State which was identified by the Roadmap as a precondition for the start of the negotiations for the final settlement of the conflict. These priorities are directly related to the EU's efforts to facilitate the Palestinian Authority's preparations for permanent status negotiations with Israel which would lead to the settlement of the Conflict. These priorities included progress on establishing a functioning judiciary and effective enforcement of legislation; strengthening the rule of law and respect for human rights; and strengthening institutions and further reinforcing administrative capacity, the holding of elections in the West Bank and Gaza Strip in accordance with international standards, building on progress made in establishing an accountable system of public finances. These priorities were related to the Palestinian political and economic reform process in the areas of the promotion of judicial independence, promotion of accountability and transparency in the fiscal system, reform of administration and the executive, the holding of free and fair elections and developing a modern education system and media based on peace, tolerance and mutual understanding.

In order to fulfil these priorities, under the heading of 'Political Dialogue and Reform-building - the Institutions of an Independent, Democratic and Viable Palestinian State', the EU and the Palestinian Authority agreed on several actions. These actions include:

- strengthening political dialogue and cooperation between the EU and the Palestinian Authority in resolving the Middle East conflict through intensifying efforts to facilitate the peace process and bring about the implementation of the Quartet Roadmap to a permanent two-state solution to the Israeli-Palestinian conflict;
- taking measures to facilitate improving the overall humanitarian situation;
- ensuring respect for international law, in particular international humanitarian law;
- fighting against terrorism;
- strengthening EU-Palestinian Authority cooperation on the Palestinian reform programme;
- establishment of an independent, impartial and fully functioning judiciary in line with international standards and strengthen the separation of powers;
- holding of transparent general and local elections according to international standards;
- acceleration of constitutional and legislative reform including finalization of work on the drafting of a democratic Constitution and consultation with wider public;
- carrying out public administration and civil service reform;

- strengthening legal guarantees for freedom of speech, freedom of the press, freedom of assembly and association in accordance with international standards;
- ensuring the respect for human rights and basic civil liberties in accordance with the principles of international law;
- fostering a culture of non-violence, tolerance and mutual understanding;
- continuing efforts to establish a modern and well-functioning system of financial control in line with international best practices;
- continuing work to improve transparency of the Palestinian Authority's finances and taking concerted action to tackle corruption within public institutions and to fight against fraud;
- developing a modern education system based on peace, tolerance and mutual understanding;
- continuing efforts to establish a modern and well-functioning system of financial control in line with international best practices;
- continuing work to improve the transparency of the Palestinian Authority's finances and taking concerted action to tackle corruption within public institutions and to fight against fraud;
- ensuring transparency of public procurement operations; putting in place a modern and financially sustainable pension system.

This action plan envisaged intensified bilateral political and economic cooperation between the EU and the Palestinian Authority for the continuation of the Palestinian political and economic reform process towards the creation of a democratic, economically and politically viable and sovereign Palestinian State. Unlike the Israeli case, beside its efforts within the multilateral framework of the Quartet, the EU effectively utilized the ENP's bilateral framework for the peaceful settlement of the Arab-Israeli conflict in the Palestinian case. However, after the Hamas victory in the Palestinian legislative elections of 2006, the EU's policy of boycotting the Hamas-led Palestinian government and then the internal conflict between Hamas and Fatah and the separation of Palestine between Hamas-controlled Gaza and

Fatah-controlled West Bank made the implementation of the ENP objectives impossible. This situation impeded the continuation of intensified bilateral political and economic cooperation between the EU and the Palestinian Authority.

ESDP Operations

The EU carried out two civilian crisis management operations under the framework of the ESDP in the Occupied Territories in order to contribute to the promotion of peace, security and stability in the region. These two missions are also directly related to the EU's commitment to assist and facilitate the implementation of the Roadmap, which the EU has regarded as the only way to the settlement of the conflict. Both ESDP operations have raised the profile of the EU in relation to the sensitive border, policing and rule-of-law dimensions of the conflict (Bulut 2009: 289).

EUBAM Rafah: The first mission, EUBAM Rafah was established upon the invitation of the two parties to the conflict, the Israeli government and the Palestinian Authority. It aimed to provide a third party presence at the Rafah Crossing Point between Gaza and Egypt in order to contribute to the opening of the Rafah Crossing Point and build up confidence between the Israeli government and the Palestinian Authority, in cooperation with the Community's institution-building efforts. The mandate of the mission was to actively monitor, verify and evaluate the Palestinian Authority's performance with regard to the implementation of the 'Agreed Principles for Rafah Crossing' and to ensure the Palestinian Authority's observance of all applicable rules and regulations concerning the Rafah crossing point and the terms of the 'Agreed Principles for Rafah Crossing'. In addition to the supervision of the implementation of the 'Agreement on Movement and Access from and to Gaza' between the Israelis and the Palestinians, the mandate of EUBAM Rafah also included contributing to building up the Palestinian capacity in all aspects of border management at Rafah through mentoring, and contributing to the liaison between the Palestinian, Israeli and Egyptian authorities in all aspects regarding the management of the Rafah Crossing Point.

In order to contribute to the Palestinian capacity building in all aspects of border management at Rafah, EUBAM Rafah tried to develop training programmes designed to meet the training needs in a variety of border management fields, and evaluation systems. In addition to actively monitoring and mentoring the Palestinian Authority's border management at Rafah, EUBAM Rafah has also provided support to the EU's other ESDP operation in the Occupied Territories, EUPOL COPPS in areas of auditing the Palestinian Civil Police and the preparation of training courses. In the area of auditing, EUBAM Rafah officers assisted EUPOL COPPS advisers to observe several Palestinian Civil Police districts, headquarters and police stations in the West Bank in order to identify training and support needs. In the area of training, EUBAM Rafah has produced Border Police and Customs input which EUBAM officers would deliver during a Public Order training course to be run by EUPOL COPPS at the Jericho Training Centre (EU Border Assistance Mission at Rafah Crossing Point 2009).

EUBAM Rafah was the EU's first ESDP operation with the specific aim of monitoring borders abroad (Sabiote 2006: 9). EUBAM Rafah was crucial for the EU's role in the MEPP as it enabled the EU to play a significant role in the security dimension of the peace process. For the first time, EU military personnel, under the command of an Italian general, supervised an area of security concern for Israel (Musu 2010c: 74). EUBAM Rafah provided benefits for both sides of the conflict and served the achievement of the objectives of the Roadmap. First of all, it contributed to confidence-building between the Israeli government and the Palestinian Authority. Secondly, it provided the Palestinians with freedom of movement of people and goods in and out of Gaza Strip which would improve their living conditions and pave the way for the creation of an economically viable Palestinian State. Thirdly, it provided the Israelis with a sense of security against threats which would come through the Rafah Crossing Point, including possible weapons transfers and the uninhibited return of exiled extremist leaders and terrorists. As the Israelis perceived Rafah as a door of danger (Lazaroff 2009), EUBAM Rafah provided them with some kind of border security. Moreover, since the creation of an independent, economically and politically viable, sovereign and democratic Palestinian State was the best guarantee for the Israeli security, EUBAM Rafah's contribution to the creation of an economically viable Palestinian State would indirectly contribute to the security of Israel.

EUPOL COPPS: The second mission, civilian police mission EUPOL COPPS was established in order to contribute to the establishment of sustainable and effective policing arrangements under the Palestinian ownership in accordance with best international standards, in cooperation with the Community's institution building programmes as well as other international efforts in the wider context of Security Sector including Criminal Justice Reform.

The mandate of the mission included assisting the Palestinian Civil Police in the implementation of the Palestinian Civil Police Development Plan by advising and closely mentoring their senior members and the criminal justice system, coordinating and facilitating EU and Member State assistance and, where requested, offering international assistance to the Palestinian Civil Police and advising on police-related criminal justice elements. The main aim behind the launch of the mission was to support the Palestinian Authority in taking responsibility for law and order in the Palestinian territories by improving the Palestinian Civil Police and law enforcement capacity.

During its mandate, EUPOL COPPS focused on two areas of activity. First of all, it contributed to the capacity building of the Palestinian police through providing infrastructures, vehicles, computers, equipment and training. Secondly, it provided public order training to the Palestine police in order to teach them how to act as a democratic and accountable police force while managing peaceful and hostile demonstrations. In public order training, the Palestinian police officers learned public order management techniques, including minimum use of force while arresting. In addition to equipping and training the Palestinian police, EUPOL COPPS coordinated and facilitated financial assistance, whether from EU countries or other international donors, to the Palestinian Civil Police.

In order to reform the Palestinian Criminal Justice System, the rule of law section of EUPOL COPPS was established alongside the advising section in October 2007. The rule of law section focused on advising, programme planning and project facilitation for the Palestinian Criminal Justice Sector. As part of the EU's aim to support to a comprehensive approach to creating security for the Palestinians, the EU decided to treat the Palestinian Criminal Justice Sector as a whole. Thus, they decided to expand the rule of law section with additional personnel in May 2008. The rule of law section worked for the development of a comprehensive strategy for the Palestinian Justice Sector in close coordination with the Palestinian partners and existing coordination mechanisms. It advised on and monitored the legal situation through the Palestinian Ministry of Justice, prosecutors' offices and courts.

EUPOL COPPS served the achievement of the objectives of the Roadmap. It was an important element of the EU's efforts to assist and facilitate the Palestinian Authority to live up to its Roadmap obligations especially with regard to institution building and security. With regard to institution building, it was an important step towards the creation of a politically viable Palestinian State, which was one of the goals of the Roadmap. EUPOL COPPS contributed to the Palestinian Authorities' efforts to create a sound Palestinian criminal justice system and a modern, democratic, accountable and effective Palestinian police organization with a clearly identified role, operating within a sound legal framework, capable of delivering an effective and robust policing service, responsive to the needs of the society and able to manage effectively its human and physical resources. With regard to security, EUPOL COPPS bestowed benefits on the security of both sides of the conflict. First of all, it made a crucial contribution to the improvement of the security of the Palestinian territories through improving the Palestinian civil police's law enforcement capacity. By consolidating the Palestinian civil police's capacity in policing and fighting crime, EUPOL COPPS contributed to the reestablishment of law and order in the Palestinian territories. In this way, it contributed to an improvement in the safety and security of the Palestinian population and served the domestic agenda of the Palestinian Authority in reinforcing the rule of law. Secondly, by contributing to the creation of politically viable Palestinian State, it would contribute to the security of Israel.

In addition to these two ESDP operations, EU Member States' significant military contribution to the expanded UNIFIL and their leading role in the UN force, which was discussed in detail earlier in this chapter, enhanced the EU's profile, presence and visibility as the promoter of peace, security and stability in the region. Beside EUBAM Rafah, EU Member States' military presence in the region through UNIFIL demonstrated the increased international recognition of the EU as a significant security player in the Middle East conflict. As EU officials have maintained, with EUBAM Rafah and UNIFIL the EU began to play a key role in Israeli security. On the one hand, EUBAM Rafah provided security for Israel's southern border; on the other hand, UNIFIL provided security for Israel's northern border.[20]

The EU's provision of financial and technical aid to the Palestinian Authority, which will be discussed in detail later in this chapter, was one of the EU's most important contributions to the promotion of peace, security and stability in the Middle East. The EU's aid to the Palestinian Authority made significant contributions to the continuation of the MEPP. First of all, this aid prevented the Palestinian Authority from collapse; without this aid the Palestinian Authority would not have been able to finance even the basic functions of governance. The prevention of the collapse of the Palestinian Authority facilitated the continuation of the peace process. Secondly, this aid enabled the Palestinian Authority to fulfil its obligations under the Roadmap. Through its aid to the Palestinian Authority the EU assisted and facilitated the creation of an independent, economically and politically viable, sovereign and democratic Palestinian State.

The EU's support for the Palestinian political and economic reform process, which will be discussed in detail later in this chapter, was another significant contribution by the EU to the promotion of peace, security and stability in the Middle East. The EU, through its support to the political and economic reform process of the Palestinian Authority towards the creation of an independent, economically and politically viable, sovereign and democratic Palestinian State, facilitated and assisted the Palestinian Authority to fulfil its obligations under the Roadmap. The EU facilitated the Palestinian Authority's preparations for permanent status negotiations with Israel, which would lead to the settlement of the Israeli-Palestinian Conflict.

In conclusion, the EU can be identified as a 'constrained' force for international peace, security and stability in the case of the MEPP. On the one hand, the EU played a significant role in the peaceful settlement of the conflict through some successful mediation efforts and diplomatic missions of EU and national representatives, as in the issue of the Siege of the Church of the Nativity in Bethlehem. It carried out two ESDP operations. It signed ENP Action Plans with both sides. It made significant military contribution to the expanded UNIFIL. It provided financial and technical aid to the Palestinian Authority and supported the Palestinian reform process towards the creation of an independent, economically and politically viable, sovereign and democratic Palestinian State. Moreover, the EU was the most active member of the Quartet on the Middle East in the promotion of the Roadmap. Nevertheless, the EU as a force for international peace, security and stability faced two kinds of constraints which prevented it from always acting as an effective mediator for the peaceful settlement of conflict, both internal and external.

Internal constraints are related to the EU's lack of both vertical[21] and horizontal[22] coherence, the EU's inability to act as a coherent actor and speak with one voice. In the area of foreign and security policy, Member States are the key players and decisions are made through consensus. Diverging national interests and preferences prevented EU Member States from agreeing on a common position and acting effectively in conflict situations. As seen in the early months of 2002, EU Member States did not agree on a common strategy to revive the stalemated peace process, hence they did not take any European initiative and finally decided to support the US initiative. Their diverging preferences constrained the EU's ability to act as an effective mediator for the settlement of the conflict. The EU's inability to act prevented it from taking an initiative which would have ended mutual violence and put the stalemated peace process back on track.

Moreover, some EU Member States' unilateral diplomacy and their diverging voices undermined the EU's effectiveness and international credibility as a force for international peace, security and stability.

The Italian government's attitude towards the Israeli construction of a security fence can be given as an example for the lack of internal cohesion within the EU. During its EU Presidency in 2003, the Italian government declared its support for the Israeli construction of a security fence through the Occupied Territories in the West Bank by declaring it as an act of self-defence on the part of Israel. However, the EU declared it as illegal under international law and identified it as an obstacle to the implementation of the Roadmap, a threat which would make the implementation of a two-state solution physically impossible and a source of misery to thousands of Palestinians. The Italian unilateral declaration undermined the EU's credibility in the eyes of the Israelis and prevented the EU from putting pressure on Israel to stop the construction of the security fence. Moreover, in order to please Israel, the Italian Prime Minister Silvio Berlusconi in June 2003 refused to meet with the President of the Palestinian Authority Yasser Arafat despite the EU's decision to maintain contacts with Arafat (Islam 2003a: 13). It is acknowledged by EU officials that the EU's Achilles' heel in the case of the MEPP was their inability to speak with one voice and thereby send a coherent message.[23] EU Member States' different interests and positions to the conflict and their diverging relations with Israel, Hamas and the Arab world made it difficult to craft a credible common EU position towards the MEPP.[24] The lack of 'vertical coherence' undermined the EU's credibility as a neutral arbiter between the parties in the eyes of the Palestinians. In two cases, Italian unilateral acts and the breaking of the Union line undermined the EU's credibility and effectiveness.

In addition, its institutional complexity resulted in a lack of 'horizontal coherence' and put a further constraint on the EU's ability to act as an effective mediator for the settlement of the conflict. A multiplicity of actors participated in the formulation and implementation of EU Foreign Policy, including the European Council, the GAERC, the European Commission and the European Parliament, and this made the development of a common foreign policy quite difficult (Dannreuther 2004: 162). Due to the complex nature of EU's institutional structure, the representatives of EU Member States, mainly the foreign ministers of the country holding the EU Presidency, the EU

High Representative for the CFSP, the EU Special Representative for the MEPP, the EU Commissioner for External Relations and European Neighbourhood Policy, were involved in the formulation and implementation of the EU's policy towards the MEPP. A clear example of this is that the EU was represented by three EU actors in the Quartet on the Middle East, including the EU High Representative for the CFSP, the EU Commissioner for External Relations and European Neighbourhood Policy and the foreign minister of the country holding the EU Presidency. Alvare De Soto, the former UN Secretary General's Envoy to the Quartet, has suggested that the representation of the EU by three actors in the Quartet hampered the EU's ability to present its position forcefully (Khaliq 2008: 285). Furthermore, in the post-9/11 era, diplomatic efforts of the EU towards the negotiated settlement of the conflict were carried out by the above mentioned three actors plus the EU Special Representative for the MEPP.

The participation of a multiplicity of actors in the formulation and implementation of the EU's policy towards the MEPP further constrained the EU's ability to act as an effective mediator for the settlement of the conflict, in the case of these actors' failure to speak with one voice and act coherently. As seen in the Italian case, governments' diverging stances from the EU in 2003 while they were holding the EU presidency undermined the EU's effectiveness and international credibility as a force for international peace, security and stability and prevented the EU from acting as an effective mediator for the settlement of the conflict. The multiplicity of diplomatic initiatives promoted by the EU High Representative for the CFSP, the EU Commissioner for External Relations and European Neighbourhood Policy and the foreign minister of the country holding the EU Presidency and the EU Special Representative for the MEPP led to confusion on the part of the Israelis and the Palestinians (Kolarska-Bobinska and Mughrabi 2008: 33). As a divided and misleading body, the EU was perceived as less efficient and harder to deal with than the USA by the Israelis and the Palestinians (ibid.). This resulted in the EU's marginalization as an effective mediator for the peaceful settlement of the conflict.

External constraints are related to the Israeli and the American reluctance towards the EU's participation in the bilateral peace negotiations as an active mediator. Israel and the USA wanted the EU's role to be supportive and complementary to the USA in bilateral political negotiations and be limited to the economic dimension of the peace process, mainly to the provision of financial and technical aid to the Palestinian Authority. For them, the EU's role should be limited to facilitating the implementation of the Roadmap, supporting Palestinian state-building and economic reconstruction. They wanted the EU to remain the payer not the player in the peace process.

Israel, which perceived the EU as pro-Palestinian, rejected the EU's participation in the bilateral negotiations as an active mediator. Israel wanted the USA to be the only mediator in the bilateral peace negotiations. Israel wanted the EU's role to be limited to the development of governmental, military and civil society institutions as part of the new Palestinian State (Newman and Yacobi 2004a: 42). Israel wanted the EU to act as an advisory body or even as a transition administration filling the vacuum between the Israeli withdrawal and full Palestinian statehood (Newman and Yacobi 2004b: 40). While perceiving the EU's role in the peace process as institution and government builder of the new Palestinian State, Israel perceived the US role as potential peacekeeper and implementer (ibid.: 41). In the words of an EU official, the Israelis did not want the EU to be around except for money.[25] In the post-9/11 era, this situation seemed to change with the US pressure on Israel. Although under US pressure, Israel began to accept the EU as an active mediator in the peace process, it still did not consider the EU as a mediator on a par with the USA.

In the post-9/11 era, the USA accepted internationalization of the MEPP through the creation of the Quartet, which provided a multilateral framework for the peace process by officially bringing other major global actors – the UN, Russia and the EU – into the peace process. However, this did not mean that the USA would share its role as the main mediator with the EU. The USA continued to act as the main mediator in the bilateral political talks between the Palestinians and the Israelis. As Nathalie Tocci has argued, the Quartet predominantly provided a multilateral cover for continuing US action in peace process (Tocci 2005a: 13). In June 2003, US President George Bush himself took the initiative to launch the Roadmap. In order to persuade the Israeli Prime Minister Ariel Sharon and the Palestinian Authority Prime Minister Mahmoud Abbas to commit to the Roadmap, Bush held a meeting with them at Aqaba in which the other members of the Quartet, including the EU, did not participate. Moreover, the EU was sidelined and excluded from the Annapolis process in November 2007. Although the EU and its Member States played a crucial role in reviving the Roadmap in early 2007 and in the run-up to the Annapolis Conference in November 2007, the EU was excluded from the preparation of the conference (Möller 2008). Although the EU, as a member of the Quartet, participated in the conference, it maintained a low profile, essentially supporting the US action (Musu 2010b). The USA played a primary role in the Annapolis Conference and the conference was primarily an American initiative (ibid.). The EU was once again sidelined and excluded from bilateral political talks by the USA and reduced to its traditional role as 'sponsor with limited political say' (Hanelt 2008: 210). In the post-9/11 era, despite the creation of the Quartet, the USA sought to reserve a primary role for itself in the bilateral talks while granting a secondary role to the EU. These two constraints put limits on the performance of the EU's role as force for international peace, security and stability in the case of the MEPP in the post-9/11 era and prevented it to act as an effective mediator for the peaceful settlement of the conflict.

The EU's Role Performance as the Provider of Development Aid

The EU's role as the provider of development aid took the form of provider of financial and technical aid in the context of the MEPP. Since Israel is a quite wealthy country, the EU's financial and technical aid was directed to the Palestinians (Youngs 2007). The EU had been the largest external donor of financial and technical aid to the Palestinian Authority and the main financial supporter of the MEPP since the signing of the Oslo Accords in 1993. The EU had been tirelessly attempting to build peace between the Israelis and the Palestinians through aid (Kolarska-Bobinska and Mughrabi 2008: 12); in Chris Patten's words, 'the Roadmap paid for in Euros' (Miller 2006: 646). The EU's status as the largest external donor of financial and technical aid to the Palestinian Authority resulted in the recognition of the EU's role in the peace process as the 'payer'. Its role has also been identified as the 'cash cow' to the Palestinian Authority (*European Voice* 2000). As identified by a Palestinian diplomat, the EU has been the banker of the Palestinian Authority.[26] In particular, the EU acted as the most prominent 'paymaster' of the Palestinian Authority and the MEPP in the post-9/11 era (Möller 2008).

In the post-9/11 era, the EU's financial and technical aid to the Palestinians was provided with the aim of alleviating the humanitarian situation of the Palestinians, preventing the collapse of the Palestinian Authority and helping it in its institutional reform towards the creation of an independent, economically and politically viable, sovereign and democratic Palestinian State, which was identified by the Roadmap as a necessary step towards the peaceful settlement of the conflict (Asseburg 2003: 180). In Chris Patten's words, the EU's financial and technical aid to the Palestinians both kept essential services in health and education in the Palestinian territories going and ensured the continuing existence of a viable negotiating partner for Israel (Patten 2001). The motive behind the EU's provision of financial aid to the Palestinians was the EU's conviction that social development, the creation of employment possibilities and the related stability and hope would result in the establishment of a conducive environment for the Palestinians to engage with their Israeli neighbours in their peaceful negotiations towards a resolution in their conflict (Pace 2007: 1046). In this part of the chapter, by evaluating the EU's role performance as the provider of financial and technical aid, I focus on how effectively the EU used this instrument for the peaceful settlement of the conflict.

The financial and technical aid was mainly used for direct budgetary support to the Palestinian Authority, support for the Palestinian infrastructure and institution building, support for the Palestinian refugees through United Nations Relief and Works Agencies for Palestinian Refugees in the Near East, humanitarian and food aid, support for pro-peace civil society and peace process and emergency support after the EU's suspension of direct aid to the Hamas-led Palestinian government. During the period between 2001 and 2006, the EU invested €1,617.78 million in the Palestinian Authority. The components of this amount of aid are shown in Table 5.1.

Table 5.1   EU's financial support for the Palestinians during the period between 2001 and 2006

	€ MILLION						
	2001	2002	2003	2004	2005	2006	TOTAL 01–06
Direct support to the Palestinian Authority	40	120	102	90.25	76		428.25 26.5 per cent
Infrastructure projects	0.97	38.3	0	0	40.55		79.82 5 per cent
Institution-building	5.76	21.50	12	6	17	12	74.26 4.6 per cent
Support to refugees through UNRWA	57.25	55	57.75	60.65	63.67	64.41	358.73 22.1 per cent
Humanitarian and food aid	41.95	69.24	61.61	61.11	65.28	104	403.19 25 per cent
Israeli/Palestinian civil society and support for peace process		10	7.50	10	10		37.50 2.3 per cent
SMEs, East Jerusalem, human rights, NGOs, other projects	2.55	11.86	30.04	26.22	5.86	17.75	94.28 5.8 per cent
Emergency support including TIM						141.75	141.75 8.7 per cent
TOTAL	148.48	325.90	270.90	254.23	278.36	339.91	1617.78

Source: http://ec.europa.eu/external_relations/palestinian_authority/index_en.htm

The EU's financial and technical aid to the Palestinian Authority made significant contributions to the survival of the MEPP. First of all, this aid prevented the Palestinian Authority from financial collapse; without this aid the Palestinian Authority would not have been able to finance even the basic functions of governance. The prevention of the collapse of the Palestinian Authority facilitated the continuation of the peace process, because the collapse of the Palestinian Authority might have resulted in the escalation of conflict and the interruption of the peace process. Secondly, this aid enabled the Palestinian Authority to fulfil its obligations under the Roadmap. The EU through its aid has laid the ground for the creation of an independent, economically and politically viable, sovereign and democratic Palestinian State. An EU official put forward the opinion that creating a functioning Palestinian State was the EU's way of facilitating the peace process.[27]

The first component of the EU's aid to the Palestinian Authority, direct budgetary support, helped the Palestinian Authority to alleviate and offset the disastrous consequences of the fiscal crisis caused by Israel's withholding of the Palestinian tax and custom revenues it had collected on behalf of the Palestinian Authority following the outbreak of the Al-Aqsa Intifada in September 2000 and the escalation of violence between the Israelis and the Palestinians. A Palestinian diplomat acknowledged that the EU's aid prevented the Palestinian Authority from collapse and thereby enabling it to remain afloat.[28] This aid enabled the Palestinian Authority to secure expenditures such as public service salaries, social, educational, health and core functions of the Palestinian Authority in the absence of regular monthly transfers of revenues from Israel to the Palestinian Authority. In Chris Patten's words, without the EU's financial and technical aid 'there would have been no Palestinian interlocutor for the negotiations now under way' (Newman and Yacobi 2004a: 31). As a British diplomat suggested, by enabling service provision by the Palestinian Authority, the EU's aid enabled the Palestinian Authority to maintain its legitimacy as a negotiating partner in the MEPP.[29]

As shown in Table 5.1, during the period between 2001 and 2006, the EU invested €428.25 million in the Palestinian Authority which constituted the highest percentage (26 per cent) of total aid directed to the Palestinians. The EU did not invest in any direct support to the Palestinian Authority in 2006. This is because the EU suspended direct budgetary support to the Hamas-led Palestinian government in March 2006 when the Hamas-led Palestinian government failed to meet and implement the three principles, the recognition of which the EU had made its future financial aid conditional on, which were non-violence including the laying down of arms, recognition of Israel's right to exist and acceptance and fulfilment of existing agreements and obligations, including the Roadmap.

The second and third components of the EU's aid to the Palestinians – support for the Palestinian infrastructure and institution building – were crucial for the creation of an independent, economically and politically viable, sovereign and democratic Palestinian State. Through its financial support for the Palestinian infrastructure and institution building the EU played the role of facilitator for the Palestinian Authority to fulfil its obligations under the Roadmap. The EU has contributed to the normalization of Palestinian Life and Palestinian institution building.

The EU's aid was the most effective instrument of the EU in its efforts to facilitate the Palestinian Authority to get ready for the permanent status negotiations with Israel which would lead to the settlement of the Israeli-Palestinian Conflict. As shown in Table 5.1, during the period between 2001 and 2006 the EU invested €74.26 million in the Palestinians in the form of support for Palestinian institution building, which constituted 4.6 per cent of total aid directed to the Palestinians.

Through its financial and technical aid to the Palestinian Authority the EU also supported infrastructure projects in the Palestinian territories, including construction, development and rehabilitation of water, wastewater and sanitation networks, public buildings and roads, procurement and replacement of solid waste containers and vehicles. The EU also funded important infrastructure projects like the rebuilding of Gaza seaport and airport. As illustrated in Table 5.1, during the period between 2001 and 2006 the EU invested €79.82 million in the Palestinians in the form of support for the Palestinian infrastructure building which constituted 5 per cent of total aid directed to the Palestinians.

The EU's support to the UNRWA has been defined by the EU as an essential component of its strategy for the MEPP (Newsletter of the European Commission Technical Assistance Office for the West Bank and Gaza 2007: 5 (henceforth Newsletter of the ECTAO)). The EU financially contributed to the regular budget of the UNRWA, which was established by UN General Assembly Resolution 302 (IV) of 8 December 1949 to carry out direct relief and works programmes for the Palestinian refugees and displaced persons who had been forced to flee their homes in Palestine as a result of the 1948 Arab-Israeli War and had started to live in the West Bank and Gaza Strip, Jordan, Lebanon and Syria. The UNRWA was the main provider of basic services such as education, health care, social, micro credit and shelter services and assistance to over 4.6 million registered Palestinian refugees in the Middle East. The European Commission and EU Member States were the largest donors to the UNRWA. The EU, through its financial contribution to the UNRWA, has contributed to the improvement of economic and social conditions of the Palestinian refugees living in the West Bank and Gaza Strip, Jordan, Lebanon and Syria since 1971. The UNRWA's specific programme towards the alleviation of poverty within the refugee population, which has provided food and cash aid to vulnerable refugees, mothers and babies, was largely funded by the EU. Moreover, the European Commission's Humanitarian Aid Directorate General (DG ECHO) was one of the main financial supporters of the UNRWA's emergency aid for the poorest Palestinian refugees, which was provided whenever crisis such as the Al-Aqsa Intifada and the Israel-Lebanon War of 2006 had occurred and consisted mainly of the provision of food aid and temporary job creation. The EU also provided support to a number of auxiliary special projects in the Palestinian territories and the region, including projects related to water and sanitation and student academic scholarships in order to improve the living conditions of refugees. As illustrated in Table 5.1, during the period between 2001 and 2006, the EU invested €358.73 million in the Palestinians in the form of support to the Palestinian refugees through the UNRWA which constituted 22.1 per cent of total aid directed to the Palestinians.

Beside its financial contribution to the UNRWA, the EU also provided humanitarian and food aid to the Palestinians in order to alleviate the humanitarian situation in the Palestinian territories. As illustrated in Table 5.1, during the period between 2001 and 2006, the EU invested €403.19 million in the Palestinians in the form of humanitarian and food aid and it constituted the second highest percentage (25 per cent) of total aid directed to the Palestinians. The EU's humanitarian and food aid was provided by the European Commission's Humanitarian Aid Office (ECHO). The amount of the EU's humanitarian and food aid gradually increased following the outbreak of the Al-Aqsa Intifada in September 2000, because the strict regime of closures and curfews imposed by Israel following the outbreak of the Al-Aqsa Intifada impeded the movement of the Palestinian people and goods and negatively affected employment and investment opportunities throughout the Palestinian territories which made the Palestinian's access to basic goods and services much more difficult. Under these conditions, in order to alleviate humanitarian crisis in the Palestinian territories, the EU gradually increased the amount of its humanitarian and food aid to the Palestinians. As was acknowledged by a Palestinian diplomat, the EU's aid prevented the emergence of a humanitarian catastrophe in the Palestinian territories.[30]

In the post-Al-Aqsa Intifada period (post-September 2000), there was a gradual shift in EU aid to the Palestinian Authorities from development projects and institutional reform to humanitarian and emergency aid (Kolarska-Bobinska and Mughrabi 2008: 13). Both withholding of the Palestinian revenue transfers by Israel and the escalation of violence between the Israelis and the Palestinians resulted in the deterioration of the humanitarian situation in the Palestinian territories. In order to alleviate the humanitarian situation of the Palestinian people and prevent the emergence of a humanitarian crisis in the West Bank and the Gaza Strip, the EU provided an increasing amount of humanitarian aid to the Palestinians in the post-Al-Aqsa Intifada period. The EU's efforts mainly focused on damage limitation exercises by striving to prevent further deterioration of the humanitarian and political situation, as opposed to improving it *per se* (Khaliq 2008: 369). As illustrated in Table 5.1, the amount of the EU's humanitarian aid to the Palestinian Authority peaked in 2006 (€104 million). The reason behind this was the deterioration of humanitarian situation in the Palestinian territories after the EU's imposition of sanctions on the Hamas-led government and withholding of direct budgetary support to the Hamas-led Palestinian government. In order to mitigate the deterioration of socio-economic and humanitarian situation of the Palestinians which resulted from sanctions imposed the EU decided to increase the amount of humanitarian aid to the Palestinians. However, this did not prevent deterioration in the socio-economic and humanitarian conditions of the Palestinians; it only represented a drop in the ocean related to the scale of socio-economic and humanitarian challenges facing the Palestinian Territories.

In order to relieve the deteriorating socio-economic situation in the West Bank and the Gaza Strip resulting from sanctions imposed on the Hamas-led Palestinian government, to ensure continued delivery of essential social public services to the Palestinian people and to facilitate the maximum level of support by international donors and the resumption of the Palestinian revenue transfers by Israel, the EU also provided humanitarian and emergency aid under the framework of a new mechanism, TIM. TIM was established in June 2006, because the EU could not deal with the Hamas-led Palestinian government at the time as Hamas refused to meet and implement the three principles of non-violence – the laying down of arms, recognition of Israel's right to exist and acceptance and fulfilment of existing agreements and obligations, including the Roadmap. TIM enabled the EU to address the basic social needs of the Palestinian people and focus on delivering aid to the poorest Palestinians, while bypassing the Hamas-led Palestinian government. TIM utilized financial resources of the European Commission, EU Member States and other donors to deliver essential services and financial support to vulnerable Palestinians (Newsletter of the ECTAO 2007: 6). The European Commission, 15 EU Member States, Canada, Norway, Switzerland and Australia contributed to TIM.

Between June 2006 and March 2008, €615.94 million was provided to the Palestinian people through TIM and €455.5 million of this amount was provided by the European Commission. The European Commission was the largest donor to TIM. In March 2008, TIM was replaced by a new mechanism called the PEGASE. TIM represented the highest point in the gradual shift in EU's aid to the Palestinian Authorities from development projects and institutional reform to humanitarian and emergency aid. Although the EU provided a significant amount of aid through TIM, the latter was not adequate to prevent a socio-economic and humanitarian crisis in the Palestinian territories. The aid provided through TIM represented a drop in the ocean related to the scale of challenges facing the Palestinian Territories (Youngs 2007).

The EU's financial support to peace-oriented NGOs in Israel and Palestine is another component of the EU's aid which was directly related to the MEPP. The main objective of the EU's financial support to peace-oriented NGOs on both sides was to create the conditions for peace, stability and prosperity in the region by providing support for pro-peace initiatives that combat violence and strengthen civil society, in particular with groups in both the Israeli and the Palestinian society that seek a solution for peace and dialogue across cultures (Douma 2006: 454).

The EU provided financial support to peace-oriented NGOs on both sides by using the European Partnership for Peace Programme. The EU, through the European Partnership for Peace Programme, supported local and international civil society initiatives that promote peace, tolerance and non violence in the Middle East in order to contribute to the rebuilding of confidence within and between the Israeli and the Palestinian societies. The main objective of the programme was to strengthen civil society actions in peace building and conflict transformation (Newsletter of the ECTAO 2007: 5). The programme focused on promoting initiatives in areas likely to have an impact on people's everyday lives and welfare, including practical activities which would promote communication and understanding by demonstrating the advantages of working together for mutual benefit and tangible results. By promoting communication and understanding through demonstrating the advantages of working together for mutual benefit and tangible results, these initiatives would broaden the base of support for the MEPP. The programme was jointly managed by the EC Delegation in Tel Aviv, the EC Technical Assistance Office to the West Bank and Gaza and the EC Delegation in Jordan. Under the framework of the European Partnership for Peace Programme, the EU funded projects with both an Israeli and Palestinian partner, including 'Building Business Bridges', 'Words Can Kill', 'Civic Action Groups for Peace and Social Justice' and 'Penultimate Jerusalem: Overcoming the Obstacles to Final Status in Jerusalem'. Through the European Partnership for Peace Programme the EU facilitated Palestinian and Israeli civil society to keep channels of communication open at a time when political dialogue was frozen. As illustrated in Table 5.1, during the period between 2001 and 2006, the EU invested €37.50 million in the Palestinian Authority in the form of financial support to peace-oriented NGOs in Israel and Palestine which constituted 2.3 per cent of total aid directed to the Palestinians.

The EU also provided financial support to the Palestinian private sector, mainly small and medium-sized enterprises (SMEs), which were in need of urgent financial assistance due to the devastating effect of the crisis that emerged after the outbreak of the Al-Aqsa Intifada; to development projects in East Jerusalem like projects for development of social services, health services and education; to projects for the promotion and protection of human rights like projects for promotion of death penalty, women's and children's rights and good governance and projects for the provision of rehabilitation to torture victims; and to numerous Palestinian NGOs and service institutions that had been assuming a number of functions in the areas of healthcare, education, housing, job creation, women's empowerment, human rights advocacy, legal aid, charity and welfare, all serving the needs and interests of the Palestinian people. As shown in Table 5.1, during the period between 2001 and 2006 the EU invested €94.28 million in the Palestinians in the framework of support for SMEs, East Jerusalem, Human rights, NGOs, other projects which constituted 5.8 per cent of total aid directed to the Palestinians.

In summary, the EU's financial and technical aid to the Palestinian Authority was its principal instrument for the peaceful settlement of the Arab-Israeli conflict in the post-9/11 era. The EU acted as the largest financial supporter of the Palestinian Authority and the MEPP. The EU successfully played the role of key donor or the largest payer of the Palestinian Authority and the MEPP. In the post-9/11 era, the EU's financial and technical aid to the Palestinian Authority made three main contributions to the MEPP.

Firstly, the EU's financial and technical aid in the form of direct budgetary support to the Palestinian Authority facilitated the latter to stay financially afloat after the Israeli withholding of the Palestinian tax and custom revenues following the outbreak of the Al-Aqsa Intifada in September 2000. By keeping the Palestinian Authority financially afloat, the EU also kept the peace process afloat, because the financial collapse of the Palestinian Authority might have resulted in the escalation of conflict, violence, chaos and the interruption of the peace process.

Secondly, the EU aid enabled the Palestinian Authority to fulfil its obligations under the Roadmap. The EU aid facilitated the creation of an independent, economically and politically viable, sovereign and democratic Palestinian State, which was identified by the Roadmap as a necessary step towards the peaceful settlement of the conflict. In particular, the EU's financial support to infrastructure projects in the Palestinian territories and the Palestinian institutional reform process was crucial. Furthermore, the EU's financial support to the Palestinian private sector – mainly the SMEs, development projects in East Jerusalem, projects for the promotion and protection of human rights and the Palestinian NGOs and service institutions – were other crucial contributions of the EU to the creation of a economically and politically viable Palestinian State.

Thirdly, through its financial aid to the peace-oriented NGOs and civil society initiatives on both sides the EU promoted communication and understanding among the Palestinians and the Israelis by demonstrating the advantages of working together for mutual benefit and tangible results. In this way the EU contributed to the creation of a positive environment for the peaceful settlement of the conflict and broadened the base of public support for the MEPP. The EU utilized its financial aid to strengthen civil society actions in peace building and conflict transformation. In addition to the EU's financial contribution, which provided direct benefit to the MEPP, the EU, through its financial support to the UNRWA, its humanitarian and food aid to the Palestinians and TIM contributed to the alleviation of socio-economic and humanitarian conditions of the Palestinian people. In particular, in the post-9/11 era, a gradual shift in the EU's financial aid to the Palestinian Authorities from development projects and institutional reform to humanitarian and emergency aid was observed. This trend reached its peak point in 2006 when the EU imposed sanctions on and withheld direct budgetary support to the Hamas-led Palestinian government.

Although the EU gradually increased the amount of humanitarian and emergency aid, it was not adequate to alleviate the dire socio-economic and humanitarian situation facing the Palestinians. The ongoing mutual violence between the Israelis and the Palestinians, the destruction of the Palestinian civilian infrastructure by the Israeli operations, the EU's withholding of direct budgetary support to the Hamas-led Palestinian government, the Israeli withholding of the Palestinian tax and custom revenues, the Israeli construction of the 'Security Fence' and the Israeli imposition of restrictions on the movement of the Palestinian people and goods through closures, checkpoints and curfews further deteriorated the scale of socio-economic and humanitarian conditions of the Palestinians to a point which the EU's humanitarian and emergency aid could not completely alleviate.

A Palestinian diplomat ascribed the deterioration of the socio-economic and humanitarian conditions of the Palestinians to the Israeli occupation. He defended the view that although the EU's aid to the Palestinians was crucial for preventing the Palestinian Authority from collapse and preventing a humanitarian catastrophe in the Palestinian territories (mainly in the case of TIM and PEGASE), it was not sufficient, as the Israeli occupation continues. According to him, under the Israeli occupation the EU's aid did not help the Palestinians build their infrastructure and institutions and create a sustainable Palestinian economy. He pointed out that the Israeli construction of the 'Security Fence' and imposition of restrictions on the movement of the Palestinian people and goods through closures, checkpoints and curfews prevented this aid from bringing sustainable development to the Palestinian territories. Therefore, owing to the Israeli occupation, the EU's huge aid was not able to prevent the Palestinians from becoming poorer.[31]

The provision of humanitarian and emergency aid to the Palestinians presented a dilemma on the part of the EU. On the one hand, the deterioration of the socio-economic and humanitarian situation of the Palestinians necessitated the EU's provision of aid due to a humanitarian imperative; non-provision would have led to a humanitarian catastrophe in the occupied Palestinian territories. On the other hand, by providing humanitarian and emergency aid to the Palestinians living in the territories under the Israeli occupation, the EU had taken over the humanitarian duties of Israel as the occupying power, under international humanitarian law[32] towards the Palestinian people as the population in the Occupied Territories (Asseburg 2003: 181). By relieving Israel of its legal obligations towards the Palestinian people, the EU inadvertently subsidized the Israeli occupation of the Palestinian territories and thus helped and facilitated Israel to continue the state of occupation, closures and curfews in the Palestinian territories, rather than working actively against it (ibid.). The EU's continuing aid to the Palestinians in the Occupied Territories due to humanitarian imperative enabled Israel to prolong its occupation in the Palestinian territories, while refraining from financial responsibilities as the occupying power. In this way, the EU's humanitarian and emergency aid acted to the detriment of the peace process.

Last but not least, the EU's financial support to the Palestinian development projects and institutional reform process towards the creation of an independent, economically and politically viable, sovereign and democratic Palestinian State is consistent with the EU's conviction that security, stability and peace can best be accomplished through development. Since the EU identified development as crucial for collective and individual long-term security and peace, the EU strove to wipe out breeding grounds for insecurity and instability, especially terrorism in the Palestinian territories, through its support to the Palestinian development projects and institutional reform process. The EU maintained that the creation of an independent, economically and politically viable, sovereign and democratic Palestinian State was the best guarantee for Israeli security since the Berlin European Council of 1999. This was later adopted by international community and was identified by the Roadmap as a precondition for the start of the negotiations for the final settlement of the conflict.

In spite of the EU's efforts, the continuation of the vicious cycle of mutual violence between the Israelis and the Palestinians in the post-9/11 era resulted in the continuation of conflict. The continuation of mutual violence led to the continuation of Palestinian underdevelopment and the continuation of Palestinian underdevelopment has provided a breeding ground for insecurity and instability, especially the prevalence of radical Islamic terrorism among the Palestinian population. Since there is an apparent correlation between economic deterioration, increasing poverty and unemployment and political radicalization, the increasing number of unemployed people in Palestine – where young jobless people constitute the majority of the population – has provided a fertile ground for radical Islamic groups who take political advantage of the suffering, need and desperation of the Palestinians (Khatib 2008: 173). The prevalence of radical Islamic terrorism among the Palestinians resulted in an increase in Palestinian terrorist attacks against Israeli targets, to which Israel made harsh responses through military operations against the Palestinian territories. The Israeli response, in some cases its disproportionate use of force, resulted in the destruction of the Palestinian civilian infrastructure and served the continuation of Palestinian underdevelopment. In addition, the Israeli construction of the 'Security Fence' and the imposition of restrictions on the movement of the Palestinian people and goods through closures, checkpoints and curfews as a countermeasure against intrusion of suicide bombers into Israeli cities hindering human and social development in the Palestinian territories, have been more factors in the continuation of Palestinian underdevelopment (Kolarska-Bobinska and Mughrabi 2008: 24). In the post-9/11 era, this vicious cycle of mutual violence and the Israeli construction of a 'Security Fence' and the imposition of restrictions on the movement of the Palestinian people and goods have been two important factors that have prevented the peaceful settlement of the conflict.

The Israeli-Palestinian case clearly demonstrated the complementary relationship between sustainable peace and sustainable development. It makes it obvious that, as identified in 'The European Consensus on Development', 'without peace and security, development and poverty eradication are not possible, and without development and poverty eradication no sustainable peace will occur' (Council of the European Union 2005). It also substantiates the view that, as identified by the European Commission, 'there cannot be sustainable development without peace and security, and sustainable development is the best structural response to the deep-rooted causes of violent conflicts and the rise of terrorism' (Commission of the European Communities 13 July 2005: 8).

The EU's Role Performance as Promoter of its Values and Norms

In the case of the MEPP, the EU's role performance as promoter of its values and norms can be evaluated through assessing to what extent the EU has promoted its foundational values and norms in relations with the two parties to the conflict, Israel and Palestine. In the case of the MEPP, since Israel is a well-governed and democratic country, the EU diverted its support to the establishment of a well-governed and democratic Palestinian State, which the EU identified as a best guarantee for the Israeli and regional security and a precondition for the peaceful settlement of the dispute. What this means in effect is that the creation of a well-governed democratic Palestinian State ensured the continuing existence of a viable negotiating partner for Israel in the peace negotiations. The continuing existence of Palestine as a viable negotiating partner for Israel would be the best guarantee for the viable peace process. This was later adopted by the international community and the creation of a well-governed and democratic Palestinian State was identified by the Roadmap as a precondition for the start of the negotiations for the final settlement of the conflict. Through its support to the Palestinian reform process the EU strove to facilitate the Palestinian Authority's preparation for permanent status negotiations with Israel, which would lead to the settlement of the Israeli-Palestinian Conflict.

Since 2002, the EU was also one of the members of the International Task Force on Palestinian Reform, which was composed of representatives of the Quartet (the USA, the EU, Russia and the UN Secretary General), Norway, Japan, the World Bank and the IMF. The International Task Force on Palestinian Reform had the role of monitoring and supporting implementation of the Palestinian civil reforms, and guiding the international donor community in its support for the Palestinians' reform agenda. In addition to its own individual support to the Palestinian reform process towards the establishment of a well-governed and democratic Palestinian State, the EU also worked within the multilateral framework of the International Task Force on Palestinian Reform.

Concerning the Palestinian Authority, the EU gave priority to the promotion of democracy and good governance. The EU supported the reform process of the Palestinian Authority towards the creation of a well-governed and democratic Palestinian State. In its efforts, the EU prioritized

- the progress on establishing a functioning judiciary and effective enforcement of legislation;
- strengthening the rule of law and respect for human rights;
- strengthening institutions and further reinforcing administrative capacity, holding of elections in the West Bank and Gaza Strip in accordance with international standards;
- building on progress made in establishing an accountable system of public finances;
- establishment of an independent, impartial and fully functioning judiciary in line with international standards and strengthening of the separation of powers;
- holding of transparent general and local elections according to international standards;
- acceleration of constitutional and legislative reform including finalization of work on the drafting of a democratic Constitution and consultation with wider public;
- carrying out public administration and civil service reform;
- strengthening legal guarantees for freedom of speech, freedom of the press, freedom of assembly and association in accordance with

international standards, ensuring the respect for human rights
and basic civil liberties in accordance with the principles of international law, and foster a culture of non-violence, tolerance and
mutual understanding;

- continuing efforts to establish a modern and well-functioning system of financial control in line with international best practices;
- continuing work to improve transparency of the Palestinian
  Authority's finances and to take concerted action to tackle corruption within public institutions and to fight against fraud;
- ensuring transparency of public procurement operations; putting
  in place a modern and financially sustainable pension system.

In 2001, the EU prepared a reform plan for the Palestinian
Authority including ratifying and enacting a Palestinian constitution,
Basic Law and the Law on the Independence of the Judiciary, establishing a Constitutional Court and a High Judicial Council, abolishing
State Security Courts, holding general elections, redistributing com-
petences between the President and cabinet, ensuring transparency
of public finances and restructuring municipalities, the civil service
and security sector (Tocci 2005a: 15). The '100-day' reform plan was
endorsed by the President of the Palestinian Authority Yasser Arafat
in June 2002.

With the adoption of the Plan, the Palestinian Authority began
to implement the reform process, aiming at strengthening good
governance and democracy. During 2002–2003, the Palestinian
Constitution, Basic Law, was adopted, a Prime Ministerial post was
established, the Cabinet was streamlined and reorganized, and a Law
on the Independence of the Judiciary was passed. In order to improve
the transparency of the Palestinian Authority's finances and to take
concerted action to tackle corruption within public institutions and
to fight against fraud, all sources of the Palestinian Authority's revenues were consolidated in a single treasury account under the Finance
Ministry, closely monitored by the IMF. The consolidation also ensured
the full and effective responsibility of the Finance Ministry for trans-
parently managing the Palestinian Authority's payroll and ensured the
maintenance of a public sector hiring freeze and strict expenditure

limit for an austerity budget. Moreover, in order to enhance transparency in public finances, the president's funds were taken under control through shifting its control from the presidency to the finance ministry (Tocci 2007: 110–11). In particular, in areas of judicial and financial reform, the EU's aid conditionality played a crucial role (Tocci 2005a: 16). During 2002–2003, the EU's threat to withhold budgetary assistance to the Palestinian Authority acted as leverage in encouraging the Palestinian Authority to carry out judicial and financial reform (ibid.). In the Palestinian case, the EU's most powerful policy instrument was the conditional promise of financial and technical aid and this exerted considerable leverage on the Palestinian Authority. In particular, concerning the democratization of Palestine, the EU tried to use its financial and technical aid as 'external democratization incentive' towards the Palestinian Authority (Stetter 2004: 154).

In 2003, the Palestinian National Security Council, which had the responsibility of supervising all of the Palestinian Security Services, was established. Moreover, in 2005, the Palestinian Security Services were reformed through the consolidation of three Palestinian security apparatuses (National Security, Interior, and Intelligence) under the Ministry of Interior, and through a facelift to the personnel service through the retirement of the Palestinian security officials, the training of forces and the recruitment of former militants.[33] Within the context of security sector reform, the EU launched a civilian police mission EUPOL COPPS. Through this mission the EU assisted the Palestinian Civil Police in the implementation of the Palestinian Civil Police Development Plan by advising and closely mentoring senior members of the Palestinian Civil Police and criminal justice system, coordinating and facilitating EU and Member State assistance and, where requested, international assistance to the Palestinian Civil Police, and advising on police-related Criminal Justice elements. The mission has facilitated the Palestinian Authority to take responsibility for law and order in the Palestinian territories by improving the Palestinian Civil Police and law enforcement capacity.

In addition to creating and empowering the post of prime minister and shifting the control of the Palestinian finances and security from the Presidency to the Ministry of Finance and the Ministry of Interior respectively, the EU also deployed election observation missions to observe the Palestinian Presidential elections of 2005 and Legislative elections of 2006 as part of its efforts to support the development of democratic institutions. Through these missions the EU enabled the Palestinian society to hold free, fair and open elections to provide democratic legitimacy for the institutions on the road to statehood.

Empirical analysis demonstrated that while the EU gave high priority to the promotion of good governance, such as security sector reform, or creation and empowerment of a prime minister, or improving transparency of the Palestinian Authority's finances, or passing of a Law on the Independence of the Judiciary, the promotion of genuine democracy was neglected in the case of Palestine. Despite the EU's rhetoric on the desirability of integrating Hamas into democratic politics, the concrete substance of EU's strategy demonstrated that the EU regarded reform in terms of strengthening Fatah against Hamas (Youngs 2006: 168). Although the EU supported the principle of Hamas's participation in the legislative elections scheduled for July 2005, it did nothing to defend that principle when elections were postponed until January 2006 by the President of the Palestinian Authority Mahmoud Abbas in 2005 (ibid.). Moreover, the EU's disinterested stance towards the non-inclusiveness of the Palestinian political system, persistent exclusion of Islamic factions from both the PLO and the Palestinian Authority and its reluctance to engage and support Islamic civil society and non-violent groups despite the fact that they represented the only credible opposition forces in Palestine, raised doubts about the EU's seriousness in promoting a genuine democracy in Palestine (Tocci 2007: 122). Although the EU supported the development of political institutions required for democracy, it did not complement this with democratic consolidation in Palestine. The EU did not press for the promotion of effective participation, party competition and pluralism in Palestine, which constituted essential elements of genuine democratization process.

The EU's ambiguous stance towards genuine democratization in Palestine was clearly seen in its reaction to Hamas's sweeping victory in the Palestinian legislative election of 2006. In the post-election period, the EU made its future financial aid to the Hamas-led Palestinian government conditional on three principles: non-violence, the laying down of arms, the recognition of Israel's right to exist and acceptance and fulfilment of existing agreements and obligations, including the Roadmap. Although the EU had previously made the provision of its direct budgetary support to the Palestinian Authority conditional on progress in areas of democracy and good governance, these three conditions did not include the standards of democratic governance or issues of civil rights in the Palestinian territories (Youngs 2007: 4). In March 2006, when the Hamas-led Palestinian government failed to meet and implement the three conditions, the EU decided to boycott Hamas and impose sanctions on the Hamas-led Palestinian government.

The EU's imposition of sanctions on a democratically elected government with a fair, free and transparent election undermined both the legitimacy of the EU's democracy promotion policy and its credibility as a promoter of democracy in Palestine and the Middle East. The EU lost much popularity and good will amongst the Palestinian people and the wider Arab world (ibid.: 1). The EU's use of sanctions increased suspicions about the sincerity of its commitment to support for the democratization of the Palestinian Authority. It negatively affected the trust of the Palestinian people and the wider Arab world in the EU's good will as well as the whole process of reform, transformation and the belief in principle of democracy (Kolarska-Bobinska and Mughrabi 2008: 13).

The Palestinians and the wider Arab world regarded the EU's refusal to deal with the democratically elected Hamas government as a clear demonstration of political insincerity (Barbé and Johansson-Nogués 2008: 94). The EU's imposition of sanctions on a government which was elected with a fair, free and transparent election was regarded by the Palestinians as its ignorance of the democratic expression of the Palestinian people (although the EU had made democracy one of the conditions for financial aid to the Palestinian Authority): in effect, it was seen as a contradiction – although Hamas had a legal mandate to govern through a fair, free and transparent vote, it was considered a terrorist organization by the EU and the USA (Pace 2009a: 46). Furthermore, the imposition of sanctions interrupted the long process of confidence building between officials of the Palestinian Authority and the EU (Kolarska-Bobinska and Mughrabi 2008: 13). Although the Palestinians took an important step towards a process of democratization, the EU's reaction to the Hamas victory stood in stark contrast to its discursive practices regarding the importance of fair, free and transparent elections as crucial dimensions of a much needed momentum towards democratization on the Palestinian side for a possible resolution to the Israeli-Palestinian conflict (Pace 2008: 214). Moreover, as discussed in detail earlier in this chapter the EU's imposition of sanctions on the Hamas-led government adversely affected the EU's image in Middle Eastern countries.

While imposing sanctions on the Hamas-led Palestinian government, the EU has continued financial aid to unelected Fatah controlling the West Bank. In particular, after the separation of Palestine into Hamas-controlled Gaza and Fatah-controlled West Bank in June 2007, the EU continued to maintain political and economic support to the Fatah administration in the West Bank in order to alienate Hamas from the Palestinians by promoting economic growth and political stability in the West Bank (Möller 2009). As it was confirmed by an EU official, the main objective of the EU's policy of 'West Bank first' was to make the West Bank a success story and a centre of attraction for those Palestinians living in Gaza by promoting economic and social well-being of the Palestinians living in the West Bank.[34] The EU channelled aid specifically to avoid dealing with the democratically elected Hamas administration while bolstering the unelected Fatah administration in the West Bank. This move illustrated that the EU pursued a policy of supporting the Fatah administration which was capable of acting as a viable negotiating partner for Israel, but did not necessarily have to be democratic. Furthermore, this move demonstrated that the EU had not developed an explicit democracy promotion strategy and underlined the apparent double standards that exist when the EU favours stable regimes in the Middle East, even if these are undemocratic, over unstable but potentially more democratic regimes (Celador et al. 2008: 17). Michelle Pace (2009b) identified the EU's policy of isolating elected Hamas while continuing its support to unelected Fatah as clear evidence of a paradox in the EU's discourse on the promotion of democracy in the Middle East.

Moreover, the EU's support to Fatah did not act as an encouraging tool for an internal reconciliation between Fatah and Hamas and the Palestinian democracy (Emerson, Tocci and Youngs 2009). The EU, through its policy of isolating elected Hamas while continuing its support to unelected Fatah, reduced its policy of supporting democracy to 'supporting our kind of democrats' (Youngs 2007: 6). The EU's policy can be identified as 'supporting reform means favouring moderate figures which are seen as the EU's allies' (ibid.: 5).

Muriel Asseburg argued that the EU's policy contributed both to the further devaluation of democratic process in Palestine and to the cementing of the Palestinian internal division. The two illegitimate governments have ruled in the West Bank and the Gaza Strip, both trying to assert and strengthen their hold on power in an authoritarian manner (Asseburg 2009b: 38). She also maintained that this policy made it impossible to realize a sustainable Palestinian institution-building. The presence of a two illegitimate governments, a defunct parliament and the security forces that are perceived to be taking sides in the power struggle made it simply impossible to build a security mechanism that would meet international standards and be under democratic control, nonpartisan, citizen-oriented and unified (Asseburg 2009a: 97).

An EU official made it clear that European politicians 'prefer the devil they know to the devil they do not know', which is why European leaders supported Mahmoud Abbas and Fatah although they had the problem of legitimacy. The EU preferred to support secular Mahmoud Abbas and Fatah rather than radical Islamist Hamas, which is already on the EU's list of terrorist organizations.[35]

After the Hamas victory, the EU also started to pursue a policy of empowering the President of the Palestinian Authority Mahmoud Abbas at the expense of the Hamas-led Palestinian government (Tocci 2006: 9). Through its support to the President Abbas the EU tried to stabilize the Palestinian leadership around him (Möller 2009). With regard to TIM, the EU preferred Abbas as its partner in order to show to the Palestinians that he could promise and deliver on assistance from the international community, whereas Hamas could not (Khaliq 2008: 393). By doing so, the EU tried to alienate Hamas from the

Palestinians. Thus, beside alleviating the Palestinian suffering, one of the aims of TIM was supporting the President Abbas and the institutions under his control while trying to isolate the Hamas-led Palestinian government (ibid.).

This move was contradictory to the EU's previous policy of creating and empowering the post of prime minister and shifting the control of the Palestinian finances and security from the presidency to the Ministry of Finance and the Ministry of Interior respectively (Tocci 2006: 9). This U-turn both undermined the views expressed by the Palestinian electorate and reconstituted a highly centralized system around the presidency, which the EU had criticized and demanded to be changed during the Arafat's presidency (ibid.). With this move, the EU equated its policy of 'supporting democracy' with 'supporting president's office' (Youngs 2007: 5). This move undermined both institutions and offices of which the EU had played a prominent role in creating and strongly financially supported like the Prime Ministerial post, which was now under the control of Hamas (Khaliq 2008: 383), and the EU's credibility as the promoter of democracy in Palestine.

Michelle Pace put forward the idea that the Hamas case clearly demonstrated the key paradox of the EU as the supporter of reform in the Middle East. According to her view, the EU harshly turned against the accomplishments of the Palestinian reform process when it resulted in unanticipated results. As Pace (2009a: 47) quoted from one of its interviewees, 'the EU likes the ideal of democracy but they do not like its results'.

The policy of boycotting the Hamas-led Palestinian government not only discredited democracy in the Middle East, but was also in violation of donor standards for security sector reform assistance and in violation of principles of good governance. With the boycott, the operations of two ESDP operations, EUPOL COPPS and EUBAM Rafah, became inoperable (Celador et al. 2008: 16).

In the Hamas case, the EU faced a difficult political dilemma. On the one hand, there was the democratically elected Hamas government. On the other hand, the democratically elected Hamas was on the EU's list of terrorist organizations[36] and refused to meet and implement the three principles put forward by the Quartet on the Middle East. EU

Member States faced a hard choice between upholding the principle of democracy and safeguarding the EU's credibility and standing as an actor in the MEPP, and maintaining its commitment not to deal with organizations that have been labelled as 'terrorist' by a number of Western countries and other bodies, including the EU itself (Barbé and Johansson-Nogués 2008: 94). The EU preferred to impose sanctions on the Hamas-led Palestinian government in order to force it to meet and implement the three principles. The EU sacrificed upholding the principle of democracy in Palestine for the sake of safeguarding its own credibility and standing as an actor in the MEPP. The EU's decision to impose sanctions on the democratically elected Hamas-led Palestinian government compromised what the EU claimed to stand for, the promotion of democracy in Palestine. This move was inconsistent with the EU's role as a promoter of its values and norms.

In addition to its failure in promoting genuine democracy in Palestine, empirical analysis demonstrated that the EU also failed to promote human rights and international humanitarian law in the case of the Arab-Israeli conflict. Although Israel routinely and systematically violated the human rights of the Palestinian people in the Occupied Territories and international humanitarian law (the Fourth Geneva Convention) through its conduct in the Occupied Territories, the EU refrained from using any kind of sanctions against Israel. Moreover, the Israeli measures in the Occupied Territories, such as the construction of the Israeli 'Security Fence' and restrictions on movement that Israel imposed on the Palestinians through closures, checkpoints and curfews, were also profoundly in contradiction to the EMP principles which aimed to foster political, social, economic and cultural links between the Mediterranean countries. Despite this fact, the EU refrained from using sanctions against Israel and preferred a method of 'discussion not threats' (Khaliq 2008: 342) when engaging with Israel, and thus failed to stand up for the very norms it was seeking to export in the Middle East (Pace 2009a: 47–48). Michelle Pace also identified the Israeli conduct in the Occupied Territories, such as the construction of the 'Security Fence' and restrictions on movement that Israel has imposed on the Palestinians, as a violation of the Palestinians' democratic right to live in an independent country. She criticized the EU's stance of indifference towards the Israeli breach of the Palestinians' democratic right by stating that the Palestinians' democratic right to live in an independent country remained absent from the EU's 'democratization' efforts – apart from some repetitive statements about the EU's aim at a Palestinian State in the context of the MEPP (ibid.: 47). Despite these facts on the ground, the EU limited itself to rhetorical condemnation of the Israeli acts and calls on Israel to stop its acts in the Occupied Territories, while refraining from directly sanctioning the Israeli violations of the Palestinians' democratic and human rights, international humanitarian law and the EMP principles in the Occupied Territories.

One of the reasons behind the EU's refraining from using sanctions against Israel was its material interests. Israel had been one of the largest EU trading partners in the Euromed area, ranking as the EU's 25th major trade partner (http://ec.europa.eu/trade/issues/bilateral/countries/israel/index_en.htm). Thus, any trade and economic sanctions against Israel would be detrimental for both sides. It would mean some kind of self-imposed punishment for the EU (Dieckhoff 2005: 60). Moreover, the EU's use of economic and trade sanctions would undermine the EU's political credibility in Israel and would result in the loss of its status as legitimate interlocutor (ibid.: 61). The EU's imposition of sanctions against Israel would result in raising the Israeli perception that the European states were biased against Israel. As a result, Israel would refuse the EU's further participation in any negotiations concerning the MEPP or at least try and relegate the EU to a secondary role (Khaliq 2008: 340). In order not to be sidelined, even as a member of the Quartet, in the peace process, the EU refrained from using sanctions against Israel, which would have detrimental effects on its status as legitimate interlocutor in the peace process. For the EU, the peace process and its role in it took priority and the possibility of maintaining some influence over Israel came first (ibid.: 341). Therefore, EU Member States, aware of the detrimental effects of sanctions on their material interests, refrained from using any sanctions or legal mechanisms of passive enforcement against Israel even when Israel routinely and systematically violated human rights and international humanitarian law. In this case, it can be argued that the EU's policy was based on the lowest common denominator which indicated that Member States could not agree to impose far-reaching sanctions that might damage their own material interests, commercial or political.

Another reason behind the EU's refraining from using sanctions against Israel was that the use of sanctions would be inconsistent with the EU's role as a force for good. The EU's role as a force for good and role as promoter of its values and norms hold incompatible role expectations. This effectively means that on the one hand, the EU's role as a force for good urged it to refrain from using sanctions against Israel; but on the other hand, the EU's role as promoter of its values and norms simultaneously urged it to promote human rights and international humanitarian law even with the use of sanctions against the violators. Faced with this kind of inter-role conflict, the EU preferred to meet the expectations of its role as a force for good, which was also beneficial for its material interests, but inconsistent with the EU's role as promoter of its values and norms. The EU's decision to refrain from using any sanctions or legal mechanisms of passive enforcement against Israel, even when it violated human rights and international humanitarian law, compromised what the EU claimed to stand for, the promotion of human rights and international humanitarian law. This undermined the EU's effectiveness and credibility as promoter of its values and norms. It also undermined the EU's credibility as an effective international actor and put it in a position of an ineffective international actor who failed to impose some sanctions in order to uphold human rights and international humanitarian law.

Another reason, put forward by one of the Ex-Commissioners of the European Commission Manuel Marin-Gonzales, is that pursuing a method of 'discussion not threats' when engaging with Israel put the EU in a better position to exercise a positive influence regarding all human rights related issues in the framework of the political dialogue (ibid.: 342). As can be clearly seen, this strategy has not worked so far.

Another reason, put forward by an EU official, is that Israel is a friend of the EU and the EU cannot take a drastic action against its friends. Therefore, it is difficult for the EU to impose sanctions on Israel.[37]

Moreover, the EU's imposition of sanctions on the democratically elected Hamas-led Palestinian government while not using any sanctions against Israel despite its violation of human rights of the Palestinian people in the Occupied Territories undermined the EU's credibility as promoter of its values and norms in the eyes of the Palestinian people. This action was interpreted by most Palestinians as the EU not being prepared to put equal pressure on Israel to recognize UN resolutions and the Palestinian rights (as well as pressure on Hamas to renounce violence, recognize Israel, and accept all previous agreements between Israel and the Palestinian Authority) (Pace 2009a: 47).

In summary, the EU played a limited role as the promoter of its values and norms in the case of the MEPP. The Israeli and the Palestinian cases clearly demonstrated the limits of EU's role as the promoter of its values and norms. In the Palestinian case, although the EU supported the reform process towards the creation of a well-governed and democratic Palestinian State through its financial and technical aid to the Palestinian Authority, there was much emphasis on the promotion of good governance, leaving aside genuine democratization. The EU's highly tolerant position towards the persistent exclusion of Islamic factions from both the PLO and the Palestinian Authority, its reluctance to engage and support Islamic civil society and non-violent groups, and its policy of isolating democratically elected Hamas while continuing its economic and political support to unelected Fatah undermined the EU's effectiveness and credibility as the promoter of democracy in Palestine. These policy moves constrained the performance of the EU's role as promoter of its values and norms.

In the Israeli case, the EU prioritized the promotion of its material interests over the promotion of humanitarian values and principles. The EU failed to act consistently with its role conception as promoter of its values and norms. Despite the Israeli violation of human rights of the Palestinian people in the Occupied Territories, the EU did not use sanctions against Israel. The EU seemed to limit itself to a certain rhetoric in favour of respect for human rights and international humanitarian law rather than directly sanctioning violations. The Israeli case demonstrated that the political and commercial interests of the EU rather than values and norms were crucial in shaping its policy towards Israel. The Israeli case also revealed that the promotion of values and norms is not always the basic principle of the EU's foreign policy, as for the sake of the promotion of the EU's material interests, it can be sacrificed.

The Israeli and the Palestinian cases clearly demonstrated that although the EU tended to consider values and norms such as respect for democracy and human rights to be at the core of its relations with the rest of the world and the universal promotion of these values and norms through the world to be one of the main objectives and priorities of its foreign policy, its promotion of these values and norms seemed more part of a political discourse than a priority of the EU's foreign policy actions. In conclusion, the Israeli and the Palestinian cases demonstrated that there existed an inconsistency between the EU's role conception as promoter of its values and norms and its actual role performance, which undermined its effectiveness and international credibility as promoter of its values and norms. It can be concluded that the EU's record in practice in the case of the MEPP demonstrated that the EU did not act as a credible sponsor of values and norms of respect for democracy and human rights.

The EU's Role Performances as Promoter of Effective Multilateralism, Partner for the UN and Builder of Effective Partnership with Key Actors

Given that the EU's role performances as promoter of effective multilateralism, partner for the UN and builder of effective partnership with key actors are closely interlinked with and overlapped each other in the MEPP, I prefer to evaluate them under the same title. In the case of the MEPP, the EU's role performances as promoter of effective multilateralism, partner for the UN and builder of effective partnership with key actors can be evaluated through assessing to what extent the EU has managed to live up to its self-proclaimed commitments and responsibilities.

In the case of the MEPP, the EU has a long established and enduring commitment to multilateralism. The EU always advocated that the Arab-Israeli Conflict should be solved within a multilateral framework. Since the 1970s the EU advocated that just and lasting settlement of the Arab-Israeli conflict could be achieved through a multilateral and comprehensive approach, such as the multilateral framework of an international peace conference with the participation of the all parties to the conflict. The EU has always emphasized that the Arab-Israeli Conflict should be solved within the multilateral framework of the UN and on the basis of UN Security Council Resolutions 242, 338, 1397 and 1515. Costanza Musu (2006: 6) argued that the reason why the EU favoured a multilateral approach to the peace process and emphasized the need for a greater role of the international community in the negotiations between the parties was possibly due to its own nature of multilateral framework and to member states' habit of negotiating over every important issue. A similar evaluation is made by Roberto Menotti and Maria Francesca Vencato (2008: 105), who argued that the EU favoured multilateralism, because the latter is naturally matched with the EU's own founding principle of multilateral cooperation and this assumption was reinforced by the explicit adoption of effective multilateralism as the hallmark of the EU's external action.

In the early 1990s, the Madrid peace process was launched and the EU had played a significant and active role in the multilateral track of the peace process. The EU acted as the chair or gavel-holder of the Regional Economic Development Working Group, one of the working groups of multilateral track of the Madrid Peace Process. In addition, the EU also launched the EMP in 1995, which was a complementary initiative to the MEPP and provided a multilateral forum for the conflicting parties, the Arabs and the Israelis to sit at the same table and discuss. In the post-9/11 era, with the creation of the Quartet on the Middle East, the MEPP was officially multilateralized. The EU, as a member of the Quartet on the Middle East, started to gain a more effective presence in the political and diplomatic dimension of the peace process.

The creation of the Quartet in April 2002 symbolized the official multilateralization and internationalization of the MEPP (Musu 2006). The Quartet provided a multilateral framework for the peace process by officially bringing other major global actors – the UN,

Russia and the EU – into the peace process in addition to the old ones – Israel, the Palestinian Authority and the USA (ibid.). Through its membership in the Quartet, the EU gained visibility and influence in the MEPP, and acquired a tool for influencing the US policies (Musu 2007a: 23). Indisputably, the EU played an increasingly important role in the peace process after the Madrid Conference of 1991, especially in the economic dimension, but participation in the Quartet arguably gave the EU's role a higher political relevance and resonance (ibid.). With its membership in the Quartet, the EU achieved its long-struggled-for aim to participate in the political and diplomatic dimension of the peace process as an equal partner alongside the USA, the UN and Russia. A Palestinian diplomat maintained that with the establishment of the Quartet, the EU became a major political actor on a par with the USA.[38] As Ben Soetendorp (2002: 293) argued, 'more than twenty years after the Venice declaration and ten years after the Madrid conference, the EU is at last fully involved in Middle East peacemaking'. EU's membership in the Quartet was an acknowledgement of the growing political role of the EU in the peace process and the legitimacy of the EU's involvement as a major contributor to funding and institution building. Moreover, the EU increased its involvement with Israel as a trusted interlocutor, not only in trade terms but also as a partner for political dialogue. Israel began to accept the EU as an active mediator in the peace process, although not on a par with the USA (House of Lords European Union Committee 2007: 32). The Quartet provided a formal framework for the EU's role in the peace process and tied it to that of the US, thus easing Israel's deep-seated reservations towards the EU's involvement in the peace process (Musu 2010b).

There are some criticisms concerning the Quartet's effectiveness as an instrument of multilateralism. According to Costanza Musu, the Quartet was a 'multilateral control framework' for bilateral negotiations, which are supposed to aim at implementing pre-established steps agreed upon by the Quartet, rather than a real multilateral framework for negotiations. She argued that although in appearance the Quartet opened the peace process to multilateralism and created a multilateral framework for the negotiations; in substance, it created a contradictory multilateral control framework for bilateral negotiations (ibid.). She argued that final goals and intermediate steps had been endorsed by the Quartet and then presented to the parties who were supposed to implement them, but the role of direct negotiations and the importance of achieving a negotiated settlement between the parties were clearly acknowledged (ibid.). As can be seen in the Roadmap, it called for bilateral negotiations aiming at implementing pre-established phases, timelines, target dates and benchmarks, aiming at progress through mutual steps by the two parties in the political, security, economic, humanitarian and institution-building fields which were agreed on by the Quartet rather than by the Israelis and the Palestinians. The two main parties to the conflict, Israel and Palestine, in fact were not involved in developing the Roadmap; rather, the Plan was published and presented to them for their approval. While looking at Musu's identification of the Quartet, it can be concluded that the Middle East Quartet can be identified as minilateral[39] cooperation among four major global actors, the USA, the EU, the UN and Russia, rather than a multilateral framework for negotiations. As can be seen in the Roadmap, the members of the Quartet agreed on the Roadmap and multilateralized their agreed plan by presenting it for the approval of the Israelis and the Palestinians.

Another criticism concerning the Quartet's effectiveness as an instrument of multilateralism came from Nathalie Tocci. She argued that the Quartet has predominantly provided a 'multilateral cover' for continuing unilateral US action in peace process (Tocci 2005a: 13). Although the USA accepted official multilateralization of the MEPP through the creation of the Quartet by officially bringing other major global actors into the peace process in addition to the existing ones, the USA continued to act unilaterally as the main mediator in the bilateral political talks between the Palestinians and the Israelis. As seen earlier in this chapter, in June 2003, the US President George Bush unilaterally took the lead in launching the Roadmap. In order to persuade the Israeli Prime Minister Ariel Sharon and the Palestinian Authority Prime Minister Mahmoud Abbas to commit to the Roadmap, Bush held a meeting with them at Aqaba in which the other members of the Quartet did not participate. Moreover, three members of the

Quartet including the EU, the UN and Russia were excluded from the Annapolis process in November 2007. The USA played a primary role in the Annapolis Conference and the conference was primarily an American initiative (Musu 2010c: 78). The other three members of the Quartet were sidelined and excluded from bilateral political talks by the USA.

In the post-9/11 era, despite the creation of the Quartet and official multilateralization of the MEPP, the USA sought to reserve primary role for itself in the bilateral talks while granting a secondary role to the other members of the Quartet. In addition to Nathalie Tocci, Costanza Musu also expressed her doubts about whether the US administration is seriously committed to the Quartet as a form of multilateral exercise or the Quartet is supposed to give an illusion of international involvement in the peace process while the USA maintains its primary role in the negotiations (Musu 2007b: 116). Moreover, Alvare De Soto, the former UN Secretary General's Envoy to the Quartet identified the Quartet as 'a group of friends of the USA – and the USA does not feel the need to consult closely with the Quartet except when it suits' (Khaliq 2008: 282). Christopher Hill also adopted a cynical perspective on the Quartet's effectiveness as an instrument of multilateralism and put forward that it was a way of keeping the EU and Russia compromised – and therefore quiet – through giving them a superficial share in US-sponsored mediation (Piana 2004: 162). Thus, American persistent unilateral actions brought the effectiveness of the Quartet as an instrument of multilateralism into question. Although the Quartet has not been an effective instrument of multilateralism, it constituted a consistency in the EU's multilateral approach to the peace process and its active participation in any kind of multilateral initiative for the peaceful settlement of the conflict.

In accordance with its commitment as the promoter of effective multilateralism, the EU strove to make international organizations and agreements more effective in the case of the MEPP. In the post-9/11 era, the EU played a prominent and active role in the preparation and the implementation of the Roadmap, which was the main plan for the peaceful settlement of the conflict. German and Danish proposals formed the basis of the Roadmap agreed by the Quartet on the Middle East in September 2002. The EU played the role of the facilitator for the Palestinian Authority to fulfil its obligations under the Roadmap. The EU contributed to the normalization of Palestinian life and Palestinian institution building. It supported the reform process of the Palestinian Authority towards the creation of an independent, economically and politically viable, sovereign and democratic Palestinian State which was identified by the Quartet members as a precondition for the start of the negotiations for the final settlement of the conflict. The EU supported the Palestinian reform process in the areas of drafting a new constitution, the promotion of judicial independence, promotion of accountability and transparency in the fiscal system, the security sector reform, reform of administration and the executive, holding of free, fair and open elections, developing a modern education system and media based on peace, tolerance and mutual understanding and the promotion of pro-peace civil society. The EU facilitated the Palestinian Authority's preparations for permanent status negotiations with Israel.

In accordance with its commitment to making international agreements more effective, the EU launched a civilian crisis management mission within the framework of the ESDP (EUBAM Rafah) in order to facilitate effective implementation of the 'Agreement on Movement and Access from and to Gaza' between the Israelis and the Palestinians. The Agreement envisaged the presence of a third party on the ground which would have the authority to ensure the compliance of the Palestinian Authority with all applicable rules and regulations concerning the Rafah crossing point and the terms of this agreement. With the consent of the two parties, the EU was assigned to the task of the 'third party monitoring role' at the Rafah Crossing Point on the Gaza-Egypt border. According to the agreement, the third party on the ground has the responsibility to ensure the compliance of the Palestinian Authority with all applicable rules and regulations concerning the Rafah crossing point and the terms of this agreement and assist the Palestinian Authority to build capacity, including training, equipment and technical assistance, on border management and customs. In order to carry out the task of the third party monitoring role, the EU launched EUBAM Rafah.

In addition to its membership in the Quartet and the decisive role played in the preparation and implementation of the Roadmap, since 2002 the EU has also been one of the members of another multilateral initiative concerning the MEPP, the International Task Force on Palestinian Reform. The Task Force has the task of monitoring and supporting the implementation of the Palestinian civil reforms, and guiding the international donor community in its support for the Palestinians' reform agenda, was composed of representatives of the Quartet (the USA, the EU, Russia and the UN Secretary General), Norway, Japan, the World Bank, and the IMF. The EU continued its support to the Palestinian reform process towards the establishment of a well-governed and democratic Palestinian State within the multilateral framework of the International Task Force on Palestinian Reform. The EU's membership of the International Task Force on Palestinian Reform constituted another example for the EU's active participation in any kind of multilateral initiative for the peaceful settlement of the conflict.

Another indicator of the EU's multilateral approach to the MEPP is the EU's insistence on the peaceful settlement of the conflict within the multilateral framework of the UN and on the basis of UN Security Council Resolutions 242, 338, 1397 and 1515 and the EU's continual support to the UN efforts towards the peaceful settlement of the conflict. This is consistent with the EU's role conceptions as a promoter of effective multilateralism and a partner for the UN. Firstly, this is consistent with the EU's commitment to making international organizations (in this case the UN) more effective as promoter of effective multilateralism. Secondly, it is consistent with the EU's commitment to upholding the universal values, norms, goals and principles enshrined in the UN Charter and supporting and strengthening the UN's efforts for the protection and promotion of regional and global peace, security, stability and prosperity. It is also congruent with the EU's self-proclaimed responsibility to support and strengthen the UN in order to fully enable the UN to fulfil its role effectively in seeking multilateral solutions to global problems on the basis of its Charter.

Since the early 1970s, the EU has strengthened and deepened its partnership with the UN in the case of the Arab-Israeli Conflict. The

EU supported and contributed to UN activities mainly in the fields of development and humanitarian assistance and peace-keeping in the case of the MEPP. In the post-9/11 era, the EU has acted as one of the most significant partners of the UN in the case of the MEPP, both within the multilateral framework of the Quartet and on a bilateral basis through its support of the UN activities.

As discussed in detail earlier, the EU – the European Commission and EU Member States – was the largest donor to the UNRWA. The EU, through its financial contribution to the UNRWA, contributed to the improvement of economic and social conditions of the Palestinian refugees living in the West Bank and Gaza Strip, Jordan, Lebanon and Syria since 1971. The European Commission's Humanitarian Aid Directorate General (DG ECHO) was one of the main financial supporters of the UNRWA's emergency aid for the poorest Palestinian refugees, during crises such as the Al-Aqsa Intifada and Israel-Lebanon War of 2006, which consisted mainly of the provision of food aid and temporary job creation. The EU's support to the UNRWA is defined as an essential component of its strategy for the MEPP. The European Commission was identified by the UNRWA's Commissioner-General, Karen Abu Zayd as a reliable partner (Newsletter of the ECTAO 2007). Through its financial support to the UNRWA the EU acted as a prominent partner for the UN in alleviating the economic and social conditions of the Palestinian refugees living in the West Bank and Gaza Strip, Jordan, Lebanon and Syria. The EU has acted as a real partner for the UN rather than only a donor to the UNRWA.

As discussed in detail earlier, EU Member States were major military contributors to the expanded UNIFIL, which was established following the Israel-Lebanon War of 2006. EU Member States made up the backbone of the force by providing 7,000 troops, crucial military components and the operational command for UNIFIL. France, Italy and Spain took the lead in taking the responsibility of the operational command of the force. Through their significant military contribution to the expanded UNIFIL and their leading role in the UN force EU Member States acted as prominent partners of the UN in the protection and promotion of regional peace, security, stability and prosperity in the Middle East. Concerning UNIFIL, the former UN Secretary General Kofi Annan declared that 'Europe (the EU and its Member States) had lived up to its responsibility and provided the backbone of the force' (Gowan 2008: 54). The EU and its Member States' support to the UNRWA and UNIFIL showed that they were strong supporters of the UN in the case of the MEPP. Their support to the UNRWA and UNIFIL demonstrated the considerable amount of inter-institutional cooperation and partnership between the EU and the UN.

The EU's membership of the Quartet and the International Task Force on Palestinian Reform, and its bilateral partnership with the UN are also consistent with its role conception as the builder of effective partnerships with key actors. The EU's search for a solution to the Arab-Israeli conflict within the framework of the Quartet and with the UN are consistent practices with the EU's belief that contemporary global and regional problems and threats are common problems shared by the entire world thus requiring multilateral initiatives. In the case of the Arab-Israeli Conflict, the EU, through its membership of the Quartet and the International Task Force on Palestinian Reform and its strong bilateral partnership with the UN, preferred to deal with a regional problem which has global repercussions through building partnerships with key global actors, including the USA, the UN and Russia. It can be said, in the post-9/11 era, that the EU has been one of the partners of a global alliance comprising the UN, the EU, Russia, and the USA, which was formed for the peaceful settlement of the Arab-Israeli conflict. In this sense, the Quartet can be called a Quartet of global partners for the peaceful settlement of the Arab-Israeli conflict.

To sum up, the empirical study of the EU's role performances as promoter of effective multilateralism, partner for the UN and builder of effective partnerships with key actors showed that it has managed to live up to its self-proclaimed commitments and responsibilities in its actual practice. Concerning the EU's role performance as promoter of effective multilateralism:

- the EU's active participation in multilateral initiatives for the peaceful settlement of the conflict;
- the prominent and active role played by the EU in the preparation and the implementation of the Roadmap;

- the EU's active participation in the implementation of 'Agreement on Movement and Access from and to Gaza' by carrying out the task of the third party monitoring role at the Rafah Crossing Point on the Gaza-Egypt border;
- the EU's insistence on the peaceful settlement of the conflict within the multilateral framework of the UN and through adherence to the relevant UN Security Council Resolutions;
- the EU's persistent support to the UN efforts towards the peaceful settlement of the conflict;

are consistent with the EU's commitment to making international organizations and agreements more effective. It is safe to assert that the EU can sustain its commitment to effective multilateralism in the case of the MEPP.

Concerning the EU's role performance as a partner for the UN, the EU's insistence on the peaceful settlement of the conflict within the multilateral framework of the organization and through adherence to the relevant UN Security Council Resolutions, and its active support for and contribution to the UNRWA and to the expanded UNIFIL are consistent with the EU's self-proclaimed responsibility to support and to strengthen the UN in order to fully enable it to fulfil its role effectively in seeking multilateral solutions to global problems on the basis of its Charter. It is safe to assert that the EU and the UN are real partners in the case of the MEPP.

Concerning the EU's role performance as builder of effective partnership with key actors, the EU's building of effective partnerships with the UN, the USA and Russia within the framework of the Quartet and its strong bilateral partnership with the UN are consistent with the EU's commitment to dealing with contemporary global and regional problems through building partnerships with key global and regional actors.

Conclusion

As can clearly be seen from the first part of the chapter, the EU's political role increased and its presence was increasingly felt in the MEPP in the post-9/11 era especially with its membership of the Quartet. As a member of the Quartet, the EU played an active role in the political and diplomatic dimension of the peace process. During this period, we observed an increase in international recognition of the EU as a significant player in the political, diplomatic, security dimensions of the Middle East conflict. The EU started to play a significant role in the realms of conflict management, crisis mediation and conflict resolution. Through its prominent and active role in the preparation and the implementation of the Roadmap the EU played an important and active role in the realm conflict resolution (Asseburg 2009b: 45). Through its representatives the EU played a crucial role in the settlement of micro-security crises, such as the issue of the Siege of the Church of the Nativity in Bethlehem. Through such successful mediation efforts and diplomatic missions of its representatives the EU played an important and active role in the realm of crisis mediation (ibid.). Furthermore, the EU started to play a prominent role in the security dimension of the peace process through its ESDP operations. Through these operations and its active support and contribution to the expanded UNIFIL it played an active role in the realm of conflict management (ibid.).

The EU's status of being the largest external donor of financial and technical aid and the prominent supporter of the reform process of the Palestinian Authority enhanced its profile and presence in the MEPP. Although the EU still played a politically and diplomatically supplementary and subordinate role to the USA, it has been more and more internationally recognized as a prominent player in the post-9/11 era. As was correctly put forward by an EU official, the EU's status of 'payer' started to change with its more involvement in political and security aspects of the peace process.[40]

On the whole, the EU's role as a foreign and security policy actor in the MEPP in the post-9/11 era can be identified as more than a modest presence, but less than a robust actor. Although the EU has moved beyond just a modest presence in the MEPP with an increase in its role, visibility, assertiveness and presence in nearly every dimensions of the MEPP, it still is not able to develop as a robust actorness in the MEPP. Despite its actions, which enhanced its role and visibility on the ground, and its presence in the political, diplomatic, economic, security dimensions of the peace process, the EU still does not have enough influence to have a robust political role in the MEPP. It has continued to play a politically and diplomatically supplementary and subordinate role to the USA, while the USA has continued to play the role of primary mediator in bilateral peace negotiations.

In the second part of the chapter, the extent to which the EU managed to measure up to its self-images as a 'force for good', a 'force for international peace, security and stability', a 'promoter of its values and norms', 'the provider of development aid', a 'promoter of effective multilateralism', a 'partner for the UN' and a 'builder of effective partnership with key actors' in its actual practice in the MEPP in the post-9/11 era was examined in order to test the congruity between EU's role conceptions and role performance. As a result of the analysis, two major conclusions emerge. First, concerning the EU's roles as a 'force for good', a 'force for international peace, security and stability' and a 'promoter of its values and norms', the EU has, to a limited extent, managed to measure up to its self-images in its actual practice. As will be discussed below, some constraints put limits on the EU's ability to live up to its self-proclaimed commitments and responsibilities. This weakened the EU's effectiveness and international credibility as a foreign and security policy actor in the case of the MEPP. Second, concerning the EU's roles as 'the provider of development aid', a 'promoter of effective multilateralism', a 'partner for the UN' and a 'builder of effective partnership with key actors', the EU has more successfully performed these roles, which has strengthened the EU's profile, effectiveness and international credibility as a foreign and security policy actor in the case of the MEPP.

In the post-9/11 era, the EU's financial and technical aid to the Palestinians, which aimed at alleviating the humanitarian situation and helping the Palestinian Authority in its institutional reform enhanced its profile as a 'force for good', 'the provider of development aid' and a 'force for international peace, security and stability'. This aid prevented the Palestinian economy from collapse; without it the Palestinian Authority would not have been able to finance even the basic functions of governance. The collapse of the Palestinian Authority might have resulted in the escalation of conflict.

Moreover, the EU's support for the reform process of the Palestinian Authority enhanced its profile as a 'force for good', a 'force for international peace, security and stability' and a 'promoter of its values and norms'. The EU identified the creation of an independent, economically and politically viable, sovereign and democratic Palestinian State as the best guarantee for the Israeli and regional security and a precondition for the peaceful settlement of the dispute. What this means in effect is that the creation of a well-governed democratic Palestinian State would ensure the continuing existence of a viable negotiating partner for Israel in the peace negotiations. It would also be the best guarantee for the viable peace process. This was later adopted by the international community and the creation of a well-governed and democratic Palestinian State was identified by the Roadmap as a precondition for the start of the negotiations for the final settlement of the conflict. The EU supported the reform process of the Palestinian Authority with the aim of paving the way for the peaceful settlement of the conflict by facilitating the creation of a well-governed and democratic Palestinian State. Through its support to the Palestinian reform process the EU strove to facilitate the Palestinian Authority's preparations for permanent status negotiations with Israel.

The EU's crisis management operations within the framework of the ESDP (EUBAM Rafah) enhanced the Union's profile as a 'force for good', a 'force for international peace, security and stability' and a 'promoter of effective multilateralism'. Through its third party presence at the Rafah Crossing Point through EUBAM Rafah the EU provided benefits for both parties and served the achievement of the objectives of the Roadmap. First of all, it provided the Palestinians with freedom of movement of people and goods in and out of Gaza Strip which would improve their living conditions and pave the way for the creation of an economically viable Palestinian State. Secondly, it provided the Israelis with a sense of security against threats which would come through the Rafah Crossing Point including possible weapons transfers and the uninhibited return of exiled extremist leaders and terrorists. As the Israelis perceived Rafah as a door to danger, EUBAM Rafah provided them some kind of border security. Moreover, EUBAM Rafah's contribution to the creation of an economically viable Palestinian State would indirectly contribute to the security of Israel. Thirdly, it contributed to the confidence-building between the Israeli government and the Palestinian Authority. Moreover, the EU, through EUBAM Rafah, facilitated effective implementation of the 'Agreement on Movement and Access from and to Gaza' between the Israelis and the Palestinians, which was one of the commitments of the EU as a 'promoter of effective multilateralism', to make international agreements more effective.

EU Member States' major military contributions to the expanded UNIFIL and their leading role in the UN force enhanced the EU's profile as a 'force for good', a 'force for international peace, security and stability' and a 'partner for the UN'. EU Member States – through their provision of the backbone of the force by providing 7,000 troops, crucial military components and the operational command for UNIFIL – significantly contributed to the promotion of peace, security and stability in the region. Through its efforts the EU acted for the benefit of the peoples in the region and international peace and stability. Their support to the expanded UNIFIL demonstrated the considerable amount of inter-institutional cooperation and partnership between the EU and the UN.

As discussed in detail previously, the EU's active participation in multilateral initiatives for the peaceful settlement of the conflict such as the Quartet and the International Task Force on Palestinian Reform, the prominent and active role played by the EU in the preparation and the implementation of the Roadmap and its active participation in the implementation of 'Agreement on Movement and Access from and to Gaza' through carrying out the task of the third party monitoring role at the Rafah Crossing Point on the Gaza-Egypt border, the EU's insistence on the peaceful settlement of the conflict within the multilateral framework of the UN and through adherence to the relevant UN Security Council Resolutions and the EU's persistent support to the UN efforts towards the peaceful settlement of the conflict, the EU's active support and contribution to the UN activities mainly in the fields of development and humanitarian assistance in the form of its significant financial contribution to the UNRWA and peace-keeping in the form of its major military contribution to the expanded UNIFIL and the EU's building of effective partnership with the UN, the USA and Russia within the framework of the Quartet enhanced the EU's profile as a 'promoter of effective multilateralism', a 'partner for the UN' and a 'builder of effective partnership with key actors'.

Although its actions and decisions enhanced the EU's profile as a 'force for good', a 'force for international peace, security and stability' and a 'promoter of its values and norms', some constraints put limits on the EU's ability to live up to its self-proclaimed commitments and responsibilities in its actual practice. Concerning the EU's roles as a 'force for good' and a 'promoter of its values and norms', the EU's imposition of sanctions on a democratically elected Hamas with fair, free and open elections while continuing its economic and political support to unelected Fatah and its refraining from using any kind of sanctions against Israel despite the Israeli violation of human rights of the Palestinian people in the Occupied Territories put limits on the EU's ability to live up to its self-proclaimed commitments and responsibilities and thus weakened its profile as a 'force for good' and a 'promoter of its values and norms'. In the Hamas case, the EU faced a political dilemma. On the one hand, there was the democratically elected Hamas government with a fair, free and open election. On the other hand, democratically elected Hamas was on the EU's list of terrorist organizations and refused to meet and implement the three principles put forward by the Quartet on the Middle East. EU Member States faced a hard choice between upholding the principle of democracy and safeguarding the EU's credibility and standing as an actor in the MEPP by maintaining their commitment not to deal with organizations that had been labelled 'terrorist' by the international community. Faced with a hard choice, the EU preferred to impose sanctions on the Hamas-led Palestinian government in order to force it to meet and implement the three principles. The EU sacrificed upholding the principle of democracy in Palestine for the sake of safeguarding its credibility and standing as an actor in the MEPP.

In the Israeli case, two main reasons prevented the EU from using any kind of sanctions or legal mechanisms of passive enforcement against it even when Israel violated human rights and international humanitarian law. The first one was the political and commercial interests of the EU. The EU refrained from using sanctions against Israel, which would have detrimental effects on its political and commercial interests. The second one was the inter-role conflict between the EU's role as a 'force for good' and role as a 'promoter of its values and norms'. On the one hand, the EU's role as a 'force for good' urged it to refrain from using sanctions against Israel; but on the other hand, the EU's role as a 'promoter of its values and norms' simultaneously urged it to promote human rights and international humanitarian law even with the use of sanctions against the violators. Faced with this kind of inter-role conflict, the EU preferred to meet the expectations of role of a 'force for good', which was also beneficial for its material interests.

Concerning the EU's role as a 'force for international peace, security and stability', two kinds of constraints put limits on the EU's ability to live up to its self-proclaimed commitments and responsibilities and prevented it from acting as an effective mediator for the peaceful settlement of the conflict: internal and external. The internal constraint was the EU's lack of both vertical and horizontal coherence – its inability always to act as a coherent actor and speak with one voice. External constraints are the Israeli and the American reluctance regarding the EU's participation in the bilateral peace negotiations as an active mediator and their insistence on limiting the EU's role merely to facilitating the implementation of the Roadmap, supporting the Palestinian State-building and economic reconstruction.

Urfan Khaliq, in his book *Ethical Dimension of the Foreign Policy of the European Union: A Legal Appraisal*, has argued that in order to understand the value of the EU's role in the MEPP better, it is better to try to envisage the situation if the EU played no role in the MEPP at all than to consider its weaknesses and shortcomings (Khaliq 2008: 403). On this basis, although due to limitations and inconsistencies outlined above the EU's effectiveness, efficiency and international credibility as a foreign and security policy actor in the case of the MEPP in the post-9/11 was weakened moderately, on the whole it can be maintained that the EU, through its decisions and actions, has enhanced its role and visibility on the ground, and its presence in the political, diplomatic, economic and security dimensions of the peace process has been increasingly felt in the post-9/11 era.

CHAPTER 6

CONCLUSION

The main purpose of this book was to explain, analyze and understand the role of the EU as a foreign and security policy actor in the post-9/11 international security environment (particularly during the period extending from 11 September 2001 to 31 December 2006). By relying on the belief that in order to explain, analyze and understand the role of the EU as a foreign and security policy actor in the post-9/11 era in a profound and critical manner, it is necessary to investigate the level of congruity between its role conceptions and role performance as a foreign and security policy actor and outcomes/consequences of (in)congruity between the EU's role conceptions and role performance on both the EU's profile as a foreign and security policy actor and the MEPP. Accordingly, this book endeavoured to discover the EU's role conceptions during the period extending from 11 September 2001 to 31 December 2006; whether there is a congruity or incongruity between the EU's self-defined role conceptions and its actual role performance during the same period; and consequences of (in)congruity between the EU's role conceptions and role performance on both the EU's profile as a foreign and security policy actor and the MEPP. In order to carry out the congruity test, this book focused on the EU's role performance in the MEPP during the same period.

Firstly, in order to find out the role conceptions of the EU, contents of the general foreign policy speeches delivered by the principal EU foreign policy officials and the EU official documents concerning foreign and security policy of the EU have been analyzed. As a result of the content analysis, seven role conceptions referring to the EU's general roles as a foreign and security actor in international context have been identified: 'force for good', 'force for international peace, security and stability', 'promoter of its values and norms', 'the provider of development aid', 'promoter of effective multilateralism', 'partner for the UN' and 'builder of effective partnership with key actors'.

Secondly, in order to uncover to what extent the EU has managed to measure up to its above-mentioned self-images in its actual practice in the MEPP in the post-9/11 era, the level of congruity between EU's role conceptions and role performance for each self-identified role in the MEPP during the period extending from 11 September 2001 to 31 December 2006 has been examined.

The EU's self-identification as a 'force for good' implies the EU's responsibility and duty to make the world a better place for everybody by making the world freer, more peaceful, fairer, more prosperous, more secure and more stable. This role conception puts emphasis on duties and responsibilities to work for the 'global common good', which implies working on the basis of the interests of the community of peoples as a whole rather than solely those of its own interests. This role conception implies that the EU as a force for good needs to pursue an ethically balanced policy, in which an equilibrium exists between its material interests and ethical considerations. The EU needs to balance both member and non-member concerns and satisfy the preferences of all actors involved.

Concerning the issue of to what extent the EU has acted congruently with its self-image as a 'force for good' in its actual practice in the MEPP, it can be concluded that to a limited extent the EU has managed to measure up to its self-image in its actual practice. On the one hand, its balanced and comprehensive approach to the conflict, its contribution to the creation of an independent, economically and politically viable, sovereign and democratic Palestinian state, its provision of financial and technical aid to the Palestinian Authority and support for the Palestinian reform process and its contribution to the mediation efforts demonstrated that the EU to some extent struck a balance between its own concerns and those of the conflicting parties.

The EU's actions and decisions in some measure can be said to be satisfactory for the preferences of all actors involved in the conflict. The EU's actions served the benefit of the peoples in the region and international peace, security and stability.

However, the EU's decision to impose sanctions on the democratically elected Hamas-led Palestinian government was incongruent with the EU's self-image as force for good. This decision acted both to the detriment of all actors involved in the conflict and did not serve the 'global common good'. The paradox that the EU faced between its policy of promotion of democracy and its refraining from using coercion against parties to the conflict and its security considerations in terms of refraining from dealing with a terrorist organization, which refused to renounce violence, prevented the EU from acting in a satisfactory manner for both the Palestinians and itself. Moreover, on the issue of using sanctions against Israel, the EU's refraining from using any kind of sanctions or legal mechanisms of passive enforcement against it even when Israel violated human rights and international humanitarian law demonstrated that the EU failed to pursue an ethically balanced policy; it was not able to find a balance between its material interests and ethical considerations. The promotion of its material interests outweighed the promotion of humanitarian values and principles. The EU refrained from imposing sanctions which would have had a detrimental effect on its commercial and political interests even when Israel violated human rights and international humanitarian law. In the Israeli case, the intra-role conflict which the EU faced on the issue of employing sanctions against Israel and its failure to pursue an ethically balanced policy on the issue of employing sanctions against Israel put limits on the EU's ability to live up to its self-proclaimed commitments and responsibilities as a force for good.

The EU's role conception of a 'force for international peace, security and stability' emphasizes the necessity of exporting the EU's stability, security and peace to both the EU's neighbourhood and the wider world in order to prevent the importing of instability from its neighbourhood. The EU identified exporting its stability, security and peace to its neighbours as its enlightened self-interest. This means that while the EU is acting to further the interests of others, ultimately it serves its own self-interest. The EU's promotion of security, stability and peace refers to a positive-sum situation in which both it and its neighbourhood mutually enjoy peace, security and stability.

As a result of analysis to find out to what extent the EU has acted congruently with its self-image as a 'force for international peace, security and stability' in its actual practice in the MEPP, it can be concluded that the EU has acted as a 'constrained' 'force for international peace, security and stability'. On the one hand, it has played a significant role in the peaceful settlement of the conflict through some successful mediation efforts and diplomatic missions of EU and national representatives, as in the issue of the Siege of the Church of the Nativity in Bethlehem. It carried out two ESDP operations. It signed ENP Action Plans with both sides. It made significant military contribution to the expanded UNIFIL. It provided financial and technical aid to the Palestinian Authority and supported the Palestinian reform process towards the creation of an independent, economically and politically viable, sovereign and democratic Palestinian state. Moreover, the EU has been the most active member of the Quartet on the Middle East in the promotion of the Roadmap.

Nonetheless, internal and external constraints put limits on the EU's ability to live up to its self-proclaimed commitments and responsibilities and prevented it from acting as an effective mediator for the peaceful settlement of the conflict. One internal constraint is the EU's lack of both vertical and horizontal coherence, its inability to act as a coherent actor and speak with one voice. As previously discussed in detail, the Italian government's attitude towards the Israeli construction of a security fence can be given as an example for the lack of vertical coherence within the EU. External constraints are the Israeli and the American reluctance towards the EU's participation in the bilateral peace negotiations as an active mediator and their insistence on limiting the EU's role merely to facilitating the implementation of the Roadmap, supporting the Palestinian state-building and economic reconstruction.

The EU's role conception as 'the provider of development aid' emphasizes the necessity to help developing countries in their fight to: eradicate extreme poverty, hunger, malnutrition and pandemics such as AIDS; achieve universal primary education; promote gender equality and empower women; reduce the mortality rate of children; improve maternal health; and achieve sustainable development, which includes good governance, human rights and political, economic, social and environmental aspects. As the EU has identified development as a precondition for security and underdevelopment as a breeding ground for insecurity and instability in the world, by helping developing countries in their fight against underdevelopment through providing development aid the EU has contributed to both its own security and international security.

In the case of the MEPP, the EU's self-image as 'the provider of development aid' reflects its actual practice. The EU's role as 'provider of development aid' took the form of 'provider of financial and technical aid' to the Palestinian Authority in the context of the MEPP. As the largest external donor of financial and technical aid to the Palestinian Authority and the main financial supporter of the MEPP, the EU has effectively used this instrument for the peaceful settlement of the conflict. The EU's financial and technical aid to the Palestinian Authority and the MEPP has made three significant contributions to the survival of the peace process.

Firstly, the EU's financial and technical aid in the form of direct budgetary support to the Palestinian Authority facilitated the latter's ability to stay financially afloat after the Israeli withholding of the Palestinian tax and custom revenues following the outbreak of the Al-Aqsa Intifada in September 2000. By keeping the Palestinian Authority financially afloat, the EU also kept the peace process afloat, because the financial collapse of the Palestinian Authority might have resulted in the escalation of conflict, violence, chaos and the interruption of the peace process.

Secondly, this aid enabled the Palestinian Authority to fulfil its obligations under the Roadmap. This aid assisted and facilitated the creation of an independent, economically and politically viable, sovereign and democratic Palestinian state. The financial support to the infrastructure projects in the Palestinian territories and the Palestinian institutional reform process has been especially crucial. Furthermore, the EU's financial support to the Palestinian private sector, mainly the SMEs, development projects in East Jerusalem, projects for the promotion and protection of human rights and the Palestinian NGOs and service institutions have been other crucial contributions by the EU to the creation of an economically and politically viable Palestinian state.

Thirdly, through its financial aid to the peace-oriented NGOs and civil society initiatives on both sides the EU promoted communication and understanding among the Palestinians and the Israelis by demonstrating the advantages of working together for mutual benefit and achieving tangible results. In this way, the EU contributed to the creation of a positive environment for the peaceful settlement of the conflict and broadened the base of public support for the MEPP. The EU utilized its financial aid to strengthen civil society actions in peace building and conflict transformation.

However, the EU's provision of humanitarian and emergency aid to the Palestinians put a serious constraint on its ability to use the instrument of aid as an effective tool for the peaceful settlement of the conflict. Although the EU has provided aid to the Palestinian people as a humanitarian imperative, this has, however, resulted in its taking over the humanitarian duties of Israel towards the Palestinian people under the international humanitarian law. Thus, by relieving Israel of its legal obligations towards the Palestinian people, the EU has inadvertently subsidized the Israeli occupation of the Palestinian territories and thus helped and facilitated Israel to continue the state of occupation, closures and curfews in the Palestinian territories, rather than working actively against it.

The EU's role conception as 'promoter of its values and norms' put emphasis on its standing as a community of shared values. This role conception emphasized the EU's commitment to the promotion of its shared values and norms and to establishing well-governed democratic states for the protection of both international security and the security of the EU and the strengthening of the international order.

As a result of analysis to discover to what extent the EU has promoted its shared values and norms in its relations with Israel and Palestine, it can be concluded that the EU faced serious limitations in performing its role as the promoter of its values and norms. In the Palestinian case, even though the EU supported the Palestinian reform process, there has been much emphasis on the promotion of good governance, leaving aside genuine democratization in its actual practice. The EU adopted a highly tolerant position towards the persistent exclusion of Islamic factions from both the PLO and the Palestinian Authority, exhibited reluctance to engage and support Islamic civil society and non-violent groups, and pursued a policy of isolating democratically elected Hamas while maintaining its economic and political support to unelected Fatah. Such a position undermined the EU's effectiveness and credibility as the promoter of democracy in Palestine.

In the Israeli case, despite the Israeli violation of the Palestinian people's human rights through its conduct in the Occupied Territories, the EU did not use sanctions against it. There are two main reasons behind the EU's refraining from using any kind of sanctions or legal mechanisms of passive enforcement against Israel even when it violated human rights. The first one is the political and commercial interests of the EU, which could be damaged by the imposition of sanctions. The second one is the inter-role conflict between the EU's role as a 'force for good' and role as 'promoter of its values and norms'. On the one hand, the EU's role as a 'force for good' urged it to refrain from using sanctions against Israel; but on the other hand, its role as 'promoter of its values and norms' simultaneously urged it to promote human rights and international humanitarian law even with the use of sanctions against the violators. Faced with this kind of inter-role conflict, the EU preferred to meet the expectations of its role as a 'force for good' which was also beneficial for its material interests. To sum up, there was a gap between the EU's role conception as 'promoter of its values and norms' and its actual role performance.

The EU's role conception as a 'promoter of effective multilateralism' emphasized its commitment to building an effective multilateral system governed by rules and monitored by multilateral institutions. The establishment of an effective multilateral system was identified as a necessity for the maintenance of both international security and the security and prosperity of the EU. In parallel with the former role conception, the EU put special emphasis on the UN as the most important partner for the establishment of an effective multilateral system and placed it at the centre of such a system. The role conception 'partner for the UN' emphasizes the EU's commitment to upholding the universal values, norms, goals and principles enshrined in the UN Charter and supporting and strengthening the UN's efforts for the protection and promotion of regional and global peace, security, stability and prosperity. This role conception emphasizes the EU's responsibility to support and to strengthen the UN in order to fully enable the UN to fulfil its role effectively in seeking multilateral solutions to global problems on the basis of its Charter. The EU's role conception as 'builder of effective partnership with key actors' emphasizes its preference for dealing with global and regional problems and threats through cooperation with other important global and regional actors. This role conception places an emphasis on the EU's preference to pursue its foreign and security policy objectives through multilateral cooperation in international organizations and through building partnership with other important global and regional actors, mainly because the EU believes that by acting in this way the EU furthers both the interests of others and its own self-interest.

As a result of analysis to discover to what extent the EU acts congruently with its self-images as 'promoter of effective multilateralism', 'partner for the UN' and 'builder of effective partnership with key actors', it can be concluded that the EU managed to live up to its self-proclaimed commitments and responsibilities in its actual practice. The below mentioned actions of the EU in the context of the MEPP confirmed that the EU acted consistently with its self-proclaimed commitments and responsibilities:

- the EU's active participation in multilateral initiatives for the peaceful settlement of the conflict;
- the prominent and active role played by the EU in the preparation and the implementation of the Roadmap;
- the EU's active participation in the implementation of 'Agreement on Movement and Access from and to Gaza' by carrying out the task of the third party monitoring role at the Rafah Crossing Point on the Gaza-Egypt border;
- the EU's insistence on the peaceful settlement of the conflict within the multilateral framework of the UN and through adherence to

the relevant UN Security Council Resolutions and the EU's persistent support to the UN efforts towards the peaceful settlement of the conflict;

- the EU's active support and contribution to the UNRWA and to the expanded UNIFIL;
- the EU's building of effective partnership with the UN, the USA and Russia within the framework of the Quartet.

In conclusion, despite limitations and constraints which resulted in a certain degree of inconsistency between some of the roles the EU proclaims it will perform and its actual role performance, it would be unfair to conclude that there exists a high degree of incongruity between its role conceptions and role performance. Evidence gathered from the EU's involvement in the MEPP in the post-9/11 era revealed that we could not talk about an apparent 'conception-performance gap' in the EU's foreign and security policy. On this basis, it cannot be maintained that the EU is an ineffective and inefficient foreign and security policy actor which totally lacks international credibility. Although the limitations and constraints the EU encountered when performing its self-proclaimed roles of a 'force for good', a 'force for international peace, security and stability' and a 'promoter of its values and norms' moderately weakened its effectiveness, efficiency and international credibility as a foreign and security policy actor in the post-9/11 era, all in all, as observed in the case of the MEPP, the decisions and actions carried out by the EU while enacting its self-identified roles outweighed its deficiencies in its role performance. Thus, even though the EU, whose foreign and security policy is in its adolescence, has encountered some inconsistency problems while performing its self-identified roles, its overall balance sheet as a foreign and security policy actor in the post-9/11 era is fairly positive.

NOTES

Chapter 1

1. The proposed EU Battlegroups consist of highly trained, battalion-size formations (1,500 soldiers each) including all combat and service support as well as deployability and sustainability assets. These should be available within 15 days notice and sustainable for at least 30 days (extendable to 120 days by rotation). They should be flexible enough to promptly undertake operations in distant crises areas (i.e. failing states), under, but not exclusively, a UN mandate, and to conduct combat missions in an extremely hostile environment (mountains, desert, jungle, etc.). As such, they should prepare the ground for larger, more traditional peacekeeping forces, ideally provided by the UN or Member States (Quille 2003).
2. In this book, congruity refers to the situation when an actor's (the EU) role performance is judged as appropriate and convincing according to the norms provided by actors' role conception. In the role theory literature, this judgement is based on a qualitative analysis of the evidence available regarding role conceptions and role performance (Walker 1979: 179).

Chapter 2

1. Purposive sampling is a deliberate and non-random sample selection method. In purposive sampling, the researcher selects a sample with a purpose in his/her mind. In accordance with this purpose, he/she attempts to obtain a sample which he/she thinks would help achieve his/her research objectives.

2. In 'The EU: A Global Military Actor' (2002), Henrik Larsen analyzed the dominant EU discourse concerning the EU's international actorness in the year 2000. In particular, he tried to find out whether the EU articulated itself as a civilian power, and whether its geographical focus was global or regional by using constructivist discourse analysis. In his study, the analytical focus was the discursive construction at the EU level. In other words, he set out to analyze EU level discourse. For that reason, he selected EU Council documents and the speeches of High Representative for the CFSP of the EU, Javier Solana, as his sample for discourse analysis.

3. Inter-coder reliability means the amount of agreement or correspondence among two or more coders (Neuendorf 2002: 71).

4. Interview with an EU official, General Secretariat of the Council of the European Union, 26 October 2009.

5. Interviews with EU officials, General Secretariat of the Council of the European Union, 26 October 2009 and Directorate-General External Relations, European Commission, 27 October 2009.

Chapter 3

1. The UN Millennium Development Goals set out in the UN Millennium Declaration were adopted by 189 UN members during the UN Millennium Summit in September 2000. The UN Millennium Development Goals are eight goals to be achieved by the year 2015 and include eradicating extreme poverty and hunger; achieving universal primary education; promoting gender equality and empowering women; reducing child mortality; improving maternal health; combating HIV/AIDS, malaria and other diseases; ensuring environmental sustainability; and developing global partnership for development.

Chapter 4

1. The Netherlands and Luxembourg adopted a pro-Israeli position; Belgium and Germany adopted an impartial or balanced position; France and Italy adopted a pro-Arab position.

2. The name came from French Minister of Foreign Affairs Maurice Schumann, who was the spiritual father of the document.

3. The Irish Foreign Minister Michael O'Kennedy, while addressing – the UN General Assembly on 26 September 1979 on behalf of all EC Member States, reemphasized the legitimate rights of the Palestinian people including the right to a homeland and the right to play its full part in the negotiations

of a comprehensive settlement through its representatives. In his speech, he referred to the PLO and it was mentioned for the first time in a text of EC Member States. He stated that in the view of all EC Member States, it was necessary that UN Security Council Resolutions 242 and 338 be accepted by all those involved – including the PLO – as the basis for negotiation of a comprehensive settlement in which all the parties would play their full part. So, EC Member States declared that they would support the participation of the PLO in peace negotiations and its role, as the representative of the Palestinian people, but only when it accepted Israel's right to exist in an internationally agreed settlement. In September 1979, EC Member States defended the mutual recognition of Israel's right to exist and the Palestinians' right to self-determination. In his speech, O'Kennedy referred to the right to self-determination of the Palestinian people by stating that 'it is essential that there be respect for the legitimate rights of the Palestinian people... who are entitled, within the framework set by a peace settlement, to exercise their right for their own future as a people'. Moreover, O'Kennedy declared that EC Member States did not accept any unilateral moves claiming to change the status of Jerusalem (Ifestos 1987: 448).

4. Begin stated that for the peace that would be achieved with the participation of that 'organization of murderers', he meant the PLO; a number of European countries were prepared to give guarantees, even military ones. Anyone with a memory must shudder, knowing the result of the guarantee given to Czechoslovakia in 1938 after Sudetenland was stolen from it, also in the name of self-determination. He asserted that any man of good will and every free person in Europe who studied the Venice declaration would see in it a 'Munich surrender', the second in our generation, to the totalitarian blackmail and an encouragement to all those elements which sought to undermine the Camp David Treaty and bring about the failure of the peace process in the Middle East (Ifestos 1987: 460; Greilsammer and Weiler 1987: 142: Dosenrode and Stubkjaer 2002: 98).

5. The first mission was the Thorn mission and it was headed by Gaston Thorn, Foreign Minister of Luxembourg and the President-in-office of the EC Council. In autumn 1980 the Thorn mission visited the countries in the region including Tunisia, Israel, Lebanon, Syria, Jordan, Kuwait, Iraq, Saudi Arabia and Egypt. Although the Arab States adopted a positive attitude towards a European peace initiative, Israel adopted a negative stance and rejected any European Peace initiative. Israel's negative stance against any European peace initiative prevented EC Member States from launching their own peace initiative. The second mission was the Van der Klaauw mission and it was headed by Christoph Albert Van der Klaauw, Foreign Minister of the Netherlands and

the President-in-office of the EC Council. Van der Klaauw visited the countries in the Middle East including Syria, Iraq, Israel, Lebanon and Egypt during the spring 1981. The Klaauw mission shared the same fate as the Thorn mission. Although most of the Arab countries approached favourably to any European peace initiative, Israel denied it completely.

6. The Fahd Plan, which was proposed by Crown Prince Fahd of Saudi Arabia on 7 August 1981, was an eight-point proposal to resolve the Arab-Israeli conflict. The plan's eight points were: Israeli withdrawal from 1967-captured territories, including East Jerusalem; dismantling of Israeli settlements in the Occupied Territories; guarantees of freedom of worship for all in the holy places; the Palestinian people's right to self-determination; indemnity for Palestinian refugees not exercising the right of return; West Bank and Gaza placed under UN control for a transitional period (a few months); establishment of an independent Palestinian state with East Jerusalem as its capital; subsequent Security Council guarantee of peace among all states in the area, including the new Palestinian state; and the Security Council guarantee of the above principles. A modified form of this plan was adopted by Arab leaders at the Fez summit on 9 September 1982.

7. During this period, the Thatcher government decided to adopt a somewhat higher profile in the Arab-Israeli Conflict. The main reasons behind this were: the British Foreign Secretary Lord Carrington's success in the settlement of the Zimbabwe issue which created both expectation of, and a greater confidence in, a more positive policy under his leadership; the invasion of Afghanistan by the Soviet Union, which inevitably gave greater attention to the Middle East than required by oil and trade; the loss of momentum in the Camp David Peace Process which created an impetus for the Europeans to launch their own initiative; and the fact that the British would take the EC Presidency in the second half of 1981 (Edwards 1984: 52).

8. Interview with an EU Official, General Secretariat of the Council of the European Union, 4 November 2009.

9. For further information please see Kaya 2004.

10. For further information please see Kaya 2004.

11. Interview with a Palestinian Diplomat, General Delegation of Palestine to the European Union, 13 November 2009.

12. The Palestinian interim self-government was to be materialized in phases. Until a final status accord was established, West Bank and Gaza would be divided into three zones: Area A would be under full control of the Palestinian Authority; Area B would be under Palestinian civil control and Israeli security control; and Area C, which covered the areas of Israeli settlements and security zones, would be under full Israeli control, except over Palestinian civilians.

13. 94/276/CFSP: Council Decision of 19 April 1994 on a joint action adopted by the Council on the basis of Article J (3) of the Treaty on European Union, in support of the Middle East Peace Process.

14. The GMP consisted of a legal framework to regulate relations between the EC and all the Mediterranean non-member countries on matters of mainly trade and aid (Bicchi 2007: 63). As the GMP was designed to establish a global approach in all the EC's relations with the Mediterranean non-member countries, it sought to put the multiplicity of bilateral relations and agreements that existed between the EC and the Mediterranean non-member countries individually into a single and coordinated framework (Piening 1997: 72). The main aim of the GMP was to regulate relations between the EC and all the Mediterranean non-member countries, with a view to the eventual creation of a Mediterranean free trade (ibid.: 74). Within the framework of the GMP, the EC concluded bilateral cooperation agreements with the Mediterranean non-member countries in the 1970s, including Algeria (26 April 1976), Morocco (27 April 1976), Tunisia (25 April 1976), Egypt (18 January 1977), Lebanon (3 May 1977), Jordan (18 January 1977), Syria (18 January 1977) and Israel (11 May 1975). These agreements aimed to set up free trade and economic cooperation between the EC and all the Mediterranean non-member countries (Dosenrode and Stubkjaer 2002: 94). These agreements envisaged cooperation in commercial, financial and economic, and social matters.

15. The mandate of the special envoy would be: to establish and maintain close contact with all the parties to the peace process, other countries of the region, the USA and other interested countries, as well as relevant international organizations, in order to work with them in strengthening the peace process; to observe peace negotiations between the parties, and to be ready to offer the EU's advice and good offices if the parties request: to contribute where requested to the implementation of international agreements reached between parties, and to engage with them diplomatically in the event of non-compliance with the terms of these agreements; to engage constructively with signatories to agreements within the framework of the peace process in order to promote compliance with the basic norms of democracy, including respect for human rights and the rule of law; to report to the Council's bodies on possibilities for EU intervention in the peace process and on the best way of pursuing EU initiatives and ongoing Middle East peace process-related EU business including the political aspects of relevant EU development projects; to monitor actions by either side which might prejudice the outcome of the permanent status negotiations.

16. In order to strengthen the cohesion in EU's external representation and give EU a single visible voice in international system, with the Treaty of Amsterdam

(signed on 2 October 1997 and entered into force on 1 May 1999) the post of High Representative for the CFSP and Secretary General of Council of the EU was introduced. The holder of the post can be viewed as 'Mr or Mrs CFSP', 'Monsieur Politique étrangère et de sécurité européenne (PESC)' or the 'telephone number of Europe'. According to Article J.16 of the Treaty of Amsterdam, 'the Secretary-General of the Council, High Representative for the CFSP, shall assist the Council in matters coming within the scope of the CFSP, in particular through contributing to the formulation, preparation and implementation of policy decisions, and, when appropriate and acting on behalf of the Council at the request of the Presidency, through conducting political dialogue with third parties'. Moreover, according to Article J.8, 'the Presidency shall be assisted by the High Representative for the CFSP'.

17. Interview with an EU Official, General Secretariat of the Council of the European Union, 26 October 2009.
18. Interview with an Israeli Diplomat, Mission of Israel to the European Communities, 13 November 2009.
19. Interview with an EU Official, Directorate-General External Relations, European Commission, 27 October 2009.

Chapter 5

1. An EU diplomat identified the Quartet as a contact group or a consultation mechanism for creating a conducive atmosphere for peace negotiations. (Interview with an EU Diplomat, General Secretariat of the Council of the European Union, 3 November 2009.) According to a British diplomat, the Quartet brings international coherence in the case of the Middle East peace process by setting up key principles of international community and bringing the views of international community together. It enables systematic cooperation of approaches (interview with a British Diplomat, UK Permanent Representation to the European Union, 11 November 2009).
2. Interview with an EU Official, General Secretariat of the Council of the European Union, 26 October 2009.
3. Interview with an EU Official, General Secretariat of the Council of the European Union, 4 November 2009.
4. Interview with an EU Official, General Secretariat of the Council of the European Union, 26 October 2009 and Interview with an EU Diplomat, General Secretariat of the Council of the European Union, 3 November 2009.
5. Joschka Fischer's 'Idea Paper for the Middle East' envisaged a peace conference to conclude negotiations on all unresolved issues within two years and

called for Israeli withdrawal from the West Bank and Gaza and the clearing of settlements. The Israelis and Palestinians would recognize each other's right to exist and 'any country which continues to support terrorism or its organizations or members will be completely isolated, politically and economically' (Castle 2002).

6. The Palestinians had concerns about the language and the emphasis on the conditionality rather than reciprocity. They feared that the Israeli government would be able to exploit the inherent ambiguities in the text to ensure that negotiations would be subject to obfuscation and delay (Hartley 2004: 300). In the meantime, Israel would continue to create the condition on the ground which would prejudice final outcomes.

7. The Israeli government had reservations concerning the absence of guarantees on conditionality. It was reluctant to engage with the process, including the demands for a settlement freeze without the Palestinian Authority's disarming and uprooting of the Palestinian militias. It was not ready to recognize the Palestinian State until Palestinians renounced their right to return (Hartley 2004: 301).

8. The 'security fence' consists of a network of fences with vehicle-barrier trenches surrounded by an on average 60 m wide exclusion area (90 per cent) and up to 8 m high concrete walls (10 per cent). At the time of writing the 'security fence' was still under construction and was expected to be completed by 2010.

9. Although the 'security fence' was intended to be built along the 'Green Line' (the 1949 armistice line which constituted the border between Israel and Jordan before 1967), due to topographic difficulties its construction route diverged from the 'Green Line' in some places. This led to criticism on the part of International Community. The reason behind this is that it encroaches and envelops Occupied Palestinian Territory. According to 2007 Report of UN Special Rapporteur on Human Rights and Counterterrorism, 80 per cent of the fence is built within the Palestinian Territory itself and in order to incorporate the Ariel settlement block, it extends over 20 km into the West Bank. Once completed, over 60,000 West Bank Palestinians will reside in a 'closed zone' – the area between the Green Line and the Fence – which also includes many of the West Bank's most valuable water resources. Nearly one-third of all the Palestinians living in the West Bank need a permit to exit to the 'closed zone', in order to tend their lands, visit relatives or to get to their places (Khaliq 2008: 327). Regarding the construction route of the fence, the International Court of Justice decided that the fence violates international law. It severely hinders the Palestinian's right to self-determination; violates a number of international human rights

and humanitarian law obligations incumbent on Israel; is tantamount to de facto annexation; and takes a route which is not necessary for security reasons (ibid.: 330).

10. There are two reasons behind the disengagement plan. The first one was to deal with the demographic challenge to the Israelis. According to demographic trends, Israeli Jews would become a decreasing minority in the area between the Jordan River and the Mediterranean Sea. The Disengagement Plan was thought to be a good way to maximize Israeli land annexation while minimizing the number of Palestinians included in it. The second reason was to find an alternative to a negotiated two-state solution. It would be unilateral and would not need a Palestinian partner. It would abandon less territory; keep Israeli effective control on the peace agenda, especially on the issues of Jerusalem and refugees (Tocci 2007: 109).

11. Interview with an EU Official, General Secretariat of the Council of the European Union, 26 October 2009.

12. EU COPPS started to work in January 2005 with four senior EU police advisors in the West Bank and Gaza. It was officially established on 20 April 2005 in Ramallah. The mandate of EU COPPS was to assist the Palestinian Authority in developing modern and effective civil police service. Its aim was to reduce crime and insecurity and help create the conditions for economic recovery. It would also help the Palestinian Authority to meet its Roadmap commitments regarding the consolidation of its security services and the reform of its institutions (http://www.delisr.ec.europa.eu/newsletter/english/default.asp?edt_id=17&id=248). EU COPPS supported the Palestinian Authority in taking responsibility for law and order and provided the Palestinian Authority with vehicles, personal protective gear, communication equipment, office equipment and infrastructure repairs. (http://www.wsibrussels.org/gaza.htm).

13. French acronym for Mecanisme 'Palestino-Européen de Gestion et d'Aide Socio-Economique'.

14. EU Member States' contributions to UNIFIL were as follows: Italy contributed up to 3,000 soldiers, the Garibaldi aircraft carrier and three disembarkation and patrol ships; France contributed 2,000 personnel and a squadron of 13 Leclerc tanks and heavy material; Spain contributed a marine infantry unit 800–1,000 strong and 30 to 40 tanks; Poland contributed 280 soldiers; Belgium contributed 400 soldiers, including de-mining experts and medical teams; Luxemburg contributed a de-mining team within the Belgian contingent; Finland contributed 250 personnel; Sweden contributed two ships; Denmark contributed three warships; Greece contributed a frigate, a helicopter and special forces; Portugal contributed a number of troops

not specified; the UK contributed two AWACS reconnaissance planes, six helicopters and a reconnaissance ship, as well as the use of its military basis in Cyprus; Germany and the Netherlands contributed ships for the surveillance of the Lebanese coast; Slovenia contributed 10 to 20 soldiers and de-mining experts; Bulgaria contributed number of troops not specified; Cyprus contributed via logistics (Pirozzi 2006: 2–3).

15. Article 1 of the Fourth Geneva Convention prevents any state or its nationals from participating in or facilitating the Convention's violation.

16. According to the World Bank, real GDP Growth in the Palestinian Territories was 0 per cent which, in the face of a rapidly increasing population, led to a further decrease in the per capita income. In mid-2008, per capita income was 40 per cent less than before the Second Intifada. The official unemployment rate was 23 per cent in the Palestinian Territories. Thirty-five per cent of the Palestinians living in Gaza have been living in absolute poverty (Asseburg 2009b: 37).

17. On 27 December 2001, the Council of the EU adopted a Common Position on the application of specific measures to combat terrorism, through with EU Member States decided to freeze funds and other financial assets or economic resources of persons, groups and entities involved in terrorist acts. The terrorist wing of Hamas, Kata'ib al-shadid Izz al-din al-Qassam, was added to the list of terrorist organizations. On 29 November 2005, the Council also added the political wing of Hamas to this list. The EU imposed sanction on the Hamas-led Palestinian government on the basis of this list of terrorist organizations (Möller 2009).

18. Interview with an EU Official, General Secretariat of the Council of the European Union, 26 October 2009.

19. Interview with a British Diplomat, UK Permanent Representation to the European Union, 11 November 2009.

20. Interview with an EU Official, Directorate-General External Relations, European Commission, 27 October 2009.

21. Vertical coherence refers to the coherence between Member States and the EU.

22. Horizontal coherence refers to the coherence within the EU, mainly the coherence between the intergovernmental CFSP and the supranational EC and the achievement of synergy between these policies.

23. Interview with an EU Official, General Secretariat of the Council of the European Union, 26 October 2009; interview with an EU Official, General Secretariat of the Council of the European Union, 4 November 2009; interview with a British Diplomat, UK Permanent Representation to the European Union, 11 November 2009.

24. Interview with an EU Official, General Secretariat of the Council of the European Union, 26 October 2009.
25. Interview with an EU Official, General Secretariat of the Council of the European Union, 26 October 2009.
26. Interview with a Palestinian Diplomat, General Delegation of Palestine to the European Union, 13 November 2009.
27. Interview with an EU Official, General Secretariat of the Council of the European Union, 26 October 2009.
28. Interview with a Palestinian Diplomat, General Delegation of Palestine to the European Union, 13 November 2009.
29. Interview with a British Diplomat, UK Permanent Representation to the European Union, 11 November 2009.
30. Interview with a Palestinian Diplomat, General Delegation of Palestine to the European Union, 13 November 2009.
31. Interview with a Palestinian Diplomat, General Delegation of Palestine to the European Union, 13 November 2009.
32. According to the Fourth Geneva Convention Relative to the Protection of Civilian Persons in Time of War, the Occupying Power is under legal obligation to provide emergency relief and basic services to civilian population living in the occupied territory. According to articles 55, 56, 59 and 60 of the Convention, Israel as the Occupying Power is under obligation to bring in the necessary foodstuffs, medical stores and other articles if the resources of the occupied Palestinian territories are inadequate; to ensure and maintain, with the cooperation of national and local authorities, the medical and hospital establishments and services, public health and hygiene in the occupied Palestinian territories; to agree to relief schemes, consisting of the provision of consignments of foodstuffs, medical supplies and clothing, on behalf of the Palestinian population, and facilitate them by all the means at its disposal if the whole or part of the Palestinian population is inadequately supplied. According to article 60 of the Convention, delivery of relief to the Palestinian population does not relieve Israel, the Occupying Power, of the above responsibilities.
33. These reforms included the firing of top security chiefs, imposing an age limit on servicemen and forcing some 1,000 ineffective members of the security forces to retire.
34. Interview with an EU Official, General Secretariat of the Council of the European Union, 4 November 2009.
35. Interview with an EU Official, General Secretariat of the Council of the European Union, 26 October 2009.
36. The presence of Hamas on the EU's list of terrorist organizations made it difficult for the EU to do business with it, because it would cause a legal

problem for the EU (interview with an EU Official, General Secretariat of the Council of the European Union, 26 October 2009).

37. Interview with an EU Official, General Secretariat of the Council of the European Union, 26 October 2009.

38. Interview with a Palestinian Diplomat, General Delegation of Palestine to the European Union, 13 November 2009.

39. Frederich Kratochwil (1993: 468) defined minilateralism as the creation of core groups and multilateralization of their agreements.

40. Interview with an EU official, Directorate-General External Relations, European Commission, 27 October 2009.

BIBLIOGRAPHY

Primary Sources

Speeches

Ferrero-Waldner, Benita, 'The Future of the UN: Results of the Kofi Annan High Level Panel on Threats, Challenges, and Change', 8 December 2004, Brussels. http://ec.europa.eu/external_relations/news/ferrero/2004/speech04_524_ en.htm. Accessed on 28.11.2007.
——, 'Press Conference to launch first seven Action Plans under the European Neighbourhood Policy', 9 December 2004, Brussels. http://ec.europa.eu/external_relations/news/ferrero/2004/sp04_529.htm. Accessed on 28.11.2007.
——, 'Commissioner Benita Ferrero-Waldner', 13 January 2005, Washington DC. http://ec.europa.eu/external_relations/news/ferrero/2005/csis_130105.htm. Accessed on 16.02.2007.
——, 'European Architecture', 17 May 2005. http://ec.europa.eu/external_relations/news/ferrero/2005/sp_coe_170505.htm. Accessed on 28.11.2007.
——, 'Working Together as Global Partners', 1 June 2005, Washington DC. http://ec.europa.eu/external_relations/news/ferrero/2005/sp05_313.htm. Accessed on 28.11.2007.
——, 'The EU, China and the Quest for a Multilateral World', 4 July 2005, China Institute of International Studies, Brussels. http://ec.europa.eu/external_relations/news/ferrero/2005/sp05_414.htm. Accessed on 28.11.2007.
——, 'The European Neighbourhood Policy: helping ourselves through helping our neighbours', 31 October 2005, London. http://europa.eu/rapid/pressReleasesAction.do?reference=SPEECH/05/658&format=HTML&aged=0&language=EN&guiLanguage=en. Accessed on 28.11.2007.

——, 'The Role of Crisis Response in External Relations – "From Needs to Solutions: Enhancing Civilian Crisis Response Capacity of the European Union", 14 November 2005, Brussels. http://ec.europa.eu/external_relations/news/ferrero/2005/sp05_684.htm. Accessed on 28.11.2007.

——, 'Quo Vadis Europa?', 14 December 2005, Strasbourg. http://europa.eu/rapid/pressReleasesAction.do?reference=SPEECH/05/797&format=HTML&aged=0&language=EN&guiLanguage=en. Accessed on 28.11.2007.

——, 'The EU in the World', 2 February 2006, Brussels. http://europa.eu/rapid/pressReleasesAction.do?reference=SPEECH/06/59&format=HTML&aged=0&language=EN&guiLanguage=enhttp://ec.europa.eu/external_relations/news/ferrero/2005/sp05_313.htm. Accessed on 28.11.2007.

——, 'Managing Globalization – the Case for a European Foreign Policy', 10 February 2006, London. http://europa.eu/rapid/pressReleasesAction.do?reference=SPEECH/06/75&format=HTML&aged=0&language=EN&guiLanguage=en. Accessed on 28.11.2007.

——, 'The EU's Role in Protecting Europe's Security', 30 May 2006, Brussels. http://europa.eu/rapid/pressReleasesAction.do?reference=SPEECH/06/331&format=HTML&aged=0&language=EN&guiLanguage=en. Accessed on 28.11.2007.

——, 'Opening Speech: Europe's Response to Global Change', 27 August 2006, Austria. http://europa.eu/rapid/pressReleasesAction.do?reference=SPEECH/06/473&format=HTML&aged=0&language=EN&guiLanguage=en. Accessed on 28.11.2007.

——, 'The European Union as A Global Power?', 25 September 2006, Texas. http://europa.eu/rapid/pressReleasesAction.do?reference=SPEECH/06/530&format=HTML&aged=0&language=EN&guiLanguage=en. Accessed on 28.11.2007.

——, 'The EU's Role in Tackling Current International Challenges', 12 November 2006. http://europa.eu/rapid/pressReleasesAction.do?reference=SPEECH/06/678&type=HTML&aged=0&language=EN&guiLanguage=en. Accessed on 28.11.2007.

——, 'A Soul for Europe', 18 November 2006, Berlin. http://europa.eu/rapid/searchResultAction.do. Accessed on 28.11.2007.

——, 'The European Union and the OSCE – Natural Partners in a Networked World', *OSCE Yearbook 2006*, http://www.core-hamburg.de/documents/yearbook/english/06/osce2006-enpdfGesamt.pdf. Accessed on 08.11.2008.

Patten, Chris, 'Coherence and Co-operation: The EU as Promoter of Peace and Development', 4 December 2001, Swedish Institute of International Affairs, Stockholm. http://www.europaworld.org/DEVPOLAWAR/Eng/Conflict/Conflict_DocD_eng.htm. Accessed on 01.12.2007.

——, 'European Union Foreign Policy & the challenges of Globalisation', 5 April 2002, Singapore. http://ec.europa.eu/external_relations/news/patten/sp04_02global.htm. Accessed on 01.12.2007.

——, 'America and Europe: an essential partnership', 3 October 2002, Chicago. http://ec.europa.eu/external_relations/news/patten/sp02_452.htm. Accessed on 01.12.2007.

——, 'Europe in the World: CFSP & its relation to development', 7 November 2003, Overseas Development Institute, the UK. http://ec.europa.eu/external_relations/news/patten/sp07_11_03.htm. Accessed on 01.12.2007.

Solana, Javier, 'The CFSP in an Enlarged Union', 1 March 2001, Paris. http://www.consilium.europa.eu/cms3_applications/applications/solana/details.asp?cmsid=246&BID=107&DocID=65840&insite=1. Accessed on 03.02.2008.

——, EU High Representative for the CFSP, 19 February 2002, Brussels. http://www.consilium.europa.eu/cms3_applications/applications/solana/list.asp?cmsid=256&BID=107&page=arch&lang=EN. Accessed on 16.06.2007.

——, 25 March 2002, Bruges. http://www.consilium.europa.eu/cms3_applications/applications/solana/list.asp?cmsid=256&BID=107&page=arch&lang=EN. Accessed on 16.06.2007.

——, 'NATO: The Next 50 Years – Cooperation for Security and Stability in South-eastern Europe', 18 April 2002, Athens. http://www.consilium.europa.eu/cms3_applications/applications/solana/list.asp?cmsid=256&BID=107&page=arch&lang=EN. Accessed on 16.06.2007.

——, 'Europe's Place in the World: The Role of the High Representative', 25 April 2002, Stockholm. http://www.consilium.europa.eu/cms3_applications/applications/solana/list.asp?cmsid=256&BID=107&page=arch&lang=EN. Accessed on 16.06.2007.

——, 'Europe's Place in the World', 23 May 2002, Copenhagen. http://www.consilium.europa.eu/cms3_applications/applications/solana/list.asp?cmsid=256&BID=107&page=arch&lang=EN. Accessed on 16.06.2007.

——, 24 July 2002, Rome. http://www.consilium.europa.eu/cms3_applications/applications/solana/list.asp?cmsid=256&BID=107&page=arch&lang=EN. Accessed on 16.06.2007.

——, 16 October 2002, Warsaw. http://www.consilium.europa.eu/cms3_applications/applications/solana/list.asp?cmsid=256&BID=107&page=arch&lang=EN. Accessed on 16.06.2007.

——, 21 May 2003, Dublin. http://www.consilium.europa.eu/cms3_applications/applications/solana/list.asp?cmsid=256&BID=107&page=arch&lang=EN. Accessed on 16.06.2007.

——, 'The EU Security Strategy: Implications for Europe's Role in a Changing World', 12 November 2003, Berlin. http://www.consilium.europa.eu/cms3_applications/applications/solana/list.asp?cmsid=256&BID=107&page=arch&lang=EN. Accessed on 16.06.2007.

——, 'The Voice of Europe on Security Matters', 26 November 2003, Brussels. http://www.consilium.europa.eu/cms3_applications/applications/solana/list.asp?cmsid=256&BID=107&page=arch&lang=EN. Accessed on 16.06.2007.

——, 8 January 2004, Dublin. http://www.consilium.europa.eu/cms3_applica-tions/applications/solana/list.asp?cmsid=256&BID=107&page=arch&lang=EN. Accessed on 17.06.2007.

——, 28 June 2004, Istanbul. http://www.consilium.europa.eu/cms3_applications/applications/solana/list.asp?cmsid=256&BID=107&page=arch&lang=EN. Accessed on 16.06.2007.

——, 27 July 2004, Rome. http://www.consilium.europa.eu/cms3_applications/applications/solana/list.asp?cmsid=256&BID=107&page=arch&lang=EN. Accessed on 06.03.2007.

——, 'Terrorism in Europe: How Does the Union of 25 Respond to this Phenomenon', 7 October 2004, Berlin. http://www.consilium.europa.eu/cms3_applications/applications/solana/list.asp?cmsid=256&BID=107&page=arch&lang=EN. Accessed on 16.06.2007.

——, 'Shaping an Effective EU Foreign Policy', 24 January 2005, Brussels. http://www.consilium.europa.eu/cms3_applications/applications/solana/list.asp?cmsid=256&BID=107&page=arch&lang=EN. Accessed on 16.06.2007.

——, 11 October 2005, Bonn. http://www.consilium.europa.eu/cms3_applica-tions/applications/solana/list.asp?cmsid=256&BID=107&page=arch&lang=EN. Accessed on 10.11.2006.

——, 31 October 2005, Cambridge. http://www.consilium.europa.eu/cms3_applications/applications/solana/list.asp?cmsid=256&BID=107&page=arch&lang=EN. Accessed on 16.06.2007.

——, 'Europe's International Role', 9 November 2005, Bratislava. http://www.consilium.europa.eu/cms3_applications/applications/solana/list.asp?cmsid=256&BID=107&page=arch&lang=EN. Accessed on 05.03.2007.

——, 27 January 2006, Salzburg. http://www.consilium.europa.eu/cms3_appli-cations/applications/solana/list.asp?cmsid=256&BID=107&page=arch&lang=EN. Accessed on 05.03.2007.

——, 17 March 2006, Stockholm. http://www.consilium.europa.eu/cms3_applications/applications/solana/list.asp?cmsid=256&BID=107&page=arch&lang=EN. Accessed on 10.11.2006.

——, 'The Role of the EU in Promoting and Consolidating Democracy in Europe's East', 4 May 2006, Villinius. http://www.consilium.europa.eu/cms3_applications/applications/solana/list.asp?cmsid=256&BID=107&page=arch&lang=EN. Accessed on 16.06.2007.

——, 'Mediating Today's Conflicts for Tomorrow's Peace', 27 June 2006, Oslo. http://www.consilium.europa.eu/cms3_applications/applications/solana/list.asp?cmsid=256&BID=107&page=arch&lang=E. Accessed on 16.06.2007.

——, 'Europe's Answers to the Global Challenges', 8 September 2006, Copenhagen. http://www.consilium.europa.eu/cms3_applications/applica-tions/solana/list.asp?cmsid=256&BID=107&page=arch&lang=EN. Accessed on 03.03.2007.

——, 6 October 2006, Paris. http://www.consilium.europa.eu/cms3_appli-cations/applications/solana/list.asp?cmsid=256&BID=107&page=arch &lang=EN. Accessed on 10.11.2006.

——, 23 November 2006, The Hague. http://www.consilium.europa.eu/cms3_ applications/applications/solana/list.asp?cmsid=256&BID=107&page=arch &lang=EN. Accessed on 18.01.2007.

——, 24 January 2007, Brussels. http://www.consilium.europa.eu/cms3_appli-cations/applications/solana/list.asp?cmsid=256&BID=107&page=arch &lang=EN. Accessed on 03.03.2007.

——, 29 January 2007, Berlin. http://www.consilium.europa.eu/cms3_appli-cations/applications/solana/list.asp?cmsid=256&BID=107&page=arch &lang=EN. Accessed on 16.06.2007.

——, 17 May 2007, Aachen. http://www.consilium.europa.eu/cms3_appli-cations/applications/solana/list.asp?cmsid=256&BID=107&page=arch &lang=EN. Accessed on 16.06.2007.

Official Documents

Commission of the European Communities, 'The European Union and the United Nations: The Choice of Multilateralism', *Communication From the Commission to the Council and the European Parliament*, 10 September 2003, Brussels.

Commission of the European Communities, 'Policy Coherence for Development: Accelerating Progress Towards Attaining the Millennium Development Goals', *Communication From the Commission to the Council and the European Parliament and the European Economic and Social Committee*, 12 April 2005, Brussels.

Commission of the European Communities, 'Proposal for a Joint Declaration by the Council, the European Parliament and the Commission', *Communication From the Commission to the Council and the European Parliament, the European Economic and Social Committee and the Committee of the Regions*, 13 July 2005, Brussels.

Commission of the European Communities, 'EU-Palestinian Cooperation Beyond Disengagement – Towards a Two-state Solution', *Communication From the Commission to the Council and the European Parliament, the European Economic and Social Committee and the Committee of the Regions*, 5 October 2005, Brussels.

Commission of the European Communities, 'Europe in the World – Some Practical Proposals for Greater Coherence, Effectiveness and Visibility', *Communication From the Commission to the European Council of June 2006*, 8 June 2006, Brussels.

Council of the European Union, 'The European Consensus on Development', *Joint Statement by the Council and Representative of Governments of the Member States Meeting Within the Council, the European Parliament and the Commission*, 22 November 2005, Brussels.

European Security Strategy: A Secure Europe in a Better World, 12 December 2003, Brussels.

European Union, 'The Enlarging European Union at the United Nations: Making Multilateralism Matter', Belgium, January 2004. http://www.medea.be/files/EU_and_UN_1_2004.pdf. Accessed on 07.02.2008.

The Treaty of Lisbon Amending the Treaty on European Union and the Treaty Establishing the European Community.

Secondary Sources

Books and Articles

Adigbuo, Richard, 'Beyond IR Theories: The Case for National Role Conceptions', *Politikon* (Vol. 34, No. 1, April 2007), pp. 83–97.

Aggestam, Lisbeth, *A European Foreign Policy? Role Conceptions and the Politics of Identity in Britain, France and Germany*, Stockholm Studies in Politics 106 (Doctoral Dissertation, Stockholm University: Department of Political Science, 2004a).

——, 'Role Identity and Europeanization of Foreign Policy: A Political-Cultural Approach', in Ben Tonra and Thomas Christiansen (eds), *Rethinking European Union Foreign Policy* (Manchester: Manchester University Press, 2004b).

——, 'A European Foreign Policy? Role Conceptions and the Politics of Identity in Britain, France and Germany' (February 2005). http://www.arena.uio.no/events/papers/AggestamFEB05.pdf. Accessed on 25.03.2008.

——, 'Role Theory and European Foreign Policy: A Framework for Analysis', in Ole Elgström and Michael Smith (eds), *The European Union's Role in International Politics: Concepts and Analysis* (Oxford: Routledge, 2006).

——, 'Introduction: Ethical Power Europe?', *International Affairs* (Vol. 84, No.1, 2008), pp. 1–11.

Al-Dajani, Ahmad Sidqi, 'The PLO and the Euro-Arab Dialogue', *Journal of Palestine Studies* (Vol. 9, No. 3, Spring, 1980), pp. 81–98.

Aliboni, Roberto, 'Re-Setting the Euro-Mediterranean Security Agenda', *The International Spectator* (Vol. 33, No. 4, October-December 1998), pp. 11–15.

Allen, David and Smith, Michael, 'The European Union's Security Presence: Barrier, Facilitator, or Manager?', in Carolyn Rhodes (ed.), *The European Union in the World Community* (Boulder, CO: Lynne Rienner Publishers, 1998).

——, 'Western Europe's Presence in the Contemporary International Arena', *Review of International Studies* (No. 16, Iss. 1, 1990), pp. 19–37.

Alpher, Joseph, 'The Political Role of the European Union in the Arab-Israel Peace Process: An Israeli Perspective' *The International Spectator* (Vol. 33, No. 4, October-December 1998), pp. 77–86.

——, 'The Political Role of the EU in the Middle East: Israeli Aspirations', in Sven Behrendt and Christian-Peter Hanelt (eds), *Bound to Cooperate: Europe and the Middle East* (Gütersloh: Bertelsmann Foundation, 2000).

Anderson, Jim, 'The European Union: Time for a Place at the Table?', *Middle East Policy* (Vol. 6, No. 3, February 1999), pp. 160–166.

Aoun, Elena, 'European Foreign Policy and the Arab-Israeli Dispute: Much Ado About Nothing?', *European Foreign Affairs Review* (Vol. 8, Iss. 3, 2003), pp. 289–312.

Asseburg, Muriel, 'The EU and the Middle East Conflict: Tackling the Main Obstacle to Euro-Mediterranean Partnership', *Mediterranean Politics* (Vol. 8, Iss. 2–3, Summer 2003), pp. 174–193.

———, 'The EU and the Middle East Conflict: Tackling the Main Obstacles to Euro-Mediterranean Partnership', in Annette Jünemann (ed.), *Euro-Mediterranean Relations After September 11: International, Regional and Domestic Dynamics* (Great Britain: Frank Cass, 2004).

———, 'The ESDP Missions in the Palestinian Territories (EUPOL COPPS, EUBAM Rafah): Peace through Security', in Muriel Asseburg and Ronja Kempin (eds), *The EU as a Strategic Actor in the Realm of Security and Defence: A Systematic Assessment of ESDP Missions and Operations* (Berlin: German Institute for International and Security Affairs, December 2009a).

———, 'European Conflict Management in the Middle East: Toward a More Effective Approach', *SWP Research Paper* (Berlin: German Institute for International and Security Affairs, February 2009b).

Asseburg, Muriel and Perthes, Volker, 'Is the EU Up to the Requirements of Peace in the Middle East', *The International Spectator* (Vol. 44, No. 3, September 2009), pp. 19–25.

Backman, Carl W., 'Role Theory and International Relations: A Commentary and Extension', *International Studies Quarterly* (Vol. 14, No. 3, September 1970), pp. 310–319.

Barbé, Esther and Johansson-Nogués, Elisabeth, 'The EU as a Modest 'Force for Good': the European Neighbourhood Policy', *International Affairs* (Vol. 84, No. 1, 2008), pp. 81–96.

Batt, Judy, et al., 'Partners and Neighbours: a CFSP for A Wider Europe', *Chaillot Papers*, no. 64 (Paris, Institute for Strategic Studies, September 2003).

Behr, Timo, 'Enduring Differences? France, Germany and Europe's Middle East Dilemma', *Journal of European Integration* (Vol. 30, No. 1, March 2008), pp. 79–96.

Behrendt, Sven and Hanelt, Christian-Peter (eds), *Bound to Cooperate: Europe and the Middle East* (Gütersloh: Bertelsmann Foundation, 2000).

Beitler, Ruth Margolies, 'The European Union and The Middle East: The Benefits of Soft Power', in Janet Adamski, Mary Troy Johnson, Christina Schweiss (eds), *Old Europe, New Security: Evolution of A Complex World* (England: Ashgate, 2006).

Benli Altunışık, Meliha, 'EU Foreign Policy and the Israeli-Palestinian Conflict: How Much of an Actor', *European Security* (Vol. 17, No. 1, March 2008), pp. 105–121.

Bertelsmann Group for Policy Research, 'Europe and the Middle East – New Ways and Solutions for Old Problems and Challenges?', *Discussion Paper of the Kroenberg Talks Reflecting the Current Middle East Crisis* (Munich: Center for Applied Policy Reseach, September 2006).

Bicchi, Federica, *European Foreign Policy Toward the Mediterranean* (New York: Palgrave Macmillan, 2007).

Bicchi, Federica and Martin, Mary, 'Talking Tough or Talking Together? European Security Discourses Towards the Mediterranean', *Mediterranean Politics* (Vol. 11, No. 2, July 2006), pp. 189–207.

Biddle, Bruce J., *Role Theory: Expectations, Identities and Behaviours* (New York: Academic Press, 1979).

——, 'Recent Developments in Role Theory', *Annual Review of Sociology* (No. 12, 1986), pp. 67–92.

Bilgin, Nuri, *Sosyal Bilimlerde İçerik Analizi: Teknikler ve Örnek Çalışmalar* (Ankara: Siyasal Kitabevi, 2006).

Bilgin, Pınar, 'A Return to 'Civilizational Geopolitics' in the Mediterranean? Changing Geopolitical Images of the European Union and Turkey in the Post-Cold War Era', *Geopolitics* (Vol. 9, No. 2, Summer 2004), pp. 269–291.

——, *Regional Security in the Middle East: A Critical Perspective* (Oxford: Routledge, 2005).

Biscop, Sven, 'Opening Up the ESDP to the South: A Comprehensive and Cooperative Approach to Euro-Mediterranean Security', *Security Dialogue* (Vol. 34, No. 2, 2003), pp. 183–197.

——, 'For a "More Active" EU in the Middle East: Transatlantic Relations and the Strategic Implications of Europe's Engagement with Iran, Lebanon and Israel-Palestine', *Egmont Paper 13* (Brussels: Academia Press, March 2007).

——, 'The European Security Strategy in Context: A Comprehensive Trend', in Sven Biscop and Jan Joel Andersson (eds), *The EU and the European Security Strategy: Forging a Global Europe* (Oxford: Routledge, 2008).

Bono, Giovanna, 'The Impact of 11 September 2001 and the 'War on Terror" on European Foreign and Security Policy: Key Issues and Debates', in Giovanna Bono (ed.), *The Impact of 9/11 on European Foreign and Security Policy* (Brussels: Brussels University Press, 2006).

Bretherton, Charlotte and Vogler, John, *The European Union as a Global Actor* (Oxford: Routledge, 2006).

Bulut, Esra, 'EUBAM Rafah (Palestinian Territories)', in Giovanni Grevi, Damien Helly and Daniel Keohane (eds), *European Security and Defence Policy: The First Ten Years* (France: EU ISS, 2009).

Carlsnaes, Walter, 'Where is the Analysis of European Foreign Policy Going?', *European Union Politics* (Vol. 5, No. 4, 2004), pp. 495–508.

——, 'European Foreign Policy', in Knud Erik Jorgensen, Mark Pollack and Ben J Rosamond (eds), *Handbook of European Union Politics* (London: Sage, 2006).

Castle, Stephen, 'EU dismisses Sanctions and Backs Powell's Peace Mission', *The Independent*, 16 April 2002. http://www.independent.co.uk/news/world/middle-east/eu-dismisses-sanctions-and-backs-powells-peace-mission-657362.html. Accessed on 24.02.2009.

Cavatorta, Francesco and Tonra, Ben, 'Normative Foundations in EU Foreign, Security and Defence Policy: the Case of the Middle East Peace Process – a View from the Field', *Contemporary Politics* (Vol. 13, No. 4, December 2007), pp. 349–363.

Celador, Gemma Collantes et al., 'Fostering an EU Strategy for Security Sector Reform in the Mediterranean: Learning From Turkish and Palestinian Police Reform Experiences', *EuroMesco Paper* (No. 66, January 2008).

Christian Century Foundation, 'Arafat Pays Visit to Church of the Nativity', 22 May 2002. Available at: http://findarticles.com/p/articles/mi_m1058/is_11_119/ai_87080208/.

Cremona, Marise, 'The Neighbourhood Policy: Legal and Institutional Issues', *CDDLR Working Papers* (No. 25, 2 November 2004).

Dannreuther, Roland, 'The Middle East: Towards A Substantive European Role in the Peace Process', in Roland Dannreuther (ed.), *European Union Foreign and Security Policy: Towards a Neighbourhood Strategy* (London: Routledge, 2004).

——, 'Europe and The Middle East: Attempting to Bridge the Divide', in Thierry Tardy (ed.), *European Security in a Global Context: Internal and External Dynamics* (London: Routledge, 2009).

Del Sarto, Raffaella A., 'Wording and Meaning(s): EU-Israeli Political Cooperation According to the ENP Action Plan', *Mediterranean Politics* (Vol. 12, No. 1, March 2007), pp. 59–75.

Dembinski, Matthias, 'Europe and the UNIFIL II Mission: Stumbling into the Conflict Zone of the Middle East', *CFSP Forum* (Vol. 5, Iss. 1, January 2007).

Dieckhoff, Alain, 'Europe and the Arab World: The Difficult Dialogue', in Ilan Greilsammer and Joseph Weiler (eds), *Europe and Israel: Troubled Neighbours* (Berlin: Walter de Gruyter, 1987).

——, The European Union and the Israeli-Palestinian Conflict', *Journal Inroads* (Iss. 16, Winter-Spring 2005), pp. 52–62.

Dosenrode, Soren and Stubkjaer, Anders, *The European Union and the Middle East* (Sheffield: Sheffield Academic Press, 2002).

Douma, Wybe Th., 'Israel and the Palestinian Authority', in Steven Blockmans and Adam Larowski (eds), *The European Union and Its Neighbours* (The Hague: T.M.C. Asser Institut, 2006).

Duchéne, François, 'Europe's Role in World Peace', in Richard Mayne (ed.), *Europe Tomorrow: Sixteen Europeans Look Ahead* (London: Fontana/Collins, 1972).

——, 'The European Community and the Uncertainties of Independence', in Max Hohnstamm and Wolfgang Hager (eds), *A Nation Writ Large? Foreign Policy Problems Before the European Community* (London: Macmillan Press, 1973).

Edwards, Geoffrey, 'Britain' in David Allen and Alfred Pijpers (eds), *European Foreign Policy-making and the Arab-Israeli Conflict* (the Hague: Martinus Nijhoff Publishers, 1984.

Elgström, Ole and Smith, Michael (eds), *The European Union's Role in International Politics: Concepts and Analysis* (Oxford: Routledge, 2006).

Emerson, Michael et al., 'The Reluctant Debutante: The European Union as Promoter of Democracy in its Neighbourhood', *CEPS Working Document* (No. 223, July 2005).

Emerson, Michael and Tocci, Nathalie, 'What Should the European Union do Next in the Middle East?', *CEPS Policy Brief* (No. 112, September 2006).

Emerson, Michael, Tocci, Nathalie and Youngs, Richard, 'Gaza's Hell: Why the EU Must Change Its Policy', *CEPS Commentary*, 13 January 2009.

Euromed Synopsis, Issue 334, 10 November 2005.

European Voice, 'Middle East Peace Process Tests EU's Foreign Policy Ambition' (Vol. 6, No. 42, 9 November 2000).

Everts, Steven, *The EU and the Middle East: a Call for Action* (London: CER, January 2003).

Ferrero-Waldner, Benita, 'The European Neighbourhood Policy: The EU's Newest Foreign Policy Instrument', *European Foreign Affairs Review* (Vol. 11, No. 2, 2006), pp. 139–142.

Fraenkel, Jack R. and Wallen, Norman E., *How to Design and Evaluate Research in Education 6. Edition* (New York: McGraw Hill, 2006).

Fraser T.G., *The Arab-Israeli Conflict* (New York: Palgrave Macmillan, 2008).

Ghose, Gauvav and James, Patrick, 'Third-Party Intervention in Ethno-Religious Conflict: Role Theory, Pakistan and War in Kashmir, 1965', *Terrorism and Political Violence* (Vol. 17, Iss. 3, 2005), pp. 427–445.

Ginsberg, Roy H. and Smith, Michael E., 'Understanding the European Union as a Global Political Actor: Theory, Practice, and Impact', in Sophie Meunier and Kathleen McNamara (eds), *The State of the European Union, Making History: European Integration and Institutional Change at Fifty* (Oxford: Oxford University Press, 2007).

Gomez, Ricardo, *Negotiating the Euro-Mediterranean Partnership: Strategic Action in EU Foreign Policy?* (Aldershot: Ashgate, 2003).

Gowan, Richard, 'The European Security Strategy's Global Objective: Effective Multilateralism', in Sven Biscop and Jan Joel Andersson (eds), *The EU and the European Security Strategy: Forging a Global Europe* (Oxford: Routledge, 2008).

Greilsammer, Ilan, 'Reflections on the Capability of the European Community to Play an Active Role in an International Crisis: The Case of the Israeli Action in Lebanon', in Ilan Greilsammer and Joseph Weiler (eds), *Europe and Israel: Troubled Neighbours* (Berlin: Walter de Gruyter, 1987).

Greilsammer, Ilan and Weiler, Joseph, 'European Political Cooperation and the Palestinian-Israeli Conflict: An Israeli Perspective', in David Allen and Alfred Pijpers (eds), *European Foreign Policy-making and the Arab-Israeli Conflict* (the Hague: Martinus Nijhoff Publishers, 1984).

——, *Europe's Middle East Dilemma: The Quest for a Unified Stance* (Boulder, CO: Westview Press, 1987).

Ham, Peter Van, 'Europe Gets Real: The New Security Strategy Shows the EU's Geopolitical Maturity', http://www.aicgs.org/c/vanham.shtml., 9.1.2004. Accessed on 10.04.2004.

Hanelt, Christian-Peter, 'After Annapolis: What is Europe's Role in Facilitating the Implementation of a Two-State Solution', in Christian-Peter Hanelt and Almut Möller (eds), *Bound to Cooperate: Europe and the Middle East II* (Gütersloh: Bertelsmann Foundation, 2008).

Hanelt, Christian-Peter and Möller, Almut (eds), *Bound to Cooperate: Europe and the Middle East II* (Gütersloh: Bertelsmann Foundation, 2008).

Hartley, Cathy (ed.), *A Survey of Arab-Israeli Relations*, 2nd edn. (London and New York: Europa Publications, 2004).

Herman, Lior, 'An Action Plan or a Plan for Action?: Israel and the European Neighbourhood Policy', *Mediterranean Politics* (Vol. 11, No. 3, November 2006), pp. 371–394.

Hermann, Charles F., 'Superpower Involvement with Others: Alternative Role Relationships', in Stephen G. Walker (ed.), *Role Theory and Foreign Policy Analysis* (Durham: Duke University Press, 1987).

Hill, Christopher, 'The Capability-Expectations Gap, or Conceptualizing Europe's International Role', *Journal of Common Market Studies* (Vol. 31, No. 3, September 1993), pp. 305–328.

Hill, Christopher and Smith, Karen E., *European Foreign Policy Key Documents* (London: Routledge, 2000).

Hollis, Rosemary, 'Europe and the Middle East: Power by Stealth?', *International Affairs* (Vol. 73, No. 1, 1997), pp. 15–29.

——, 'The Israeli-Palestinian Road Block: Can Europeans Make a Difference?', *International Affairs* (Vol. 80, No. 2, 2004), pp. 191–201.

Holsti, Kalevi Jacque, 'National Role Conceptions in the Study of Foreign Policy', *International Studies Quarterly* (Vol. 14, No. 3, September 1970), pp. 233–309.

——, *International Politics: A Framework for Analysis* (New York: Prentice-Hall Inc., 1972).

——, 'National Role Conceptions in the Study of Foreign Policy', in Stephen G. Walker (ed.), *Role Theory and Foreign Policy Analysis* (Durham, NC: Duke University Press, 1987).

House of Lords European Union Committee, 'The EU and the Middle East Peace Process', *26th Report of Session 2006–07* (London: The Stationery Office Limited, 24 July 2007).

Howorth, Jolyon and Keeler, John T.S., 'The EU, NATO and the Quest for European Autonomy', in Jolyon Howorth and John T.S. Keeler (eds), *Defending Europe: The EU, NATO and the Quest for European Autonomy* (London: Palgrave-Macmillan, 2003).

Ifestos, Panayiotis, *European Political Cooperation: Towards a Framework of Supranational Diplomacy* (Aldershot: Avebury, 1987).

Islam, Shada, 'Plans on the Table', *Middle East International*, 8 February 2002a.

——, 'EU Blueprint on Ice', *Middle East International*, 22 February 2002b.

——, 'Falling Short Again', *Middle East International*, 19 April 2002c.

——, 'Enter Berlusconi', *Middle East International*, 11 July 2003a.

——, 'Mixed Messages', *Middle East International*, 24 October 2003b.

——, 'Talking Tough', *Middle East International*, 19 December 2003c.

Joffé, George, 'Relations Between the Middle East and the West', *Middle East Journal* (Vol. 48, No. 2, Spring 1994), pp. 250–267.

Jönsson, Christer and Westerlund, Ulf, 'Role Theory in Foreign Policy Analysis' in Christer Jönsson (ed.), *Cognitive Dynamics and International Politics* (London: Frances Pinter Publishers Limited, 1982).

Jupille, Joseph and Caporaso, James A., 'States, Agency and Rules: The European Union in Global Environment Politics', in Carolyn Rhodes (ed.), *The European Union in the World Community* (Boulder, CO: Lynne Rienner Publishers, 1998).

Jünemann, Annette (ed.), *Euro-Mediterranean Relations After September 11: International, Regional and Domestic Dynamics* (London: Frank Cass, 2004).

Kahraman, Sevilay, 'The European Neighbourhood Policy: The European Union's New Engagement Towards Wider Europe', *Perceptions* (Vol. 10, Winter 2005), pp. 1–28.

——, 'The European Neighbourhood Policy: A Critical Assessment', *Ankara Avrupa Çalışmaları Dergisi* (Ankara Review of European Studies) (Vol. 5, No. 3, Spring 2006), pp. 13–46.

Kaya, Taylan Özgür, *The Common Foreign and Security Policy: The European Union's Quest for Being a Coherent and Effective Actor in Global Politics* (unpublished MSc thesis, Middle East Technical University: The Graduate School of Social Sciences, 2004).

——, 'Constituting the Common Foreign and Security Policy: The European Union's Pursuit of Being a Coherent and Effective Foreign and Security Policy Actor in Global Politics', *Akdeniz İİBF Dergisi* (Vol. 5, No. 9, May 2005), pp. 123–153.

——, 'A Coherent and Effective Foreign and Security Policy For the European Union?: The Cases of the Yugoslav Crisis and the Iraq Crisis', *Journal of Yaşar University* (Vol. 3, No. 12, October 2008), pp. 731–747.

Keukeleire, Stephan and MacNaughtan, Jennifer, *The Foreign Policy of the European Union* (New York: Palgrave Macmillan, 2008).

Khader, Bichara, 'Europe and the Arab-Israeli Conflict 1973–1983: An Arab Perspective' in David Allen and Alfred Pijpers (eds), *European Foreign Policy-making and the Arab-Israeli Conflict* (the Hague: Martinus Nijhoff Publishers, 1984).

Khaliq, Urfan, *Ethical Dimension of the Foreign Policy of the European Union: A Legal Appraisal* (Cambridge: Cambridge University Press, 2008).

Khatib, Ghassan, 'The Arab Peace Initiative as a Vision for Peace with the State of Israel: Steps Toward Realization', in Christian-Peter Hanelt and Almut Möller (eds), *Bound to Cooperate: Europe and the Middle East II* (Gütersloh: Bertelsmann Foundation, 2008).

Kolarska-Bobinska, Lena and Mughrabi, Magdelena, 'New Member States' Policy Towards the Israeli-Palestinian Conflict: The Case of Poland', EuroMesco 2008.

Krahmann, Elke, *Multilevel Networks in European Foreign Policy* (Aldershot: Ashgate, 2003).

Kratochwil, Frederick, 'Norms versus Numbers: Multilateralism and the Rationalist and Reflectivist Approaches to Institutions – a Unilateral Plea for Communicative Rationality', in John Gerard Ruggie (ed.), *Multilateralism Matters: The Theory and Praxis of an Institutional Form* (New York: Columbia University Press, 2003).

Laatikainen, Katie Verlin and Smith, Karen E., 'Introduction – The European Union at the United Nations: Leader, Partner or Failure?', in Katie Verlin Laatikainen and Karen E. Smith (eds), *The European Union at the United Nations: Intersecting Multilateralisms* (New York: Palgrave Macmillan, 2006).

Laipson, Ellen, 'Europe's Role in the Middle East: Enduring Ties, Emerging Opportunities', *Middle East Journal* (Vol. 44, No. 1, Winter 1990), pp. 7–17.

Larsen, Henrik, 'The EU: A Global Military Actor?', *Cooperation and Conflict: Journal of the Nordic International Studies Association* (Vol. 37, No. 3, 2002), pp. 283–302.

Lazaroff, Tovah, 'EUBAM Head: Keeping Rafah Open is the Trick', *The Jerusalem Post*, 6 February 2009. http://www.jpost.com/servlet/Satellite?pagename=JPost%2FJPArticle%2FShowFull&cid=1233304702298. Accessed on 25.06.2009.

Le More, Anne, 'The Dilemma of Aid to the PA After the Victory of Hamas', *The International Spectator* (Vol. 41, No. 2, April-June 2006), pp. 87–94.

Lennon, David, 'The European Union and the Middle East', in Robert J. Guttman (ed.), *Europe in the New Century: Visions of an Emerging Superpower* (Boulder, CO: Lynne Rienner, 2001).

Le Prestre, Philippe G., 'Author! Author! Defining Foreign policy Roles after the Cold War', in Philippe G. Le Prestre (ed.), *Role Quests in the Post-Cold*

War Era: Foreign Policies in Transition (Quebec: McGill-Queen's University Press, 1997a).

——, 'The United States: An Elusive Role Quest after the Cold War', in Philippe G. Le Prestre (ed.), *Role Quests in the Post-Cold War Era: Foreign Policies in Transition* (Quebec: McGill-Queen's University Press, 1997b).

Manners, Ian, 'Normative Power Europe: A Contradiction in Terms?', *Journal of Common Market Studies* (Vol. 40, No. 2, 2002) pp. 235–258.

Manners, Ian and Whitman, Richard G., 'The "Difference Engine": Constructing and Representing the International Identity of the European Union', *Journal of European Public Policy* (Vol. 10, No. 3, June 2003), pp. 380–404.

——, 'Towards Identifying the International Identity of the European Union: A Framework for Analysis of the EU's Network of Relationship', *Journal of European Integration* (Vol. 21, No. 3, 1998), pp. 231–249.

Martin-Diaz, Alicia, 'The Middle East Peace Process and the European Union', *European Parliament Working Paper* (POLI-115 EN, May 1999).

Menotti, Roberto and Vencato, Maria Francesca, 'The European Security Strategy and the Partners', in Sven Biscop and Jan Joel Andersson (eds), *The EU and the European Security Strategy: Forging a Global Europe* (Oxford: Routledge, 2008).

Miller, Rory, 'The PLO Factor in Euro-Israeli Relations, 1964–1992', *Israel Affairs* (Vol. 10, No. 1–2, January 2004), pp. 123–155.

——, 'Troubled Neighbours: The EU and Israel', *Israel Affairs* (Vol. 12, No. 4, October 2006), pp. 642–664.

Möller, Almut, 'A Time to Take Action: Europe's Responsibility in the Middle East', *Spotlight Europe* (Bertelsmann Stiftung Center for Applied Policy Research, September 2007).

——, 'Europe and the Annapolis Process: Israelis and Palestinians are Back at the Negotiating Table', *CAP News*, 23 February 2008. http://www.cap-lmu. de/aktuell/positionen/2008/annapolis.php. Accessed on 25.02.2008.

——, 'After Gaza: A New Approach To Hamas', *AIES Focus*, February 2009.

Musu, Costanza, 'European Foreign Policy: A Collective Policy or a Policy of "Converging Parallels"?' *European Foreign Affairs Review* (Vol. 8, No. 1, 2003), pp. 35–49.

——, 'The Madrid Quartet: An Effective Instrument of Multilateralism?', in Roby Nathason and Stephan Stetter (eds), *The Monitor of EU-Israel Action Plan* (Berlin: Fredrich Ebert Stiftung, 2006).

——, 'The EU and the Middle East Peace Process: A Balance', *Studia Diplomatica, The Brussels Journal of International Relations* (Vol. 60, No. 1, 2007a), pp. 11–28.

——, 'The EU and the Arab-Israeli Peace Process', in Nicola Casarini and Costanza Musu (eds), *European Foreign Policy in an Evolving International System: The Road to Convergence* (New York: Palgrave Macmillan, 2007b).

——, 'European Security and the Middle East Peace Process: An Unavoidable Entanglement?', in Frederic Merand (ed.), *European Security since the Fall of the Berlin Wall* (Toronto: University of Toronto Press, 2010a).

——, 'The Middle East Quartet: A New Role for Europe?', in Daniel Möckli and Victor Mauer (eds), *A Strained Partnership: European-American Relations and the Middle East from Suez to Iraq* (London: Routledge, 2010b).

——, *European Union Policy towards the Arab-Israeli Peace Process: The Quicksands of Politics* (New York: Palgrave Macmillan, 2010c).

Müller, Patrick, 'Europe's Role in the Israeli-Palestinian Peace Process – a Comparison of the Foreign Policies of the 'Big-Three' EU Member States vis-avis the Peace Process', paper presented at BISA Conference 2006, Cork, 18–19 December 2006.

Neuendorf, Kimberly A., *The Content Analysis Guidebook* (New York: Sage Publications, 2002).

Newman, David and Yacobi, Haim, 'The EU and the Israel/Palestine Conflict: An Ambivalent Relationship', *EU Border Conflicts Studies Working Paper No. 4*, January 2004a.

——, 'The Role of the EU in the Israel/Palestine Conflict', *EU Border Conflicts Studies Working Paper No. 12*, 2004b.

Newsletter of the European Commission Technical Assistance Office For the West Bank and Gaza (Iss. 1, January–March 2007). Available at: http://www.delwbg.ec.europa.eu/en/whatsnew/previous_editions.htm. Accessed on 20.09.2008.

Newsletter of the European Commission Technical Assistance Office For the West Bank and Gaza (Iss. 3, July–September 2007). Available at: http://www.delwbg.ec.europa.eu/en/whatsnew/previous_editions.htm. Accessed on 20.09.2008.

Nuttall, Simon J., *European Political Cooperation* (Clarendon Press: Oxford, 1992).

——, 'Two Decades of EPC Performance', in Regelsberger, Elfriede, de Schoutheete de Tervant, Philippe and Wessels, Wolfgang (eds), *Foreign Policy of the European Union: From EPC to CFSP and Beyond* (Boulder, CO: Lynne Rienner Publishers, 1997).

——, *European Foreign Policy* (New York: Oxford University Press, 2000).

O'Donnell, Clara Marina, 'The EU's Approach to Israel and the Palestinians: A Move in the Right Direction', *CER Policy Brief* (June 2009).

Özcan, Mesut, 'European Union's Middle East Policy and Turkey', *Avrasya Etüdleri* (No. 27–28, Sonbahar-Kış 2005), pp. 153–172.

Pace, Michelle, 'The Construction of EU Normative Power', *Journal of Common Market Studies* (Vol. 45, No. 5, 2007), pp. 1041–1064.

——, 'The EU as a "Force for Good" in Border Conflict Cases?', in Thomas Diez, Mathias Albert and Stephan Stetter (eds), *The European Union and Border Conflicts: The Power of Integration and Association* (New York: Cambridge University Press, 2008).

——, 'Paradoxes and Contradictions in EU Democracy Promotion in the Mediterranean: The Limits of EU Normative Power', *Democratization* (Vol. 16, No. 1, February 2009a), pp. 39–58.

——, 'Interrogating the European Union's Democracy Promotion Agenda: Discursive Configurations of "Democracy from the Middle East"', paper presented at EUSA Conference 2009, Los Angeles, 23–25 April 2009b.

Patokallio, Pasi, 'European Union Policy on the Israeli-Palestinian Conflict: From Payer to Player?', 8 April 2004.

Perthes, Volker, 'The Advantages of Complementarity: US and European Policies towards the Middle East Peace Process', *The International Spectator* (Vol. 35, No. 2, June 2000), pp. 41–56.

——, 'America's 'Greater Middle East' and Europe: Key Issues for Dialogue', *Middle East Policy* (Vol. 11, No, 3, Fall 2004), pp. 85–97.

Peters, Joel, *Pathways to the Peace: The Multilateral Arab-Israeli Talks* (London: The Royal Institute of International Affairs, 1996).

——, 'The Arab-Israeli Multilateral Peace Talks and the Barcelona Process: Competition and Convergence?', *The International Spectator* (Vol. 33, No. 4, 1998), pp. 63–76.

——, 'Can the Multilateral Middle East Talks be Revived?', *Middle East Review of International Affairs (MERIA) Journal* (Vol. 3, No. 4, December 1999a), pp. 90–99.

——, 'Europe and the Middle East Peace Process: Emerging from the Sidelines' in Stelios Stavridis, Theodore Couloumbis, Thanos Veremis and Neville Waites (eds), *The Foreign Policies of the European Union's Mediterranean States and Applicant Countries in the 1990s* (London: Macmillan Press Ltd, 1999b).

——, 'Europe and the Arab-Israeli Peace Process: The Declaration of the European Council of Berlin and Beyond', in Sven Behrendt and Christian-Peter Hanelt (eds), *Bound to Cooperate: Europe and the Middle East* (Gütersloh: Bertelsmann Foundation, 2000).

Piana, Claire, *Foreign Policy Analysis and the EU CFSP – Understanding the Formal and Informal Decision-making Processes* (doctoral dissertation, University of Pittsburgh: The Graduate School of Public and International Affairs, 2004).

Piening, Christopher, *Global Europe: The European Union in World Affairs* (Boulder: Lynne Rienner Publishers, 1997).

Pirozzi, Nicoletta, 'UN Peacekeeping in Lebanon: Europe's Contribution', *European Strategic Review* (No. 30, September 2006).

Quille, Gerrard, '"Battle Groups" to Strengthen EU Military Crisis Management', *European Security Review* (No. 22, April 2003).

Rieker, Pernille, 'Europeanization of Nordic Security: The European Union and the Changing Security Identities of the Nordic States', *Cooperation and Conflict: Journal of the Nordic International Studies Association* (Vol. 39, No. 4, 2004), pp. 369–392.

Research Group on European Affairs, 'The Political Role of the European Union in the Middle East', *University of Munich Working Papers* (Munich: University of Munich, January 1998).

Robin, Philip, 'Always the Bridesmaid: Europe and the Middle East Peace Process' *Cambridge Review of International Affairs* (Vol. 10, No. 2, Winter/ Spring 1997), pp. 69–83.

Rosenau, James N., 'Roles and Role Scenarios in Foreign Policy', in Stephen G. Walker (ed.), *Role Theory and Foreign Policy Analysis* (Durham, NC: Duke University Press, 1987).

Sabiote, Maria A., 'EUBAM Rafah: A Test for the EU's Role in the Middle East', *CFSP Forum* (Vol. 4, Iss. 4, July 2006).

Sakellariou, Jannis and Keating, Tamara, 'Safeguarding Multilateralism: The Urgency of European Defence', *The Brown Journal of World Affairs* (Vol. 9, Iss. 2, Winter/Spring 2003), pp. 83–93.

Salamé, Ghassan, 'Torn Between the Atlantic and the Mediterranean: Europe and the Middle East in the Post-Cold War Era', *Middle East Journal* (Vol. 48, No. 2, Spring 1994), pp. 226–249.

Sarbin, Theodore R. and Allen, Vernon L., 'Role Theory', in Gardner Lindzey and Elliot Aronson (eds), *The Handbook of Social Psychology*, Vol. 1, 2nd edn (Reading, MA: Addison-Wesley Publishing Company, 1968).

Schmid, Dorothee and Braizat, Fares, 'The Adaptation of EU and US Democracy Promotion Programmes to the Local Political Context in Jordan and Palestine and Their Relevance to Grand Geopolitical Designs', *EuroMesco Papers* (No. 50, October 2006).

Schmid, Dorothee et al., 'Mapping European and American Economic Initiatives towards Israel and the Palestinian Authority and their Effects on Honest Broker Perceptions', *EuroMesco Papers* (No. 61, October 2006).

Schulz, Michael, 'The European Union as an Important (Low-profile) Actor in the Israeli-Palestinian Conflict', in Valeria Bello and Belachew Gebrewold (eds), *A Global Security Triangle: European, African and Asian Interactions* (Oxford: Routledge, 2010).

Sjursen, Helene, 'The CFSP: An Emerging New Voice in International Politics?', *Arena Working Papers* (99/34) http://arena.uio.no. Accessed on 20.05.2004.

Smith, Hazel, *European Union Foreign Policy, What it is and What it Does* (London: Pluto Press, 2002).

Smith, Karen, *European Union Foreign Policy in a Changing World*, 2nd edn (Cambridge: Polity Press, 2008).

Smith, Michael, 'The Shock of the Real? The Trends in European Foreign and Security Policy Since September 2001', in Giovanna Bono (ed.), *The Impact of 9/11 on European Foreign and Security Policy* (Brussels: Brussels University Press, 2006).

Smith, Michael E., *Europe's Foreign and Security Policy: The Institutionalization of Cooperation* (Cambridge: Cambridge University Press, 2004).

Soetendorp, Ben, *Foreign Policy in the European Union* (Oxford: Pearson Education Limited, 1999).

———, 'The EU's Involvement in the Israeli-Palestinian Peace Process: The Building of a Visible International Identity', *European Foreign Affairs Review* (Vol. 7, Iss. 3, 2002), pp. 283–295.

Stavridis, Stelios and Hutchene, Justin, 'Mediterranean Challenges to the EU's Foreign Policy', *European Foreign Affairs Review* (Vol. 5, Iss. 1, 2000), pp. 35–62.

Steinberg, Gerald M., 'The European Union and the Middle East Peace Process', *Jerusalem Letter/Viewpoints* (No. 418, 15 November 1999).

Stetter, Stephan, 'Democratization Without Democracy? The Assistance of the European Union for Democratization Process in Palestine', in Annette Jünemann (ed.), *Euro-Mediterranean Relations After September 11: International, Regional and Domestic Dynamics* (Great Britain: Frank Cass, 2004).

———, *EU Foreign and Interior Policies: Cross-pillar Politics and the Social Construction of Sovereignty* (Oxford: Routledge, 2007).

Şenyücel, Sabiha, et al., 'Factors and Perceptions Influencing the Implementation of the European Neighbourhood Policy in Selected Southern Mediterranean Partner Countries', *EuroMesco Paper* (No. 49, October 2006).

Tessler, Mark, *A History of the Israeli-Palestinian Conflict* (Bloomington: Indiana University Press, 1994).

Tocci, Nathalie, 'The Widening Gap Between Rhetoric and Reality in EU Policy Towards the Israeli-Palestinian Conflict', *CEPS Working Document* (No. 217, January 2005a).

———, 'Conflict Resolution in the Neighbourhood: Comparing EU Involvement in Turkey's Kurdish Question and in the Israeli-Palestinian Conflict', *Mediterranean Politics* (Vol. 10, No. 2, July 2005b), pp. 125–146.

———, 'Has the EU Promoted Democracy in Palestine…and Does it Still?', *CFSP Forum* (Vol. 4, Iss. 2, March 2006).

———, *The EU and Conflict Resolution: Promoting Peace in the Backyard* (London: Routledge, 2007).

——— (ed.), *Who is a Normative Foreign Policy Actor? The European Union and its Global Partners* (Brussels: CEPS, 2008).

Tomkys, Roger, 'European Political Cooperation and the Middle East: a Personal Perspective', *International Affairs* (Vol. 63, No. 3, Summer 1987), pp. 425–437.

Tonra, Ben, 'Conceptualizing the European Union's Global Role', in Michelle Cini and Angela K. Bourne (eds), *Palgrave Advances in European Union Studies* (Basingstoke: Palgrave Macmillan, 2006).

Walker, Stephen, 'National Role Conceptions and Systemic Outcomes', in Lawrence S. Falkowski (ed.), *Psychological Models in International Politics* (Boulder, CO: Westview Press, 1979).

——— (ed.), *Role Theory and Foreign Policy Analysis* (Durham, NC: Duke University Press, 1987a).

——, 'The Relevance of Role Theory to Foreign Policy Analysis', in Stephen Walker (ed.), *Role Theory and Foreign Policy Analysis* (Durham, NC: Duke University Press, 1987b).

——, 'Role Theory and Foreign Policy Analysis: An Evaluation', in Stephen G. Walker (ed.), *Role Theory and Foreign Policy Analysis* (Durham, NC: Duke University Press, 1987c).

——, 'Role Theory and the Origins of Foreign Policy', in Charles F. Hermann, Charles W. Kegley and James Rosenau (eds), *New Directions in the Study of Foreign Policy* (Boston: Allen and Unwin, 1987d).

Wallace, William, 'Looking After the Neighbourhood: Responsibilities for the EU-25', *Notre Europe Policy Papers* (No. 4, July 2003).

Weidenfeld, Werner, *Europe and the Middle East* (Gütersloh: Bertelsmann Foundation Publishers, 1995).

Whitaker, Brian and Agencies, 'European States Offer Middle East Peace Plan Without UK', *Guardian*, 17 November 2006. Available at http://www. guardian.co.uk/world/2006/nov/17/israel.eu. Accessed on 13.04.2009.

White, Brian, 'The European Challenge to Foreign Policy Analysis', *European Journal of International Relations* (Vol. 5, No. 1, 1999), pp. 37–66.

——, *Understanding European Foreign Policy* (New York: Palgrave, 2001).

——, 'Foreign Policy Analysis and the New Europe', in Walter Carlsnaes, Helene Sjursen and Brian White (eds), *Contemporary European Foreign Policy* (London: Sage, 2004).

Wish, Naomi Bailin, 'Foreign Policy Makers and Their National Role Conceptions', *International Studies Quarterly* (Vol. 24, No. 4, December 1980), pp. 532–554.

——, 'National Attributes as Sources of National Role Conceptions: A Capability-Motivation Model', in Stephen G. Walker (ed.), *Role Theory and Foreign Policy Analysis* (Durham, NC: Duke University Press, 1987).

Youngs, Richard, 'The European Union and Democracy in the Arab-Muslim World', *CEPS Working Papers* (No. 2, November 2002).

——, *Europe and the Middle East in the Shadow of September 11* (Boulder, CO: Lynne Rienner, 2006).

——, 'The EU and the Middle East Peace Process: Re-engagement?', *FRIDE Comment*, March 2007.

Internet Sources

http://ec.europa.eu/external_relations/human_rights/eu_election_ass_observ/ westbank/ip04_1462.htm. Accessed on 10.04.2009.

http://www.delisr.ec.europa.eu/newsletter/english/default.asp?edt_id=17&id=248. Accessed on 22.04.2009.

http://www.wsibrussels.org/gaza.htm. Accessed on 20.05.2009.

EU description of the outcome of permanent status talks at Taba.

http://www.haaretz.com/hasen/pages/ShArt.jhtml?itemNo=130196&contrass ID=2&subContrassID=5&sbSubContrassID=0&listSrc=Y. Accessed on 10.03.2009.

http://ec.europa.eu/external_relations/human_rights/eu_election_ass_observ/ westbank/legislative/index.htm. Accessed on 20.02.2009.

http://ec.europa.eu/trade/issues/bilateral/countries/israel/index_en.htm. Accessed on 14.04.2009.

EU Border Assistance Mission at Rafah Crossing Point, *European Union Factsheet*, March 2009. Available at http://consilium.europa.eu/showPage. aspx?id=1022&lang=en. Accessed on 25.05.2009.

Interviews

Interview with an EU Official, General Secretariat of the Council of the European Union, 26 October 2009.

Interview with an EU Official, Directorate-General External Relations, European Commission, 27 October 2009.

Interview with an EU Diplomat, General Secretariat of the Council of the European Union, 3 November 2009.

Interview with an EU Official, General Secretariat of the Council of the European Union, 3 November 2009.

Interview with an EU Official, General Secretariat of the Council of the European Union, 4 November 2009.

Interview with a British Diplomat, UK Permanent Representation to the European Union, 11 November 2009.

Interview with a Palestinian Diplomat, General Delegation of Palestine to the European Union, 13 November 2009.

Interview with an Israeli Diplomat, Mission of Israel to the European Communities, 13 November 2009.

INDEX